Sons of Heaven
——Stories of Chinese Emperors Through the Ages

by Cheng Qinhua

Foreign Languages Press   Beijing

First Edition 2000
Translated by Huang Youyi

Home Page:
http://www.flp.com.cn
E-mail Addresses:
info@flp.com.cn
sales@flp.com.cn

ISBN 7 - 119 - 02047 - 1
Published by Foreign Languages Press
24 Baiwanzhuang Road,Beijing 100037,China
Printed by Beijing Foreign Languages Printing House
19 Chegongzhuang Xilu,Beijing 100044,China
Distributed by China International Book Trading Corporation
35 Chegongzhuang Xilu,Beijing 100044,China
P.O. Box 399,Beijing,China

Printed in the People's Republic of China

Contents

Preface

Preface

For centuries, the life stories of Chinese emperors, their wives and concubines and the ministers and officials who served them have been surrounded by a sense of mystery, provoking curiosity and the urge to unveil the true inside tales.

Just how many emperors were there?

According to historical documents, from the inauguration of the First Emperor of the Qin Dynasty in 221 BC to the abdication of the last emperor Puyi of the Qing Dynasty in 1911, 406 emperors ruled the country over a period of more than 2,100 years.

This special group of people included diligent founding fathers who devoted their life to the building of the nation, tyrannic rulers who did not hesitate to assassinate their fathers in order to usurp supreme power, enlightened leaders who enlisted the help of loyal and wise officials and maintained their position on the basis of collective effort and wisdom, chieftains who relied on villains and treacherous aides, heroes from low and poor backgrounds who founded their dynasties through hard work and gallantry, and figure heads who clung to their own luxury by kowtowing to foreign forces or selling out the country. Under enlightened rulers, the situation of an affluent economy, prosperous lives and strong national defence emerged. A fatuous and self-indulgent national leader could throw the prosperous country into misery. Consequently, some emperors went down in history with respect while others became the subject of continued condemnation. Along the footprints of the emperors, we can trace the reasons for the rise and fall of the various dynasties and gain an insight into the change of power and the development of culture and economy in ancient China.

This book presents stories about dozens of emperors, beginning with the First Emperor of the Qin Dynasty and ending with the Qing rulers who were most typical among the emperors in Chinese history. Focusing on the political centre of the royal court, the stories describe the lives and death, rise and fall, as well as the influence and impact of the emperors who left strong historical imprints on Chinese society. Historical events, interesting anecdotes and thought-provoking tales in which the emperors were the actors and heroes are vividly told. Readers will be able to meet with figures of all descriptions, and come across breath-taking events and historical cases yet to be answered.

I have tried to place all the persons in these stories in their actual historical context, in an attempt to present realistic and true pictures of the emperors so that the stories will shed light on the history and culture of China. I have also tried to write in popular language so as to make the plots of the stories interesting to read. It is my goal that the book will offer readers an opportunity to gain a better understanding of China's culture and history, and I hope that it will achieve just that.

by the author
December 1997

I The First Emperor of the Qin Dynasty and His Empire

Before the founding of the Qin Dynasty (221 – 207 BC), China was divided and ducal states fought with each other for supremacy. Out of many, seven of these states, namely the Qin, Chu, Qi, Wei, Zhao, Yan and Han, were more powerful than others and hence were known as the "powerful seven."

The king of the Qin, Ying Zheng (246 – 210 BC), pursued a policy of sowing discord among other states and then conquering them one by one. He successfully annexed the six states of Han, Zhao, Wei, Chu, Yan and Qi, thus putting an end to more than eight hundred years of separate rule of the country by different states and finally, in 221 BC, establishing the first centralized feudal state in China's history——the empire of Qin. Ying Zheng declared himself the First Emperor of Qin and in doing so became the creator of the system of feudal rule by emperors that lasted for over two thousand years, from 221 BC to 1911.

1. "A rare commodity worth the effort of investing"

Yi Ren, a grandson of the king of Qin, was sent to the State of Zhao when he was only a child. Why was he sent? Qin and Zhao were neighbouring states and they had agreed that a grandson of the each ruling king would be sent to the other state as a hostage so as to prevent any sudden war between them. At the time, Qin often found excuses to bully Zhao, and so Yi Ren, Qin's hostage in Zhao, was often in danger.

Yi Ren's father, Lord An'guo, was the crown prince of King Zhao of Qin (306 – 249 BC). Lord An'guo had more than twenty sons and Yi Ren was a son by his concubine Xia, who was not really a woman in favour. Under such circumstances, Yi Ren's chances of ever succeeding to the throne were quite slim.

Any dramatic turn in a person's life, however, may occur. Purely by accident, businessman Lü Buwei got to know Yi Ren at Handan, capital of Zhao. With his particular businessman's shrewdness, he concluded that Yi Ren was "a commodity worth the effort of hoarding."

Lü Buwei consulted his own father, asking, "How much profit can you make by farming?"

"About ten times your investment," was the father's answer.

"What about trading jewelry?" Lü Buwei went on.

His father responded, "You can made about hundred times your investment by trading jewelry."

"How much profit can you make if you help somebody become the ruler of a country?" Lü asked again.

His father said, "Unlimited profits."

So Lü said, "Yi Ren has a chance of becoming a ruler and is a rare commodity worth all the effort of investing. It will pay me handsomely if I put my stake on him."

Lü went to discuss the matter with Yi Ren in secret, saying, "You have more than twenty brothers and your mother is not in Lord An'guo's favour. There is no chance for you to rely on your mother. If you want to make it to the top, you'd better lean on Lady Huayang, who is now your father's favourite woman. She is childless and if you win her favour, you have a good chance of succeeding to the throne over your twenty brothers."

Yi Ren, who had been living away from home and was always in low spirits because he was a hostage, was greatly enlightened and encouraged by this. He said to Lü, "I see your point and will do as you say. If I ever become the king of Qin, I'll share the country with you."

Lü provided Yi Ren with five hundred taels of gold and told him to use the money to make friends, publicize himself and build up his influence. He spent another five hundred taels of gold to buy expensive gifts and travelled westward to personally present them to Lady Huayang through the help of her sister. He made it known to Lady Huayang that Yi Ren was an exceptionally virtuous man who, although living in Zhao, missed Lady Huayang so much that he cried for her all the time. Lü also had Lady Huayang's sister persuade her: "You're in favour because you're young and beautiful. But one's youthfulness will not last. You would be better off if you would adopt one of the twenty sons of your husband as your own so that you will have somebody to rely on when you're old." These words rang well with Lady Huayang who could not give birth to any children. She made a request of Lord An'guo that she be able to adopt Yi Ren and soon her request was granted. Yi Ren thus became her adopted son. As a result, Yi Ren now rose in status among all the princes and dukes.

One day, Lü Buwei invited Yi Ren to drink with him. During the dinner, a beautiful woman named Zhao danced and sang for their pleasure. Yi Ren liked her and could not take his eyes off her. Finally he proposed marriage to her. Zhao was actually the favourite concubine of Lü's and so Lü was immediately enraged by Yi Ren's request. However, on second thought, he reasoned to himself that since he had put all his property at stake on this man, what difference did it really make if he presented him with one of his women? He gritted his teeth and agreed to the marriage. By then Zhao was already pregnant with Lü's child, a secret known only to Zhao and Lü. In due course, Lady Zhao gave birth to a baby boy.

This was no ordinary baby boy, for he was the person who would later become the First Emperor of Qin, a boy with the personal name of Ying Zheng. He was considered to be the son of prince of Yi Ren alright, but he was the flesh and blood of Lü Buwei. Having given birth to a son, Lady Zhao was designated the chief wife of Yi Ren.

In 257 BC, Qin launched an attack on Handan, the capital of Zhao. Zhao was ready to imprison Yi Ren, Qin's hostage, but Yi Ren sought help from Lü Buwei, who bribed officials of Zhao to let Yi Ren escape and safely return to Qin.

On Yi Ren's departure, Lü said to him repeatedly: "Once back in Qin, the first thing you should do is to visit Lady Huayang, and remember to wear the Chu style of clothes when you do so because she is originally from the State of Chu."

Yi Ren did as he was told. When Lady Huayang saw him in her native state's attire, she was delighted and said, "I like to see you wearing Chu clothes. Why don't I change your name into Zi Chu?" The name not only contained the word and meaning of Chu, her native land, but also had a word Zi, which meant son.

After the death of King Zhao of Qin, Lord Anguo succeeded to the throne, but he died a year later. As Lü had predicted, Yi Ren, now called Zi Chu, became the ruler and ran the country from 249 to 246 BC with the reign title of King Zhuangxiang of Qin. Once in power, he made Lü Buwei his prime minister snd gave him Luoyang, Henan, as his enfeoffed land. It had one hundred thousand households that payed him their taxes. Thus Lü's investment paid off and his profits were too great to measure.

2. Keeping a firm grip on all power

King Zhuangxiang of Qin was also a short lived ruler as he died three years after ascending to the throne. He was succeeded by Ying Zheng, a son borne by Lady Zhao from the State of Zhao. Since Ying Zheng was just thirteen years old at the time, it was only natural that all power would fall into the hands of Lü Buwei.

As was said earlier Lady Zhao had been a favourite concubine of Lü Buwei and the two maintained an illicit relationship after the death of King Zhuangxiang, the official husband of Lady Zhao. As Ying Zheng grew up, Lü Buwei began to fear that his illicit relationship with the queen-dowager might bring him harm. He thus began to distant himself from the woman. Lady Zhao, however, was just in the prime of her life and her sexual desire was hard to saturate. Not wanting to live as a widow, she often summoned Lü Buwei to the palace

for her pleasure. Lü eventually recommended a substitute for himself to the queen-dowager and was thus able to escape her pestering.

The substitute was called Lao Ai. At that time, it was impossible for a man of ordinary status to enter the living quarters of the palace unless they were eunuchs who had been castrated. Lü and the queen-dowager secretly discussed how to bring Lao Ai into the palace. They decided to have Lao Ai accused of a crime that deserved castration. But what they did was simply to pluck his beard and then they had him smuggled into the palace. Young and strong, Lao Ai served the queen-dowager every night and she doted on him. Later they produced two children.

One day, Lao Ai was drinking and playing chess with some of the nobles. He drank too much and quarrelled with one of them. Thinking he had the backing of the queen-dowager, Lao Ai swore at his opponent, saying, "I'm the step-father of the king. How dare you contradict me and fight with me?"

So the nobles, in anger, reported to the king that Lao Ai had not been properly castrated and that he had committed adultery with the queen-dowager. The king ordered an investigation. Scared, Lao Ai launched a coup, taking advantage of the king's absence from the palace on an excursion and forging the seals of the king and the queen-dowager. The king led his troops to fight back and killed several hundred rebels. Lao Ai fled and the king issued a wanted circular that read: "Whoever captures Lao Ai alive will be awarded one million strings of cash and whoever kills him will be awarded half of a million strings of cash." A few days later, Lao Ai was captured along with over twenty of his die-hard conspirators. At Xianyang, the capital of Qin, the king ordered that he be put to death by tying his arms and legs to four horse-drawn carriages that were made to pull in different directions and tear him into four pieces. His relatives were also killed. And the heads of over twenty of his close followers were hung in the street as a warning to future conspirators. Altogether over four thousand families were involved. Some were stripped of their official posts and others were exiled to Shu (present-day Sichuan) in the southwest.

Because it was Lü Buwei who had introduced Lao Ai to the queen-dowager, he was also implicated. At first the king wanted to kill Lü, but remembering that Lü was a close follower of his father, King Zhuangxiang, and had performed meritorious deeds for his father, the king decided to be lenient with him by sending him to serve as the Marquis of Wenxin in Lü's enfeoffed land at Luoyang, Henan.

Lü was an influential man in the State of Qin. At one time, three thousand people lived in his house as his personal guests. Lü had the writings of his guests compiled into a book entitled *Master Lü's Spring and Autumn Annals*, which has been preserved to this day. Once in Luoyang, there was an endless line of visitors to his house. Many people also appealed on his behalf to the king. They did not realize that this only made matters worse, as it further revealed to the king the influence of Lü. Fearing disadvantageous consequences, the king exiled Lü and his family to a more distant place in Shu.

After repeated demotions and exile, Lü recognized that his days were numbered. He killed himself by drinking a cup of poisoned wine. It was a great tragedy for Lü that he died at the hands of the king who was actually his son by birth.

With Lao Ai killed and Lü Buwei out of the way, the king took all authority into his own hands. He worked hard at state affairs. In those days all reports and documents were written on bamboo strips because paper had not yet been invented. The bamboo strips that he had to read every day weighed over sixty kilogrammes.

3. Annexing the six neighbouring states

Being the most powerful of the seven states, Qin occupied the western part of China with a territory more than half the size of the country at the time, covering present-day Shaanxi, Ningxia, Gansu, Sichuan, the northern part of Hubei, the western part of Henan and the southern part of Shanxi. King Ying Zheng was determined to wipe out the other six states and to unify the nation under the banner of Qin.

Thus the king of Qin began his massive offensive in the year 230 BC, picking his close neighbour, the State of Han, as his first target. Soon Qin troops took Han and captured King An of Han, reducing that empire into Yingchuan Prefecture of the powerful kingdom of Qin.

Zhang Liang, a veteran official of Han, sold all his property to hire a warrior to assassinate the king of Qin in order to revenge his country. This robust warrior, using an iron hammer of over sixty kilogrammes as his weapon, tried to kill the king of Qin while the latter was touring Bolangsha in the southeast part of today's Yuanyang County, Henan. As the king's fleet of chariots were passing by, the warrior charged with all his might but hit the wrong chariot, allowing the king of Qin a narrow escape.

Qin next dispatched its general Wang Jian to attack the State of Zhao, which put up a stubborn resistance under the generals Li Mu and Sima Shang. The two opposing armies each held their ground for two years. In 228 BC, the king of Qin went to the front to confer with General Wang Jian. He told this general that General Li Mu was gallant and good at fighting. To defeat him, force should not be used, but a stratagem of sowing distrust might do the job. So some of Zhao's officials, who had already been bought over by Qin, pleaded with the king of Zhao, saying that Li Mu and Sima Shang were plotting to surrender to Qin and were at the moment negotiating the conditions of surrender.

The ruler of Zhao was muddle-headed and easily believed these lies. He killed Li Mu and stripped Sima Shang of his command. The soldiers of Zhao were demoralized by this development and within three months were defeated by Wang Jian of Qin, who charged right into Handan, capital of Zhao, where the king surrendered holding onto a valuable piece of jade as the token of his subordination. Examining this valuable piece of jade, the king of Qin said to his ministers and generals: "The former king, my father, wanted to trade fifteen cities for this jade, but he could not obtain it. Now I have it." His happiness was beyond description. Next, he gave an order to make the former State of Zhao the Julu Prefecture of Qin.

The Qin troops, now in high spirits and invincible, directed their next attack on the State of Yan on the Yishui River. Prince Dan of Yan, who once was held hostage by Qin, was well aware of the strength of the Qin army. He believed that even if the entire country of Yan was mobilized, it would still be no match for the Qin military. To save Yan, the prince sent Jing Ke to Qin to assassinate the king.

Crossing the Yishui River on his mission of assassination, Jing Ke knew he would never return. To his relatives and the friends seeing him off, he bravely composed these lines: "Wind blows and the water of Yishui is cold. The gallant soldier is taking a mission of no return."

To save his country, Jing Ke was ready to give up everything. Upon arriving at Qin, he took two gifts to give to the king in order to get near to him: one was a map showing a region of Yan covering today's Zhuoxian, Yixian and Gu'an counties, and the other the head of Fan Yuqi, a Qin general who had surrendered to Yan, something the king desperately wanted. Fan Yuqi had willingly committed suicide so that Jing Ke could have his head to take to the king of Qin. Wrapped in the map was a sharp dagger, the tip of which was covered with poison. The king of Qin was happy to see that the envoy of Yan had brought a map. When the map was unrolled to reveal the dagger, Jing Ke snatched it in his right hand and grabbed at the clothes of the king with his left, charging forward to stab the king in his chest. The king tried to flee and his palace doctor threw his bag of medicine at Jing Ke. This gave the king time to pull out a sword and cut down the assassin.

Jing Ke failed to kill the king and was instead instantly put to death. The king of Qin immediately launched a massive attack on Yan. In 226 BC, Qin troops rolled into the capital of Yan, today's Beijing but then called Ji. The king of Yan was compelled to kill the prince, Dan, and offer his head to the king of Qin in exchange for peace. But the king of Qin was not about to stop his attack and ordered the offensive to continue. The king of Yan had to flee north to eastern Liaoning.

During the following year, Qin began its attack on the State of Wei. The capital of Wei, today's Kaifeng, Henan, then called Daliang, was well protected by a tall and thick city wall. The unscrupulous Qin troops dug an opening in the dike of the Yellow River and flooded the Wei capital. Thus Wei also met its demise.

Having successively taken over the states of Han, Zhao, Yan and Wei, the Qin army now turned on the State of Chu, which was the most powerful of the six. At a meeting held by the king of Qin before their attack, veteran general Wang Jian said that an army of 600,000 men would be needed to take Chu because of its vast expanse of territory and strong military force. General Li Xin, young and aggressive, disagreed and said that all that would be needed was an army of 200,000 men. The king decided that veteran general Wang Jian was getting too old and timid and so he gave the command to Li Xin with an army of 200,000. Wang Jian resigned and went home on grounds of poor health.

Once the battle began, Li Xin was indeed brave and quickly took a number of towns. The State of Chu, however, was not a weak force. Turning defence into attack, the Chu soldiers subjected the arrogant troops of Li Xin to total failure. This was the most severe setback the Qin troops had ever suffered in their efforts to annex the six states. At the end of his resources, the king of Qin had to bring back veteran general Wang Jian to take over the command.

Wang Jian led a force of 600,000 to besiege Chu without launching any attack. He only began his attack a year later in 223 BC and soon captured Chu capital of Shouchun, now Shouxian County in Anhui Province. The king of Chu was captured and his kingdom fell under the rule of Qin.

The following year, the Qin troops attacked the escaped king of Yan in eastern Liaoning. Unable to resist the strong invading force, whatever remained of the former State of Yan was quickly crushed.

Now only the State of Qi out of the six still existed. Qi never helped any of the other five when they were attacked by Qin and, in fact, had never even made any preparations to defend itself. Renegades in Qi accepted heavy bribes from Qin and secretly assisted Qin in taking over Qi. In 221 BC, the Qin troops marched southward, after wiping out the remaining forces of Yan. As they progressed, they met no strong resistance and so they quickly occupied the capital of Qi, Linzi, in today's Shandong Province. The king of Qi was taken captive and the territory was overrun by Qin.

In a decade's time from his attack on Han in 230 BC to his defeat of Qi in 221 BC, the king of Qin put an end to the separate rule in China and succeeded in unifying the country.

The king of Qin did not wait but marched his army to the southwest, the southeast coast and the southern coast, eventually establishing a unified power and multi-ethnic feudal kingdom, an achievement previously unprecedented in China's history.

4. Centralization of power

Once the smoke of battle dispersed, the king of Qin began to take measure so as to consolidate the country.

King Ying Zheng believed that his achievements so far exceeded those of his predecessors that his position should be higher and more esteemed. Therefore he styled himself the First Emperor and expected that state power would be held within his family and be passed on to the second, third, and all subsequent generations.

The First Emperor of Qin took all the power into his own hands and insisted that all major decisions could be made only by himself. He was assisted by officials in three offices: a prime minister in charge of government administration, a censor-in-chief in charge of supervision, and a commander-in-chief in charge of the military. Under the three offices, there were nine department heads: a chamberlain for attendance, whose job was to defend the emperor; a chamberlain for the palace garrison; a chamberlain in charge of the horses and chariots of the royal family; a chamberlain for ceremonies; a chamberlain for judicial affairs; a chamberlain for grain; a chamberlain for palace revenues; a chamberlain for minority affairs, and a chamberlain for religious affairs. All the heads of these offices and departments were appointed by the emperor and their positions were not hereditary.

What about local government? Some people stood for the traditional method of enfeoffing the land to princes of the emperor's family. Prime Minister Li Si was of the view that the past system of enfeoffing the land had resulted in separate rules by the dukes and had thus led to continual wars. Now a system of prefectures and counties should be introduced, in his opinion, with prefectural governors and county magistrates who would also be appointed by the emperor. This plan was adopted by the emperor and a highly centralized political system was established in the country. The rulers of subsequent dynasties all more or less continued this system. In the rest of the world at the time most countries were still functioning under a slave system or even more primitive forms of society. It wasn't until the early 9th century in Britain and the late 19th century in Russia that unified feudal states took shape in countries other than China.

The emperor also took many other measures to consolidate the country. For example, the rich and powerful families of the six former states were all moved to the central capital of Xianyang, away from their homelands and under the watch of the central government. All the weapons captured from the six states and those collected from civilians were smelted and cast into twelve copper statues of men. These were placed on both sides of the Xianyang Palace to symbolize the power and strength of Qin. Each of the dozen copper statues weighed 120 tons and was gilded in golden magnificence. In later years, one of the statues was pushed into the Yellow River and never recovered. The rest were smelted and cast into coins by later rulers. The emperor also unified currency, script and measurement. He had roads built to facilitate transportation throughout the country.

To ward off invasion by the northern Xiongnu tribe, the emperor employed half a million labourers to build the Great Wall. Previously, during the Spring and Autumn and Warring States periods (770 –221 BC), the states of Yan, Zhao and Qin had built protective walls along their borders. Now, after unifying the country, the emperor had those walls repaired and connected into one. The newly-completed Great Wall stretched more than 2,500 kilometres between today's Liaoyang in Liaoning Province in the east and Minxian in Gansu Province in the west. At an age when only swords, spears, bows and arrows were used for battle, the Great Wall served as an effective defence against the enemy.

The construction of the Great Wall, however, increased people's burdens and took the toll of many lives. The story of "Meng Jiangnü Crying at the Great Wall" tells how Wan Ziliang, husband of

Meng Jiangnü, was drafted to build the wall when the couple was still on their honeymoon. For years, the wife received no news about her husband. One chilly autumn, Meng Jiangnü travelled miles and miles to look for her husband. It was only after she arrived at the construction site of the Great Wall that she learned that her husband had been worked to death years before. Overwhelmed with grief, she cried and her tears fell like torrents in a downpour of rain. The wall, itself, seemed to be moved by her sorrow and sections of it crashed. Today, a temple to her memory stands at the east end of the Great Wall, in the Beidaihe Scenic Zone of Hebei Province.

For his own pleasure, the ruthless emperor had many grand and magnificent palaces built. In Xianyang alone, there were as many as 270 palaces in which he kept beautiful girls brought from all over the country for his personal enjoyment. Rare treasures were displayed in those palaces for his own appreciation or use. Efang Palace, the most magnificent of all, extended for 700 metres from east to west and over 100 metres from north to south with a capacity for housing 10,000 people at a time.

The emperor also spared no effort in preparing for his final resting place, a luxurious mausoleum on Lishan Hill. To build this structure, people worked for thirty-six years. The base of the mausoleum contained a deep pit filled with liquid bronze. The various halls of the underground tomb were filled with all kinds of treasures. An automatic bow and arrow device was installed in the tunnel leading to the tomb which could release an arrow at any person who dared to attempt to rob the tomb. When the emperor was buried, the Second Emperor of Qin had the workers who had taken part in the building of the tomb buried alive in the tunnel in order to keep secret the entrance into the tomb.

Today, more than 2,000 years later, the tomb remains a mystery. In recent years, archaeologists have just begun to unveil its secrets. What is now known is that each of the four sides of the mausoleum measures 7.5 kilometres with a total area of 56.25 square kilometres. Three burial pits in the mausoleum have been opened, revealing thousands of life-size, vivid-looking pottery warriors and battle horses. According to studies, the Number One Pit alone contains some 6,000 pottery warriors and horses. The discovery of these surprised the world and people often refer to these pottery warriors as the eighth wonder of the world.

5. Hu Hai usurping power

In 210 BC, the First Emperor of Qin went on a grand inspection tour of Hunan, Jiangxi, Jiangsu, Zhejiang and Shandong provinces. The emperor fell ill when his entourage reached Pingyuanjin (present-day Pingyuan County, Shandong) and his health quickly deteriorated. Accompanying the ruler were three important officials: Prime Minister Li Si; Hu Hai, the emperor's youngest son; and Zhao Gao, Chamberlain for Palace Chariots. Zhao Gao, a eunuch who understood judicial laws, was also part of the entourage. He had long been a trusted aide of the emperor. Realizing he could not last much longer, the emperor ordered Zhao to write a will for him, ordering his eldest son, Fu Su, who was then supervising the army on the border, to pass his command to General Meng Tian while he himself was to rush back to Xianyang to ascend the throne.

Before the will was sent, however, the First Emperor of Qin died when his party reached today's Julu, Hebei. Li Si, the prime minister, decided to keep the death a secret, fearing that the more than twenty children of the emperor might immediately start competing for the throne as soon as they learned the death of their father and thus result in great disorder. As before, petitions were made to the emperor and food was prepared for him everyday while the entourage marched towards Xianyang, the capital. In all there were no more than five to six people at that time who knew of the death. The weather was hot and the corpse grew smelly. Li Si put abalone on the emperor's chariot to give people the impression that the smell came from the fish.

Zhao Gao was a cunning politician with great ambitions. He showed the will to Hu Hai and sowed disorder by saying, "The late emperor said in this will that your brother, Fu Su, should succeed him. Once Fu Su has arrived at the capital, there will be no chance for you to become emperor. What do you plan to do?"

Not knowing what to do, Hu Hai simply replied, "It's my father's will. What can I do?"

Zhao Gao answered mischievously, "The will has not been sent out and only three of us, you, Li Si and I know this. If there is an agreement reached among the three of us, you can take over the sovereign power and be the emperor." Finding Zhao Gao's plan irresistible, Hu Hai accepted his suggestion.

Zhao then went to persuade Li Si, who at first rejected the idea. Zhao had an eloquent tongue and was very persuasive. He said, "You should realize, Li Si, that in learning, you are no match for General Meng Tian, and in merits, you're also no match for him. Do you think your relationship with the crown prince can compare with that between the prince and Meng Tian?"

This hit Li Si hard and he replied, somewhat reluctantly, "Of course, I'm no match to Meng Tian in those three aspects."

Zhao Gao then pushed his point further, saying, "If Fu Su becomes the emperor, he is sure to make Meng Tian the prime minister. All you can do then is to retire to your home. Forget all the luxury and power you now have. On the other hand, if Hu Hai becomes the emperor, both you and I are in for good things, given the relationship between him and us."

Li Si finally agreed to enter the clique with Zhao and Hu Hai. The first step was for Li Si to reveal a forged will of the emperor, making Hu Hai the crown prince. They had another imperial decree forged and sent to Fu Su, the First Emperor's eldest son, denouncing him for having performed no merits whatsoever and at the same time for being full of complaints. He was ordered to kill himself. General Meng Tian was accused of harbouring disloyalty and was told to die together with the eldest prince.

Fu Su was dumbfounded by the forged decree from his father, the emperor. He, however, was not about to disobey his father and so he committed suicide. General Meng Tian was suspicious of the document and refused to die. He was therefore imprisoned.

Once Hu Hai reached the capital, he made public his father's death. He ascended the throne under the reign title of the Second Emperor of Qin. It was the seventh month of the year 210 BC. The first thing he did in his capacity as emperor was to promote Zhao Gao to the position of chamberlain for attendance, a post that put him in charge of all palace affairs. Soon, the Second Emperor plotted together with Zhao and put more than twenty of his brothers and sisters to death so as to rid himself of any possible contention.

Zhao Gao who had masterminded the enthroning of Hu Hai was, of course, not satisfied with being just the chamberlain for attendance. He lied that Li Si was plotting a coup and the Second Emperor believed him. So the death of Li Si was ordered along with his entire family, and Zhao Gao was put in the position of prime minister.

In that powerful position, Zhao Gao revealed his tyrannical and vicious nature. He knew some of the senior officials did not accept his rule in their hearts and so he found some way to test their loyalty. One day he had a deer brought to the court and said to the Second Emperor, "Here is a great horse for you, my Emperor!"

Not realizing that this was a plot, the emperor smiled and said, "Prime Minister, you're really good at making jokes. This is a deer. Why do you call it a horse?"

Zhao Gao put a stern look on his face and replied, "This is indeed a great horse. If you don't believe me, ask the ministers and generals."

Those who agreed with Zhao that it was a horse had a secure position in the court from then on, while those who dared to say it was a deer soon fell victims to Zhao's wrath. After this incident, everyone was scared to go against Zhao.

6. The declining years of the Qin

Not satisfied with what he had accomplished, Zhao Gao plotted to seize supreme power. The story about "pointing at a deer and calling it a horse" was his test for realizing this ambition. Knowing clearly that Zhao Gao killed senior officials who dared to stand for the truth, the Second Emperor did not dare to expose him and let Zhao run roughshod over the court.

All day long, the Second Emperor wallowed in a debauched life, pursuing only his personal pleasure. To consolidate his power, he employed cruel punishments and people lived in dire hardship. Consequently, peasant uprisings against the cruelty of the Qin court broke out sporadically. The most noticeable of these were those led by Liu Bang and Xiang Yu, which spread like a prairie fire across the country and were directed at Xianyang, the capital.

When urgent messages concerning the situation reached the court from all over the country, Zhao Gao deliberately kept them away from the emperor. He himself took to hiding on the grounds of illness. It was only when the rebellious troops reached the suburbs of the city that the Second Emperor became really worried. He ordered Zhao to lead the force of resistance. Knowing little about warfare, Zhao suffered a series of defeats on the battleground. To protect himself, Zhao hatched one of his most vicious schemes: a plot to kill the emperor and put all blame on him while trying to negotiate for peace with the rebels. Zhao called his third brother, Zhao Cheng, and his son-in-law, Yan Le, to a secret meeting. It was decided that Zhao Cheng would help from inside the palace, while Yan Le would attack the palace from outside. Afraid that Yan might reveal his scheme, Zhao Gao had Yan's mother held as a hostage, thus compelling Yan to do what he was told.

Thanks to the help from inside the palace, Yan fought his way into the palace, killing and demonstrating force at every turn. The Second Emperor, as if he had just woken from a nightmare, called his guards for protection. The guards, however, were busy fleeing. Helpless, the emperor tried to hide in his bedroom. The only person he found there was a palace eunuch, so he asked the man, "Why didn't you tell me earlier about Zhao Gao's plot?" The eunuch replied:"I didn't dare to say anything and precisely because of this I have been able to live till today. Otherwise, I would have been killed long ago."

Just then Yan Le came in and roared at the emperor, "You've been living in luxury and pleasure, killing innocent people at random, and so you have caused national hatred. This is the end for you and so you'd better kill yourself right away."

The emperor asked him, "Who sent you?"

Yan told him, "Prime Minister Zhao Gao!"

The emperor asked to see Zhao but this was rejected. He pleaded, saying, "I guess the prime minister wants me to abdicate. I'll do it and be content with the post of a prefectural governor."

Yan put his hand on his sword and cut him short. "No way!" he said. Crying his heart out, the emperor pleaded, "Let my wife, concubines and me be ordinary citizens. The only thing I ask is that you spare our lives."

Yan, angry, shouted at the top of his voice, "Stop giving me any crap. I've been sent by the prime minister to take your life and end your tyrannical rule!" So saying, he ordered his soldiers to move on to the emperor. Realizing he was at the end of his resources, the Second Emperor pulled out his sword and killed himself.

Zhao was overjoyed to receive news of the emperor's suicide. He rushed into the palace to take hold of the imperial seal, which was the symbol of the emperor. By putting it in his own pocket, Zhao laid bare his intension of seeking the supreme power of the country. Yet Zhao decided to take his time in making his way to the throne. He called all officials together, saying, "The Second Emperor was despotic and cruel. He was unable to preserve his country and so has just killed himself. I now recommend that Zi Ying, the grandson of the First Emperor, ascend the throne. I hope you will agree to this."

Once put on the throne, Zi Ying thought to himself that Zhao Gao, who had brought the death of the Second Emperor, should be punished severely as soon as possible. Otherwise, Zhao might usurp the supreme power at any time. Secretly he called his two sons into the palace and they conversed together. Zi Ying, the father, said to them, "Since Zhao Gao went so far as to kill the Second Emperor, I'm nothing to him. He has put me in this position to serve as a puppet simply because he is not ready to take the throne himself. If I don't take him on, he will soon kill me."

So Zi Ying and his confidants decided to take action on the day when the young emperor was to officially accept the imperial seal. When that day came, Zhao sent people several times to ask Zi Ying to go and accept the seal at the ancestral temple, but the latter refused to appear at the ceremony on the excuse of bad health. Zhao Gao had to come personally to urge Zi Ying. Zhao said, "No matter what, you have to make your presence at such an important ritual."

Before he could finish speaking, three men jumped out in front of him, waving their swords and yelling, "You wicked devil, this is the end of you!" Zhao, who had been so clever at hatching plots, was killed instantly.

Court officials cheered at the death of the cunning Zhao Gao, but the powerful kingdom of Qin was already beseiged by rebel forces. Unable to stand the rebel attacks, it soon fell apart. In October 207 BC, Zi Ying, with a rope tied around his neck, went out of the capital city and turned over the imperial seal to the rebel leader, Liu Bang. Zi Ying had been on the throne for only forty-six days. With his surrender, the Qin Dynasty ended.

II Commoner Emperor Liu Bang and the Founding of the Great Han Dynasty

The Han Dynasty is divided into the Western Han (202 BC – AD 8) and the Eastern Han (25 – 220). In between, there was a short dynasty that lasted from 8 to 23. Liu Bang (256 – 195 BC), the founding father of the Western Han, was a rebel leader who had been a commoner. He experienced many turbulent events in his career before he finally ascended the throne. Many stories about him hold people in suspense.

1. A "scoundrel"

Born into a farmer's family in Fengyi, Peixian County (today's Fengxian County, Jiangsu), he was a loafer who loved wine and women in his early life. His father, in anger and disappointment, called him a "scoundrel."

A Mr. Lü, from a prominent family in Shanfu County (today's Shanxian, Shandong), was a close friend of the magistrate of Peixian County. Escaping from a family enemy, Mr. Lü came to live in Peixian. All prominent people and local gentry in the county turned out to congratulate him on his arrival and settling in their hometown. Xiao He, a county secretary who was there on the day registering gifts received by Mr. Lü, told the guests, "All those with gifts worth less than a thousand yuan please sit outside!" Liu Bang, who had by then become a minor official, had no money to offer as a gift, but he walked into Mr. Lü's new home with a great air, announcing loudly, "Here is a ten thousand yuan gift for the host!"

Such great gift aroused Mr. Lü's attention. He hurried out of the sitting hall to greet the guest. Finding the man with a high nose bridge, long beard and drinking wine from great cups, Mr. Lü was impressed by his heroic style. He was convinced that the guest was not a person who would remain low for very long. After the feast, Mr. Lü asked Liu Bang to stay and said to him, "I've met many people but have never run into anyone as bold, uninhibited and heroic as you are. If you don't mind, I'd like to marry my daughter, Lü Zhi, to you."

Liu Bang, then helplessly poor, immediately accepted the offer. Lü Zhi, because of her family background, had many pursuers who had all been rejected by her father. Now her father wanted her to marry a poor and lowly minor official. Even her mother could not understand why, and so she complained to her husband, "The magistrate of Peixian County is your friend but you refused to marry our daughter to him. Now you want to marry her to a scoundrel!" Mr. Lü reprimanded her, saying,

"You're simply short – sighted. Stop meddling in the affair!" Mr. Lü was indeed a man of vision. Later Liu Bang rose to become the emperor and Mr. Lü's daughter, Lü Zhi, naturally became the empress.

Writing about Liu Bang's early life, historians agree that when he was young, Liu had great aspirations. One story is told about when he was serving in his youth as a hard labourer in Xianyang, capital of Qin. He was very much impressed with the pomposity of the guards of honour who accompanied the First Emperor of Qin on his inspection tours. Liu is said to have remarked at the time, "What a way to be a man!"

2. Launching a rebellion

After unifying China, the First Emperor of Qin employed the services of over 700,000 men to build his mausoleum. Liu Bang, in his capacity as a local official, took labourers to the construction site. Half of the men who were drafted fled on the way. According to the law of Qin, the people who escorted the labourers would be beheaded for if they lost any of their men. After drinking a great deal of wine, Liu announced, "Whoever wants to leave, go now." So most of the drafted labourers fled.

There were a dozen men who were still willing to follow Liu. While travelling, an advance guard reported, "There is a huge snake lying on the road.

What's to be done?"

Acting under the influence of alcohol, Liu yelled, "What's there to be afraid of?" He took out his sword and cut the snake in two. His followers made up a story to praise him. They said that after Liu killed the snake, an old woman was seen crying by the road while saying, "My son is the child of the White Emperor and was lying by the road taking a rest in the form of a snake. But he was killed by the son of the Red Emperor."

Liu was happy to hear himself referred to as the "son of the Red Emperor." He was even eager to have the story spread far and wide so that people would seriously treat him as the "son of heaven." After killing the snake, Liu took his men to prepare for rebellion in the Mang and Jie mountains (in present-day Henan and Anhui).

It was a time of sporadic revolts against the cruel rule of the Qin Dynasty. Seeing that rebels were quickly gaining in strength and the Qin Empire was on the verge of falling, the magistrate of Peixian County decided to join the rebel forces. He asked his secretary, Xiao He, for his opinion. Xiao had been a friend of Liu Bang, so he advised, "You're a county magistrate appointed by the Qin court and so if you lead a revolt, people will not follow you. Your best choice is to call Liu Bang back and join forces with him so that together you can lead the revolt." The magistrate, deciding this idea was reasonable, immediately sent for Liu Bang. When Liu arrived at the front of the county town with several hundred people on horseback, he found the gate locked. Soon Xiao He ran up and panting, said, "The county magistrate had changed his mind and I have narrowly escaped. What shall we do now?"

Liu had people write posters with these words on them: "We've had enough of Qin's cruel rule." He attached these to arrows and shot them into the town. The people inside the town were so enraged by the magistrate's having turning back on his promise that they killed the magistrate and opened the gate to let Liu Bang in.

Liu was met with a warm reception by the people, who slaughtered animals to offer sacrifices to their ancestors. They made bright red flags in response to the tale about the "son of the Red Emperor." They also chose him to be the Lord of Peixian. Liu was forty-eight years old that year.

Young people joined Liu's rebel force which soon grew to three thousand people strong. Liu was assisted by Xiao He and Cao Can. His rebel army fought bravely, taking many towns and cities, and it continued to grow in size and strength.

3. The new rule

Among the rebels against the rule of Qin, Chen Sheng was most powerful. Rebel forces under the command of Liu Bang, Xiang Liang, and his nephew Xiang Yu, regarded Chen Sheng as their common leader. During a coup, however, Chen was murdered by his chariot driver, Zhuang Jia. After conversing with one another, the various rebel forces agreed to name a man called Qin, the grandson of King Huai of Chu, as their new leader and they began to refer to him with the same title of King Huai of Chu.

Xiang Liang and Xiang Yu were from Xiaxiang (present-day Suqian, Jiangsu). During his youth, Xiang Yu, together with his uncle, fled to Huiji (present-day Suzhou, Jiangsu). Big and strong, Xiang Yu could never learn how to write. So he tried fencing, but failed to grasp this skill either. In the words of his uncle, Xiang Liang, he was "good for nothing."

Xiang Yu thought otherwise, however, saying, "All you need to learn in writing is how to put down your own name, and all you need to learn in fencing is how to defend yourself in a one-to-one fight. What I really want to learn is the art of war so as to be able to fight against 10,000 people." His uncle, therefore, began to teach him military strategy.

Once, when the First Emperor of Qin was passing Huiji on an inspection tour, Xiang Yu saw the awe-inspiring guards of honour accompanying the emperor. He could not help but claim, "There's nothing to it. Any one can easily replace him!"

At the beginning of their rebellion, Xiang Liang won successive victories and soon grew conceited. Never did he expect that Zhang Han, a veteran general of Qin with rich experience and very resourceful, would launch a surprise attack on his troops on a dark evening, when he was drinking merrily in his camp. Taken by surprise, Xiang Liang's army was defeated at Dingtao (in present-day Shandong) and he died during the fight.

With his arch enemy Xiang Liang dead, the Qin general, Zhang Han, marched north and surrounded a rebel force at Julu (present-day Pingxiang, Hebei). King Huai of Chu sent Xiang Yu to Julu to break the seige and then to march west through the Han'gu Pass into the heartland of Qin. Meanwhile, he also dispatched Liu Bang westward to attack Xianyang, the capital of Qin.

Before they left on their missions, King Huai of Chu invited Xiang Yu and Liu Bang to a send-off feast. During the dinner, the king made the two rebel army leaders cement a bond of sworn-brother-hood and agree that the first to fight his way into the heartland of Qin would become the new emper-or.

Xiang Yu took his army across Zhanghe River and made preparations for a decisive battle at Julu. Once having crossed the river, Xiang Yu gave an order to sink all the ferry ships and to break into pieces all cooking pots. Each soldier was allowed to carry only a ration of food for three days. In this way, he left no hope of retreat and so his men had to fight forward.

Once the battle began, Xiang took the lead

and, riding a black horse, was the first to charge at the enemy. Encouraged by the bravery of their commander, all the soldiers charged forward and, in three days, won nine battles, lifting the enemy's seige on Julu. This battle made Xiang Yu a hero known far and wide.

In the meantime, Liu Bang fought his way westward, enlisting men to expand his army on the way. Passing through Gaoyang (southwest of present-day Qixian County, Henan), he asked who was the most outstanding talent in the county. A man called Li Shiqi was recommended to him.

When Li came to meet with Liu Bang, however, the latter was washing his feet while sitting on the edge of his bed. On each side was a female attendant helping him do the washing. Li, offended by this reception, asked Liu Bang, "Do you want to help Qin to wipe out dukes and princes or do you want to lead the dukes and princes to crush Qin?"

Enraged at this question, Liu roared, "You foolish scholar! Everyone has been suffering under the rule of Qin. Why should I help Qin?"

Li said, in reply, "If you really want to unite the forces of the dukes to fight Qin, you should not meet me as arrogantly and impolitely as you do now!"

Hearing this, Liu immediately stopped washing his feet and apologized for his impoliteness. He had a feast prepared to entertain Li.

Li was a man well-versed in the classics. He

said to Liu Bang: "Under your command, you have less than 10,000 men and they are poorly trained. How are you going to fight Qin westward? The magistrate of Chenliu County is a friend of mine and I would like to help you by going to Chenliu to persuade the magistrate to surrender to you. If he refuses to surrender, you can attack him and I'll help you from the inside." So Liu sent Li Shiqi to Chenliu while he led his forces in following. Soon he took Chenliu County, which greatly boosted the morale of the troops and Liu's reputation. After that, Li became Liu Bang's envoy, lobbying for Liu wherever he went.

Liu adopted a flexible strategy, avoiding the main forces of Qin and pushing speedily towards Xianyang. Finding Liu Bang's army just outside the capital, the Qin Prime Minister, Zhao Gao, had the Second Emperor killed and sent people to negotiate for peace with Liu, agreeing to share the region of Guanzhong (west of present-day Han'gu Pass) with Liu, each as his own king. Liu absolutely rejected this and continued to march on Xianyang. When this plot of Zhao Gao failed, Zhao resorted to another by making Zi Ying, the son of the brother of the Second Emperor, the new ruler. Zi Ying took the opportunity of the ceremony to accept the imperial seal as a time to kill Zhao Gao. Zi then sent forces to guard Yaoguan (southeast of present-day Lantian, Shaanxi). Liu did not try to take Yaoguan but cleverly detoured to attack Lantian (west of present-day Lantian), inflicting heavy casualties there on the Qin forces.

In October 206 BC, Liu Bang's army took Bashang (southeast of present-day Xi'an, Shaanxi) and so came even closer to Xianyang. Zi Ying, the last ruler of the Qin Dynasty, surrendered by personally delivering the imperial seal to Liu Bang. The Qin empire, which the First Emperor of Qin had built and hoped would last forever, fell after existing for only fifteen years.

Liu Bang and his army marched into Xianyang. Seeing the majestic palace buildings, beautiful palace maids and many rare treasures, he wanted to remain there. Fan Kuai, a butcher from Liu's hometown of Peixian, who had fought all the way with Liu Bang and who was now a gallant general, criticized Liu in these frank words: "Do you want to be the leader of the entire country or do you want to be a man of wealth? In my view, all the wealth and luxury are not enough to keep us here. We'd better return and station our forces at Bashang."

Liu remained motionless after hearing these words, so Fan Kuai asked Zhang Liang to go to Liu Bang and persuade him. Zhang Liang, who had earlier planned to assassinate the First Emperor of Qin when he was a senior official in the State of Chu, now worked as an adviser to Liu Bang. He said to Liu, "The Qin emperor surrendered to you simply because he was wallowing in luxury and pleasure. If you pay that much attention to wealth and comfort, you will soon meet the same fate. Why do you neglect the great cause of taking the whole country by engaging in pleasure at this moment?"

These words woke up Liu Bang, who then ordered that the palaces be sealed. He took his army out of Xianyang to station it in Bashang, encouraging himself all the time with the aspiration of "taking over the whole country."

Back in the barracks, Liu called a meeting of local representatives and prominent figures, saying, "I have an agreement with Xiang Yu that whichever of us arrives at the heart of the Qin's rule first will become the king. Now I'm the king. You have all suffered a great deal under the cruel rule of the Qin court. I now declare an abrogation of all laws and regulations issued by the Qin court. But I want to make a new rule: those who have killed people are to be punished with death and those who have wounded others and stolen things will also be dealt with according to the seriousness of their offences." People who had suffered under the Qin were delighted to hear this. They brought oxen, sheep and wine to entertain Liu's army. Liu thanked them but refused to accept the gifts, saying, "There is grain in the granary for the soldiers. Thank you for your kindness." This won the hearts of the local people, who were more than glad to keep Liu Bang there as their leader.

4. The dinner at Hongmen

It was over a month after Liu Bang entered Guanzhong that Xiang Yu, who led the victorious battle at Julu, came marching towards Xianyang with his army. When he reached Hongmen (northeast of present-day Lintong, Shaanxi), a town not far from Han'gu Pass, Xiang Yu learned that Liu Bang had already entered Xianyang. His anger rose as he thought that a nobody such as Liu Bang should have been so lucky as to take Xianyang before he could do so. A traitor from Liu's camp called Cao Wushang informed Xiang Yu that Liu had already styled himself as the new ruler and was ready to take possession of all the treasures in the Qin palace. Fan Zeng, Xiang Yu's chief adviser, said that Liu was a man only interested in wealth and women. He had not yet taken possession of the treasures and women in the palace only because he must be harbouring some scheme for taking over the whole country. He told Xiang Yu that the latter should be on guard against Liu Bang and should try to get rid of him because Liu was now the opponent of Xiang Yu in their bid for power over the country.

Convinced by these words, Xiang Yu decided to launch what came to be known as the Xiang-Liu War. At that time, Xiang commanded some 400,000 men, while Liu's army was only a quarter of this. Liu's army was thus far outnumbered.

There was also a man from Xiang's army who became an informant for Liu Bang. This man was Xiang Bo, an uncle of Xiang Yu. Since this uncle was a long-time close friend of Zhang Liang, he rode a fast horse during the night to Liu Bang's camp and told Zhang Liang, "Leave immediately for there will be disaster tomorrow."

Zhang Liang took Xiang Bo to see Liu Bang.

Liu respectfully toasted to Xiang Bo and tried to win his good will by saying that though this was their first meeting, seeing him was like seeing an old friend and that they should cement their friendship by marrying their children to each other. He told Xiang that, as soon as he entered the Guanzhong region, he had the warehouses of Qin sealed and had been waiting for Xiang Yu's inspection, while he did not take a single grain or inch of cloth. He would not betray General Xiang Yu, he said, and pressed the visitor to take that message to Xiang Yu.

Xiang Bo immediately agreed to do so, but he wanted Liu Bang to go personally the next day and meet with and apologize to Xiang Yu.

Returning to his camp, Xiang Bo went to see Xiang Yu, saying, "Because Liu Bang first took Guanzhong, you were able to enter Guanzhong smoothly. He is a meritorious man and to kill him is not being righteous and benevolent."

Xiang Yu, who believed he was invincible and

therefore took Liu Bang lightly, decided to call off the planned attack.

Liu Bang came the next morning to pay a visit to Xiang Yu. He took along over a hundred people, including the resourceful Zhang Liang and the gallant Fan Kuai.

During the banquet, Liu Bang said to Xiang Yu, "You and I had a common goal and that was to overthrow Qin. You fought first in Hebei while I started with Henan and then came to Guanzhong. Unfortunately someone has tried to sow disorder between us, which has made you suspicious of me."

Xiang Yu was a direct and simple man, and he replied in a straightforward manner, "It was General Cao Wushang from your army who told me about your plans, otherwise how could I have any suspicions?"

Fan Zeng, Xiang's adviser, raised his jade ring three times as a signal, suggesting that Xiang should take this chance and kill Liu Bang. Xiang, however, was rather hesitant and ignored Fan's suggestion. Fan had to bring in Xiang Zhuang, Xiang Yu's cousin, into the banquet hall to produce a scheme to kill Liu Bang. As soon as he entered, Xiang Zhuang said, "I'd like to demonstrate my fencing skills to add amusement to your feast." So saying, he began to display his fencing skills, inching towards Liu Bang.

Noticing the tense atmosphere, Xiang Bo, Xiang Yu's uncle who had gone to Liu Bang's camp during the previous night, got up and also began to demonstrate his own fencing skills, thus shielding Liu Bang with his own body. Old as he was, Xiang Bo soon grew tired. The resourceful Zhang Liang then said to the gallant Fan Kuai, "Xiang Zhuang's fencing demonstration was aimed at killing Liu Bang." Fan Kuai immediately crashed into the banquet room, brandishing his weapon. His sudden arrival surprised Xiang Yu who asked, "Who is this guy?"

Zhang Liang replied, "He is General Fan Kuai, the personal guard of Liu Bang."

Xiang Yu ordered that a huge cup of wine and raw pork be given to Fan Kuai, who drank the wine in one gulp, cut the meat with his shield as a chopping board and his sword as the chopper, and ate it in great mouthfuls.

Xiang Yu then asked him, "Can you drink any more?"

General Fan Kuai said in a very loud voice, "I'm not afraid of death, why should I be afraid of wine? In the past, the emperor ruled by cruelty, torturing and killing people, arousing national opposition. Liu Bang fought all the way against the Qin troops and his merits are quite convincing. General Xiang Yu, you have believed lies and want to punish a man of merit. Are you tracking the old path of the former emperor?"

Xiang Yu was speechless as the atmosphere at the banquet grew ever more intense. Liu Bang went out of the camp on the excuse of visiting the toilet. Zhang Liang and Fan Kuai followed. Liu wanted to leave immediately but was troubled that he might be impolite in doing so. Fan Kuai stared at him, saying, "Under the circumstances, we're the fish and meat to be cooked while they are the chopping board. Why bother with sham courtesies?"

Liu Bang agreed and told Zhang Liang to stay behind to resist any troops that might pursue them. Liu did not dare to ride in his carriage and hurried home on horseback. With the protection of Fan Kuai, Liu returned to his barracks by a short-cut.

Knowing that Liu Bang was now far away, Zhang Liang returned to the banquet hall, saying, "Liu Bang drank too much and is rather drunk. Unable to make a formal goodbye, he wants me to present you with this piece of white jade. Here is also a pair of jade objects for Fan Zeng."

Xiang Yu took the white jade while Fan Zeng broke the jade objects he was given into pieces, yelling loudly at Xiang Yu: "I cannot work together with you on major endeavours. Just wait and see. Liu Bang will be the only one to challenge you."

The first thing Liu Bang did after returned to his barracks was to kill Cao Wushang, who was the informant for Xiang Yu.

The story about this banquet at which the killing was planned has been handed down over the ages and has spread far and wide.

5. The contention between the Chu and the Han

Several days after the banquet at Hongmen, Xiang Yu's army, like a huge tide, rolled into Xianyang, the former capital of Qin. They looted and killed at random, without sparing the life of Prince Zi Ying of Qin who had already surrendered. Xiang Yu also gave the order to set the magnificent Efang Palace on fire, a fire that, according to historical documents, "did not go out for three months." The barbarian army also took away all the treasure and women from the palace. These actions formed a sharp contrast to what had happened when Liu Bang and his army entered the capital earlier. Naturally the savage behaviour caused deep resentment in the populace.

In January 206 BC, Xiang Yu enfeoffed princes, dukes, generals and officials as though he was the supreme leader. First, he discarded the agreement he had made with King Huai of Chu that the first one who fought his way into Xianyang would be the king, and then he sent Liu Bang as Prince of Han to remote Bashu (present-day Sichuan) and Hanzhong (south of present-day Qinling area in Shaanxi). He further divided the original Hanzhong region into three areas, sending three people, including the surrendered Qin general

Zhang Han, to be stationed in these areas so as to keep a close watch on Liu Bang in fear that Liu might make a comeback in the region. Xiang Yu designated himself Lord of Western Chu, the supreme leader above all the princes and dukes, and he made Pengcheng (present-day Xuzhou in Jiangsu) his capital.

A man named Han Sheng tried to talk with Xiang Yu, suggesting that the Guanzhong region was fertile and easy to defend so that if Xiang Yu made Guanzhong the capital, it would facilitate his plan to bring the entire country under his rule. Xiang Yu, short-sighted and attaching too much sentiment to his homeland, thought otherwise. "If you don't go back to your hometown when you are rich and noble," he said, "it is like wearing the best clothes to walk in the night when nobody can see you." In secret, Han Sheng mockingly compared Xiang Yu to a "monkey with a hat," who is seeking ostensible appearances without really grand aspirations. When Xiang Yu learned of this, he ordered that Han Sheng be chopped into pieces and boiled in a big container.

Liu Bang was very resentful of Xiang Yu's making him a regional ruler, and he wanted to fight it out with Xiang for better or for worse. Xiao He persuaded him not to, reasoning that a fight with Xiang Yu just then would only mean total defeat. The best strategy was to exercise restraint and build up strength for a final battle later on.

While taking his troops to Bashu, Liu Bang, following the suggestion of his chief adviser, Zhang Liang, burned all the planks (used to pave the path chiselled out on the cliffs along the mountains), thus creating an impression that he had no plans of going back to the Central Plains to contend with Xiang Yu.

As new arrivals in Bashu, many of his soldiers fled back towards the east because they were so unaccustomed to the local living conditions. One day Liu Bang received a report that even his prime minister, Xiao He, had fled. Xiao, a close comrade-in-arms, had fought alongside Liu ever since they together launched the rebellion in Peixian. His flight broke Liu Bang's heart. Two days later, however, Xiao He came back. With a mixed feelings of anger and joy, Liu Bang questioned him, "Why did you, as prime minister, also flee?"

Xiao He replied, "I did't run away, but I went to chase after somebody else and brought him back."

"Who is it that you had to go after personally?" Liu Bang asked, growing interested.

Xiao He said with solemnity, "It was Han Xin."

Han Xin, a native of Huaiyin, was well-versed in warfare and was a rare strategist. He had first joined Xiang Liang, then Xiang Yu, but he was never given any important posts and so he finally came into the ranks of Liu Bang, who only appointed him to a minor post as an officer of logistics to look after grain and grass.

While travelling to Bashu, Han Xin could not help sighing and remarking, "Who knows the worth of gold and jade? Why is there no bosom friend who understands me?" In such a state of mind, he fled one evening in the dark.

Xiao He was well aware that Han Xin was an indispensable talent for Liu Bang in his eventual bid to seize the whole country. Learning that Han had fled, Xiao didn't have time to report this to Liu Bang and went right after Han on a galloping horse. The story of this incident showing how enlightened officials enlist the help of talented people has been passed down for many generations in "Xiao He Running After Han Xin in the Night."

Hearing Xiao out, Liu said, somewhat lightly, "Well, in that case, I'll make Han a general."

Shaking his head, Xiao He replied, "Making such a rare talent a general is not putting him in a position important enough!"

Liu Bang now changed his decision and said, "Let him then be the grand general."

Xiao He responded emphatically, "My Lord, you always treat your subordinates arrogantly and this time you should not order him about like a child. An auspicious date should be chosen and a rostrum terrace built. You should fast and bathe and then solemnly announce your decision of the appointment."

Liu Bang took his advice and did accordingly.

Once the news that Liu Bang was going to hold a ceremony to appoint a grand general spread, quite a few of the generals secretly calculated that they might be the candidate. When it turned out the newly-appointed grand general was Han Xin, a minor officer of logistics, everyone was taken by surprise.

After the ceremony, Liu conferred with Han Xin on ways for taking over the whole country. Han first asked Liu, "If you march towards the east to contend with Xiang Yu, how do you compare your strength with his?"

"Certainly I'm no match to Xiang Yu," Liu replied.

Han Xin then said, "You, My Lord, should be congratulated for understanding your own strength. I also think Xiang Yu is stronger. However Xiang Yu is not good at enlisting people and putting them in positions where they can do the best job. So he is a lonely, gallant man. Ostensibly he respects people and is polite, but when his generals have fought meritoriously, he does not promote them. He was not playing fair even when he enfeoffed people, which has left seeds of discontent. His army is badly disciplined and the populace is very disgusted with them. But you, My Lord, maintained strict discipline in your army when you first entered the Guanzhong region and the local people wanted you to be their king."

Liu was overjoyed to hear what Han Xin said.

In August 206 BC, Liu Bang ordered his army to march northward. Employing a ruse suggested by Han Xin, Liu sent people to rebuild the plank road he had burned so as to attract the attention of Zhang Han, who was guarding the road leading to Guanzhong. At the same time he secretly instructed his army to make a surprise detour and march forward to their destination through Chencang (east of present-day Baoji City, Shaanxi).

Not knowing Liu Bang's real intention, Zhang Han placed his army at the end of the plank road, believing that not a single soldier from Liu's camp would be able to pass through. Never did it ever occur to him that the Han troops might suddenly arrive in front of his territory after they passed Chencang. When this happened, he hurriedly redeployed his troops, but it was already too late. To make his defence even more difficult, the homesick Han soldiers were exceptionally brave because they believed they were fighting on their way home. Zhang Han, unable to stop the advance of Han troops, committed suicide. A fierce four-year-long contention between Liu Bang and Xiang Yu, known in Chinese history as the contention between Han and Chu, now began.

At the beginning of this war, Xiang Yu, the Lord of Western Chu, won many victories. The battle at Pengcheng nearly cost Liu Bang of his entire army. At one point the two armies stood against each other across a small mountain stream in the Guangwu Mountains (northeast of present-day Xingyang, Henan). Xiang Yu had Liu Bang's father and wife, whom Xiang had seized as hostages, pushed in a wheelbarrow to the front of the battle line. The two armies were so close to each other that they could see and hear each other clearly. Xiang Yu shouted across the river that unless Liu surrendered, his father would be made into mincemeat as ingredient for soup.

Liu was taken by surprise. He pretended to be calm and replied, in the tone of a rascal, "We became sworn brothers when we entered that agreement at King Huai's place. As we are brothers, my father is your father too. If you dare to boil my father, don't forget to send me a bowl of the soup."

These words made Xiang Yu even angrier, but before he gave the order to kill the old man, Xiang Bo told him, "No man who intends to take the country is going to be stopped by considerations for his family. Killing the old man will not help you. If you keep him alive, it will perhaps leave you an edge over your opponent!"

The war went on and on and Xiang Yu grew weary. He sent a letter of challenge to Liu Bang in which he said, "Our contention leaves the country in chaos. To put an end to this situation as soon as possible, I am willing to fight with you on a one to one basis so we can have a quick outcome. How about that?"

Liu laughed at the letter, and said to the envoy who delivered it, "Go and tell Xiang Yu. I am only interested in fighting with brains, not physical strength!"

Xiang Yu then dispatched soldiers to challenge Liu Bang who shut himself and his troops in the barracks and would not let anyone out to engage the enemy in hand-to-hand combat. Instead, he told his army to shoot arrows at the soldiers from the opposing army.

Without other alternatives, Xiang Yu personally came to challenge Liu who, in turn, listed ten great crimes of Xiang Yu. Enraged, Xiang Yu suddenly released an arrow that hit Liu Bang on the chest. But Liu hurriedly bent to cover his toe with his hand and said loudly, "You mean scoundrel, Xiang Yu. How dare you to shoot and hit me on my toe?" Thus Liu cleverly avoided any shaking of confidence within his army because of his injury.

Thanks to the able administration of Xiao He, Liu Bang's army enjoyed a stable rear and adequate supply of food for both the men and their horses. As for Xiang Yu, the sporadic contention between the various dukes and princes he had enfeoffed gave him no peace. Liu Bang then sent Han Xin to surround Xiang Yu from the rear and to successfully persuade Ying Bu, Prince of Jiujiang, to jointly fight Xiang Yu. The change in strength brought quick success to Liu's forces. Under these circumstances, Xiang Yu had to adopt a realistic attitude and he proposed that the two of them divide the country with the Honggou (now the Jialu River in Henan) as their border. Xiang Yu would have the territory east of the river as Lord of Chu, while the west of the river would be the territory of the Lord of Han, Liu Bang. When this agreement was reached, Xiang Yu released Liu's father and wife, Lü Zhi.

As Liu Bang began to pull back westward, his advisers Zhang Liang and Chen Ping, suggested to him, "Xiang Yu is moving eastward because he wants to preserve his forces and he is sure to try to make a comeback later on. The best thing for you to do is to take advantage of his retreat and wipe his army out. If you let go of this golden opportunity, it will mean that you are releasing a ferocious tiger back into the mountains and there will be dire consequences."

So, under the command of Han Xin, the Han troops attacked the retreating Chu army and, with an ambush at Gaixia (southeast of present-day Lingbi County, Anhui), trapped the Chu army in a tight seige. A fierce battle ensued without any clear winner. The Han troops then brought some people who could sing the folk songs of Chu to teach them to all their soldiers. The ensuing psychological warfare worked like a miracle. When night fell, the folk songs of Chu coming from all directions were heard by the Chu troops under the command of Xiang Yu. This sent the Chu troops into great alarm. Why was it so? It must mean that the Han troops have occupied Chu and familiarized themselves with the region, otherwise how could so many Han soldiers sing the local songs? The singing thus greatly reduced the morale of Chu soldiers.

All night long, Xiang Yu sat and drank in his camp without arriving at any solution as to how to break the seige. Only his beautiful concubine, Lady Yu, kept his company. Outside, his horse called Zhui whinnied. Xiang Yu was gripped with a sense of sorrow and loss as he chanted a tragic tune, the words of which he made up himself: "My strength uprooted mountains, my spirit overtopped the world; but the times are against me, and Zhui can gallop no more. When Zhui can gallop no more, what can I do? And what is to become of Lady Yu?" To show her total devotion to Xiang Yu, Lady Yu killed herself, a tragedy that later gave rise to a classic Chinese opera *Lord Xiang Yu Bidding Goodbye to Lady Yu*, which is still staged today.

In the dark of night, Xiang Yu mounted his horse and took his remaining troops of eight hundred men in an attempt to break through the enemy lines. They fought and fled with five thousand Han soldiers in hot pursuit. When he came to the bank of the Wujiang River (in present-day Hexian County, Anhui), a quick head count by Xiang Yu showed that there were only twenty-eight soldiers left. A station master at the river, who happened to know Xiang Yu, urged him to come on board his boat and sail across the river. But Xiang Yu replied, "Thank you for your good will. However, I used to command eight thousand soldiers from east of the river and now I have come back alone. How can I face the elders who made me their king?"

He presented his horse to the station master and engaged the pursuing Han troops for a final combat. Not wanting to be a captive of Liu Bang, Xiang Yu cut his own throat.

In the sixth month of 202 BC, Liu Bang brought the whole country under his unified rule and ascended the throne as the founding emperor of Western Han, with the title of Gaozu (Supreme Founder) of Han.

While entertaining his generals and officials at a grand banquet after he took the throne, Liu Bang posed this question: "My beloved generals and officials, what do you think that made me defeat the powerful Xiang Yu and become the only emperor of the country?"

Wang Ling, a minister, was the first to speak. "My Highness," he said, "though you treat your subordinates arrogantly and rudely, you know whom to put in what position so that they can do what they are best at. You maintain a clear and explicit system of rewards and punishments so that people work for you willingly. Xiang Yu, on the other hand, appeared to be courteous and polite, but deep in his heart he was conceited and arrogant. He only trusted his kinsmen who, even when they turned out to be useless, were still placed in important positions. Those who were not related to him by blood were never put in important posts, even when they had rare talents. After his men won victories, he never rewarded them nor shared the profits from his land with them. I believe these are the factors that brought his doom."

Liu Bang said, after he heard Wang Ling out, "There is truth in what you say. However your answer is not complete. In making a long-term military plan, I'm no match for Zhang Liang; in running a country and providing food and payment, I'm no match for Xiao He; in commanding the army and fighting on the battlefield, I'm no match for Han Xin. But when these three rare talents worked for me, how could I not succeed? Look at Xiang Yu. All he had was Fan Zeng and, more often than not, he refused to accept Fan's suggestions. These are the reasons for his failure."

Everybody at the banquet was impressed by Liu Bang's ability to know his subordinates well enough to assign them jobs commensurate to their abilities.

Eight years of warfare, first against the Qin and then between the Han and Chu, left the country weak and its people poor. Like a person with a serious illness, it was hard to see any quick recovery. When Liu Bang went on an inspection tour as the founding emperor of the Western Han Dynasty, people could not even find four horses of matching colour to pull his carriage. When his ministers came to the court in the morning, they had to settle for using ox-pulled carts. A man of extreme courage and insight called Lu Jia reminded Liu Bang that, "He won the country by military force, but he could not run it by force. He should thus maintain order by the rule of culture and learning."

Liu Bang, who was born into a poor family and hitherto had spent his entire career on the battle-field, despised scholars. A typical example of this was that he once took the hat of a scholar to serve as his urinal so as to deliberately put the scholar to shame. Now, as emperor of the country, he totally changed his behaviour. He praised Lu Jia for his theory of "rule by learning" and had him write *The New Politics* in which he emphatically illustrated the point of abrogation of tyrannical rule, abolishing of cruel torture, reducing people's burden of taxation, and the theories of "letting people recover their normal life" and "governing by doing nothing that goes against nature." Lu Jia wrote twelve chapters and everyone of them received high commendations from Liu Bang. The book is still available today in Chinese. The theories in the book were adopted by Liu Bang, who further improved them and they eventually became the guiding principles for govern-ing the newly-established Western Han Dynasty. The theories were applied during the next fifty to sixty years.

In the early days after the founding of the Western Han, Liu Bang was also greatly influenced by another scholar, Shu Suntong. Those who had fought with Liu Bang during the war years had little sense of respecting the dignity of the emperor and observing court rituals. Often they drank at court and argued with each other about who was the most distinguished in the war. When they couldn't agree on certain things, they would pull out their swords to cut a pillar in order to intimidate their opponents. Liu felt there was a need to put an end to such disorder and to tighten discipline. So he made Shu the chief administrator of the erudite and asked him to draw up a new set of court rituals by comparing the ancient ones with those of the previous Qin Dynasty. Then Liu Bang trained his court ministers and generals according to the new rituals. After that, when the court met, no one was heard making loud noises and everyone behaved courteously. Only then did Liu Bang remark with great satisfaction, "Now I really know what esteem and dignity an emperor enjoys."

6. Eliminating the meritorious aides

After Liu Bang rose from a peasant rebellion leader to the position of emperor, he did all he could to preserve his rule. In order to draw support for his fight with Xiang Yu, Liu Bang had enfeoffed seven princes who were not related with him by blood. These included Han Xin as Prince of Qi, Ying Bu as Prince of Huainan and Peng Yue as Prince of Liang. These princes gradually grew to be powerful after they were enfeoffed and this led to conflicts with the central court. Liu Bang decided to deal with the three one by one.

The first one he took on was Han Xin, Prince of Qi, who was a "man of extreme merits" and controlled great military power.

In 201 BC, Zhongli Mei, who had originally served Xiang Yu, went to see his old friend Han Xin who kept him at his court and thus protected him. When this was reported to Liu Bang, the emperor secretly sent people to verify the matter. The agents happened to see Han Xin as he went out on an inspection tour. Noting the impressive procession Han Xin had, the agents did not bother to make any further investigation, but went back and reported that Han Xin was indeed preparing for rebellion.

Liu Bang, now Emperor Gaozu, wanted to take his army and fight Han Xin immediately, but his counsellor, Chen Ping, offered the opinion that it was not good tactics to deal with Han Xin by force, since the latter was so powerful in military might. The counsellor suggested that the emperor make a trip to the Yunmeng Marshes, supposedly for sightseeing at this scenic spot and summon all the princes to come to see him. Han Xin would have to come also and he could then be arrested by a few armed soldiers. To this suggestion, Liu Bang exclaimed, "Good idea!"

Han Xin had doubts about being summoned for a tour to Yunmeng, but his aides told him, "You've done nothing wrong except for allowing Zhongli Mei to take refuge here. This has aroused the suspicions of Emperor Gaozu. If you have Zhongli Mei killed and take his head to the emperor, the emperor will be happy and put the matter behind him."

So Han Xin summoned Zhongli Mei and beat about the bush as he let him know what was bothering him. Understanding the message, Zhongli Mei said, "The reason that Liu Bang dares not send troops here is because we are together and we can put up joint resistance. If you kill me to make the emperor happy, the next one to be killed will be you." Yet Han Xin expressed no regrets about his decision, sending Zhongli Mei out to shout at the top of his voice, "I should not have come to you, a changeable mean coward!" So saying, Zhongli Mei took his own life.

Han cut his head off and went with it to see the emperor, accompanied by only a few aides.

As soon as Han Xin arrived, Liu Bang had him arrested and bound up. Han then said, with great indignation, "Now that the hare is dead, the hunting dog is to be killed and cooked. When the birds are gone, the arrows and bows can be put away. When the enemy is crushed, the loyal generals are to be killed. Now that you have become secure as emperor, it is of course time you killed me." He was pushed onto a prison cart and taken to Luoyang, the capital.

Later someone tried to persuade Emperor

Gaozu to release Han, saying that Han Xin's merits far exceeded his mistakes. So in the end, the emperor released him and demoted him to Marquis of Huaiyin.

During the fight with Xiang Yu, there was need for such a military talent as Han Xin. If he had resigned and retired after the establishment of the Western Han, he could have survived easily. Han Xin, however, was not a man who could live in solitude and this had created the tension between him and his emperor. Once during a chat, Emperor Gaozu asked him, "How many soldiers can I command, given the abilities I have?"

Han Xin said, without carefully thinking about the matter, "The most Your Majesty can command is 100,000 men."

Liu Bang then asked him, "How many can you command?"

Han Xin, with overdue confidence, answered, "The more, the better."

Liu Bang could not help being sarcastic at this remark. "If that's the case, how come I have you as my subordinate?"

Sensing the displeasure in the tone of the emperor, Han Xin hurriedly replied, "Your Majesty may not be good at commanding soldiers, but you are certainly good at commanding generals. That's why you have captured me. Besides, what you do is ordained by heaven and you don't have to solely depend on the number of soldiers you have."

Liu Bang smiled at this answer, but his displeasure was already registered. Whenever he took an outing, the emperor trusted palace affairs to his wife and the court affairs to Xiao He.

His wife, Empress Lü, liked to abuse her power when her husband was away on an outing. At one point someone secretly reported that Chen Xi was plotting a rebellion. After conferring with Xiao He, the prime minister, the empress had an imperial edict from Liu Bang forged, saying that Chen Xi was a rebellious general and had been caught, and that everyone should come to the court to offer their congratulations. Han Xin was the only official who refused to come.

Xiao He personally went to see Han Xin who then agreed to go to the court. When he arrived, soldiers, who had been hiding, rushed out and bound him up. Han yelled for help from Xiao He, who quietly slipped away. The empress, sitting in the Eternal Pleasure Palace, repudiated Han and gave the order to kill him, allowing him no chance to explain himself.

While fighting Chen Xi, Emperor Gaozu sent for the Prince of Liang, Peng Yue, to come and help. Peng refused on the excuse that he was sick. The emperor later had him arrested and imprisoned at Luoyang. Then the emperor decided to strip him of his noble title and send him to serve in the army in Shu.

On his way to exile, Peng ran into Empress Lü.

He pleaded his innocence and asked to be allowed to return to his home in Shandong instead of serving in the army in the western province of Shu. The empress agreed to his request and brought him back to the capital.

Back at Luoyang, the empress said to the emperor, "To send Peng Yue to Shu is like releasing the tiger into the mountains. I have brought him back and he should be killed immediately." The emperor accepted his wife's suggestion and had Peng killed. He even had Peng's head hung on the city gate tower to scare disloyal officials.

Realizing that he would be the next victim now that Han Xin and Peng Yue had been eliminated, Ying Bu, Prince of Huainan, decided wage a rebellion of his own. In 196 BC, the emperor personally led an army to put down that rebellion. On the battlefield, Liu repudiated Ying Bu by saying to him, "I made you a prince, so why do you revolt against me?"

Ying Bu answered back by asking a question of Liu. "Xiang Yu once made you the Prince of Han, so why did you rise to fight him?"

No longer able to suppress his anger, the emperor ordered his troops to charge at the enemy. In the confusion that followed, Liu Bang was hit in the chest by an arrow. Luckily he was wearing very thick armour and narrowly escaped death. He pulled out the arrow and continued to fight despite pain in the chest, inflicting a total defeat on Ying

Bu. Ying Bu was then assassinated as he tried to escape to Changsha.

In the third month of 195 BC, the emperor's chest injury from the arrow wound worsened. He called in the court officials and made them drink the blood from a white horse that had just been slaughtered as part of a swearing ceremony. They murmured these words as they swore: "Whoever, other than a descendant of the Liu family, dares to take supreme power should be fought by all under heaven." This rule, however, was soon broken by Empress Lü.

7. Empress Lü takes over the supreme power

On his death bed, Emperor Gaozu discussed with Empress Lü the arrangements to be made after his death.

The empress asked him, "After you die and after Xiao He dies, who should be the next prime minister?"

The emperor answered, "Cao Can." He was one of those who launched the rebellion in Peixian together with the dying emperor years before.

The empress further asked, "Then who should succeed Cao Can?"

The emperor replied, "It should be Wang Ling. Wang is honest and straightforward. Chen Ping should be asked to assist Wang. Chen is resourceful but cannot run the court as a prime minister. General Zhou Bo is strong-willed but lacks cultural learning. Yet you must rely on him to maintain political stability. He should be made the supreme commander."

His wife wanted to ask more, but Liu Bang waved his hand to stop her, saying, "You won't live long enough to need to know any more from then on."

These last instructions of Liu Bang proved to be correct according to later political events, which was a further example of his ability to know people and put them in proper posts.

In the fourth month of 195 BC, Emperor Gaozu died at the age of sixty-two in the Eternal Pleasure Palace.

Four days after his death, the empress still did not allow the release of his obituary, for she was busy plotting with her trusted aides. Her plan was to keep the death a secret so she could wipe out all the long-time loyal followers of the dead emperor. Since two of the generals, Zhou Bo and Chen Ping, were stationed away from the capital, she feared her actions might cause contrary consequences. Eventually she decided to implement her plan and have her own son, Liu Ying (211 – 188 BC), succeed the throne with the title of Emperor Hui.

Emperor Hui took the throne at the age of seventeen. As he was a timid person, virtually all state affairs fell under the control of the empress, who was an extremely jealous and cruel person. She directed her first attack on Lady Qi who was both her arch rival for the emperor's love and a major political opponent.

Young and beautiful, Lady Qi had won the deep love of Emperor Gaozu. She once succeeded in convincing the emperor to remove Liu Ying as the crown prince so that her own son could take over the vacated position. Now with the emperor dead, the empress gave vent to her long-suppressed anger and hatred and began to retaliate against Lady Qi. She had her imprisoned, cut her hair, put handcuffs and shackles on her and made her work at husking rice.

Though Lady Qi's son had been named the Prince of Zhao, he was only twelve years old and away in Hebei at the time. So he could not protect his mother.

While husking rice, Lady Qi sang songs to express her sorrow and the words in the songs further enraged the empress. She summoned the Prince of Zhao to the capital in the hope that she could have both the mother and son killed.

However, before his death, Emperor Gaozu had entrusted the protection of his youngest son, now the Prince of Zhao, to a trustworthy general, Zhou Chang, who simply ignored the summons of the empress. Later the empress used a ruse to take Zhou Chang away from the young prince. Then she summoned the prince again so that he was compelled to come to the capital.

The broad-minded and kind-hearted Emperor Hui went out of the capital to personally meet his half brother, the Prince of Zhao, after he realized that his own mother was harbouring ill towards the half brother. The emperor brought his brother, who had nearly taken away the throne, with him to his palace. They ate and slept together, making it difficult for the empress to take action.

One morning the emperor went to practise archery, but the young Prince Zhao wanted to sleep in. Seizing this opportunity, Empress Lü sent people to murder the young prince with poisoned wine. All the emperor could do on his return was to cry his heart out.

Next, the empress had Lady Qi's four limbs chopped off and two eyes gouged out. She fed her some poison to make her lose her voice. Then she had her thrown into a toilet and called her a "human pig." She took the emperor to look at this "human pig." Upon learning that what he had been taken to see was Lady Qi, the beautiful woman whom his father loved so much when he was alive, Emperor Hui was so terrified that he became sick. After that he was no longer able to attend court affairs. Soon afterwards he died. Now the empress stepped forward to "personally administer the court," becoming China's first de facto woman emperor. To consolidate her power, she placed her relatives of the Lü clan in important positions and enfeoffed them as princes in different regions.

Now the right prime minister, Wang Ling, spoke out. He said bluntly, "When he was alive, Emperor Gaozu made us drink the blood of a white horse and swear to attack anyone not from the Liu clan who wanted to take state power. We should not go back on our pledge."

Chen Ping and Zhou Bo, however, said, "It was right for Emperor Gaozu to enfeoff his brothers and sons and it is also right now for Empress Lü to enfeoff her nephews."

After the court was dismissed, Wang Ling indignantly reasoned with Chen Ping and Zhou Bo as to why they had gone back on their pledge to the late emperor.

Chen and Zhou replied, "We're not your match when it comes to face-to-face argument with the empress. But in restoring Liu's rule, you're not going to be our match."

Ignoring Emperor Gaozu's instructions to attack whoever not from the Liu clan wanted to become princes, the empress made her four nephews, Lü Tai, Lü Chan, Lü Lu and Lü Tong, princes and six other members of the Lü clan marquises. She also married women from the Lü clan to members of the Liu clan. Ostensibly she wanted to make the relationship closer. In reality, she was tightening her control over the Liu clan.

In the seventh month of 180 BC, Empress Lü became fatally ill. She arranged to make Lü Chan the prime minister and commander of the northern army, and Lü Lu the first general and commander of the southern army. On her death bed, she urged these two, again and again, saying, "Emperor Gaozu made people pledge not to allow any members outside his Liu clan to be princes and run the state. Now that we Lüs are in power, the generals and ministers are resentful. They are sure to make trouble after my death. You should keep a strong grip on the army and protect the palace. You should not leave the palace even for a single step during my funeral."

After the death of the empress, the Lüs held military and political power. Though called the supreme commander, Zhou Bo held no real power, neither did Chen Ping, who was the left prime minister. After a secret conference, they decided to make use of Li Ji's close relationship with Lü Lu. Li Ji tried to convince Lü Lu, saying, "You should consider giving up your military power and serve as the Prince of Zhao so that people won't suspect you of taking advantage of the emperor's young age for your own purposes, after the death of the empress."

Lü Lu thought Li Ji meant this for his own good and so he turned over his military power to Zhou Bo. With power in hand, Zhou Bo gave the order: "Those who support the Lüs roll up your right sleeves and those supporting the Lius roll up your left sleeves." All the people in the military rolled up their left sleeves to show their support of the Liu clan. Led by Zhou Bo, Chen Ping, and Lu Jia, other veteran officials of the Western Han court and the princes of the Liu clan represented by Liu Zhang were mobilized. They caught all the Lüs and put an end to their lives.

In 180 BC, Liu Heng, formerly the Prince of Dai, was made Emperor Wen in a bid to revitalize the Western Han Dynasty. History proved exactly what Emperor Gaozu had predicted: "It has to be Zhou Bo who will restore the rule to the Lius."

III Liu Xiu, the "Bronze Horse" Emperor Who Revived the Han Court

In AD 8, Wang Mang (45 BC – AD 23), a distant relative of the royal family of Western Han, proclaimed himself emperor and set up a new dynasty. Liu Xiu (6 BC – AD 57), was a ninth generation descendant of Liu Bang, the founding emperor of the Western Han Dynasty. To restore the Han Dynasty, Liu Xiu launched a revolt in Nanyang and, after over a dozen years of war, re-established Han rule in AD 25. He took the throne with the reign title of Emperor Guangwu and made Luoyang his new capital. Since Luoyang is east of Chang'an, the original capital of the Western Han, historians refer to the newly-revived Han Dynasty as the Eastern Han. It became the third most powerful unified kingdom in the history of China.

1. The de facto emperor, Wang Mang

To discuss Liu Xiu, we have to deal with Wang Mang first. Wang entered the palace in the capacity of being the nephew of Wang Zhengjun, wife of Emperor Yuan of the Western Han. Ostensibly, Wang was a modest and courteous person, who was diligent, honest and often gave his own family property to help the poor and needy, thus winning praises far and wide. However, Wang Mang was a careerist at heart. All the time he was trying to win support of others so as to gradually realize his goal of becoming the emperor.

In the sixth month of 1 BC, Emperor Ai died and Wang Zhengjun, grandmother of the deceased emperor, took control of state affairs. She made her nephew Wang Mang the chief minister at court. From then on, Wang surrounded himself with a group of close followers. Whenever he had a demand, he would send one of his followers to appeal for this to the empress dowager. And once she had given her consent, Wang Mang would pretend to decline the offer before he accepted it. In return, he promoted his followers and placed them to important posts in the government apparatus.

In the ninth month of the same year, after conferring with his aunt, the empress dowager, Wang put the nine-year-old Liu Kan on the throne with the title of Emperor Ping. The boy emperor was too young to make any decisions and so the court was still presided over by his grandmother. But, in effect, Wang Mang was running the court. People throughout the country knew that their fate was in the hands of Wang Mang, and few people even knew that there was an Emperor Ping.

At the age of fourteen, the young emperor, who had then been on the throne for five years and was beginning to understand how things worked, began to develop a dissatisfaction with Wang Mang's tyranny. Whenever he saw Wang, the young emperor showed his displeasure. Often he was briefed about the wrongdoings of Wang Mang. Wang, however, had planted his trusted agents in the emperor's palace and every action of the emperor was faithfully reported to Wang. Wang realized that young as he was, the emperor was already openly resentful of him. It would likely be a terrible situation for him once the emperor grew up. Consequently, Wang began to harbour the idea of having the emperor killed.

Wang one day proposed a toast to Emperor Ping who, after drinking the poisoned wine offered by Wang, became fatally ill during the night. The next day, news came out of the emperor's palace that his highness was seriously ill and none of the palace doctors knew what to do. Very happy to hear the news, Wang pretended to be struck by deep sorrow and personally went to the palace to visit the emperor. He had someone write a message of prayer in which he went so far as to say that he would himself rather die if it might help the emperor recover. Several days later, the fourteen-year-old emperor died.

Wang then put a two-year-old boy called Liu Ying on the throne, while he himself served as regent. Three years later, he made the young emperor abdicate and proclaimed himself the new emperor in the eleventh month of AD 8. He named his dynasty Xin and proclaimed the end of the Western Han.

Putting away his courteous pretensions, Wang sent his cousin Wang Shun to demand the imperial seal from his aunt, the empress dowager. The jade seal had been made under the supervision of Prime Minister Li Si of the Qin Dynasty, after Bian He, a native of the State of Chu, offered a piece of beautiful jade to the would-be First Emperor of Qin during the Warring States Period (475 – 221 BC). When Zi Ying, the last emperor of the Qin Dynasty, surrendered, he presented the jade seal to Liu Bang, founder of the succeeding Western Han Dynasty. And thus the seal was passed on from emperor to emperor throughout the Western Han Dynasty. Hearing of the death of Emperor Ai, Empress Dowager Wang Zhengjun immediately went to Weiyang Palace, residence of the emperor, and took the seal to her Eternal Pleasure Palace. She kept it for nine years. Now, to demand the imperial seal that was the symbol of state power from the empress dowager, meant that Wang Mang was pressuring her to give up her power. Wang Zhengjun, who had brought this nephew to the centre of power, never expected to be pressured by the person she had so pampered and supported. Crying, she angrily told Wang Shun, "It is I who has made it possible for the Wang clan to enjoy their power and luxury. Instead of thanking me, you want now to take the power away from me. You're worse than pigs. If you want to be the emperor, go and make a seal for yourself. I don't have much time left and, as a widow of the Liu family, I will take the imperial jade seal to my tomb."

Wang Shun was struck with grief by her aunt's situation. Also crying, he reasoned with her, "Wang Mang will have the seal at whatever cost. As his subordinate, there is nothing I can do to help you. You will have to give it to him sooner or later."

Realizing she was now no match for Wang Mang, Wang Zhengjun threw the seal on the floor, breaking off part of its dragon – shaped handle. Wang Shun picked up the pieces and took them to Wang Mang, whose eyes radiated with excitement when he saw this symbol of supreme power. He called his followers to the Weiyang Palace and held a big celebration.

2. Liu Xiu rises in revolt

After usurping state power, Wang Mang implemented a reform of the political system. Instead of adopting measures in response to real needs, he looked for ways of governing in ancient books. Thus his reform only created disorder. The rules were such that the common people were always committing offences against the law. Frequent legal penalties and natural disasters threw the people into dire hardship. Wang himself began to realize that he was in difficulty.

One day someone asked one of the palace attendants, "What does Wang Mang look like?"

The man who attended Wang in his everyday life described him in this way: "He is short and fat, with bulging eyes and a giant mouth, and his voice is hoarse." He added, "In effect, he has an eagle's eyes, a tiger's mouth and a wolf's voice. He looks like killing and eventually he will be killed by others."

When these words were reported to Wang Mang, the servant was immediately put to death. After this incident, however, Wang became more cautious than ever against any attempted assassination. All day long he shielded himself behind a screen made of a mica sheet and wouldn't let anybody get near to him.

Still, peasant rebellions broke out all over the country against Wang Mang.

In AD 17, 50,000 rebels gathered at the Lulin Mountain (present-day Dahong Mountain in Hubei) under the command of Wang Kuang and Wang Feng, both natives of Xinshi (now Jingshan County in Hubei). These rebels were known as the Green Grove Army.

In AD 18, a revolt led by Fan Chong of Langya (present-day Zhucheng, Shandong) spread to the neighbouring counties in Shandong and Jiangsu. These rebels dyed their eyebrows red and were thus known as the Red Brow Army. Quickly this force grew to tens of thousands in size.

At the same time, several dozen rebel forces were active on the vast plain areas on both banks of the Yellow River.

It was not just the peasants who revolted, rich landlords also built private armies to fight the Xin Dynasty of Wang Mang. At Nanyang, Liu Yan and Liu Xiu, brothers who were descendants of the Western Han royal family, decided there was now a good chance to restore the rule of Han. So they gathered eight thousand family members and young men of local rich families to announce their revolt in Chongyang (east of present-day Zaoyang County, Hubei). They were called the Chongling Army.

There is a legend about Liu Xiu. He was said to have been born into the family of Liu Qin, magistrate of Jiyang County (northeast of today's Lankao County, Henan) in the last month of 6 BC. As soon as he came to the world, a bolt of red lightning turned the dark room as bright as in day. It was also said that in the fields that year, wheat and rice crops of nine ears on a single stem were spotted. So his father named him Xiu, which means sturdy crops.

His father died when he was only nine years of age and so his uncle brought him up. Tall, with a broad forehead and beautiful beard, Liu Xiu was a smart and handsome man. Working in the fields at a young age, he become a diligent and experienced farmer. It was not until after he was more than twenty years old that he went to study at Chang'an. Then he returned home to tend his farmland.

During the initial days of their revolt, the rebels from the Liu clan were rather hesitant, fearing suppression. They blamed Liu Yan for acting too hastily without careful planning. But when they saw that Liu Xiu was also wearing a red robe and a wide-rimmed hat as one of the leaders of the rebel force, they felt assured, saying, "Liu Xiu is always careful, honest and kind. Now that he has joined the rebels, we will follow him. There will be no regrets."

Liu Xiu and his men first took the county seat of Zaoyang where they captured a great quantity of booty. When dividing this booty, people from the Liu clan took the largest share, causing discontent among the other rebels and leading to infighting. When Liu Xiu learned of this, he persuaded his clan members to divide their booty with the others, thus avoiding splits and fighting within the ranks.

3. The battle at Kunyang

Wang Mang regarded peasant rebels such as the Red Brow Army as a bunch of "starved bandits," but he took the Chongling Army, also known as the Han Army, seriously. It was led by Liu Yan and Liu Xiu, descendants of the Han royal family, and was an army that mobilized people under the slogan of restoring the Han Dynasty, disseminated lists of

Wang's crimes, and called on the people to fight him. This army designated Liu Xuan as sovereign ruler with the title of Emperor Gengshi, and chose Wancheng (now Nanyang City, Henan) as their capital. They successively took Kunyang (present-day Yexian County, Henan), Dingling (northeast of today's Yancheng County, Henan) and Yancheng (present-day Yancheng County, Henan), demonstrating that they were ready to win back the power of the state from Wang Mang.

Though worried by the situation, Wang Mang pretended that he was not at all troubled. Then sixty-eight years old, he still searched for beauties in the country and made one young woman his empress. To look youthful as a bridegroom, he had his hair and beard dyed black. It was not until after the elabourate wedding was over that he dispatched a force of 420,000 to Kunyang for a decisive battle with the Han Army.

Kunyang was guarded by a force of merely 8,000 to 9,000 men. The army of Wang Mang, which seemed to stretch out endlessly, sent many of the defending army scattering. Most of them wanted to flee the city.

Liu Xiu now stood up and said, "We must stand firm at this critical junction. The last thing we should do is to lose our confidence." Hearing this, the defending soldiers calmed down and were ready to carry out the orders of Liu Xiu, who told them, "The city wall here at Kunyang is tall and thick.

Our enemy will find it very difficult to break into the city. You should guard it without going out to engage the enemy. Meanwhile, I will break out and try to bring assistance."

Liu took thirteen guards and dashed out of the city in the dark of night to solicit help from the armies at Dingling and Yancheng.

It was the sixth month of AD 23 when Wang Mang's army besieged Kunyang, encircling it tightly and raining arrows into the city. The defending forces had to carry door boards to protect themselves against the incoming arrows whenever they went outdoors to get water. Wang Mang also used war chariots to bang against the city wall and nearly completed a tunnel dug to lead his forces into the city.

At that point, Liu Xiu charged Wang Mang's forces with three thousand cavalrymen. Three thousand was a small number indeed, but they charged into the enemy ranks at such lightning speed that they were able to kill the enemy commander Wang Xun. The besieged soldiers and residents rushed out and Wang Mang's army, now sandwiched between the two forces and without a commander, was thrown into confusion. They fled in all directions, falling over each other and inflicting casualties onto themselves. Then they were caught in a rainstorm, and as Wang Mang's army hurried to cross the swelling river thousands were drowned. Those who were still alive ran towards Luoyang as fast as their legs could carry them. This battle, the battle at Kunyang, came to be known in Chinese military history as a typical example of a small army wiping out a large army.

The battle at Kunyang inflicted a fatal blow to Wang Mang's army. Under the attack of rebel forces all over the country, the Xin Dynasty quickly fell. Only Luoyang and Chang'an were still held in its control.

While Liu Xiu was winning the decisive battle at Kunyang, his brother, Liu Yan, was fighting his way into Wancheng. These battles made the two brothers known far and wide, and led to jealousy on the part of Emperor Liu Xuan. Liu Xuan was a weak and totally incompetent person. When he was made emperor by the Han Army, he "was so shy that he was sweating all over and speechless." When he reached Chang'an and saw the magnificent palaces and well-dressed palace officials and attendants, he did not dare to raise his head. All day long, he sought pleasure from women and wine in the residential quarters. He, however, was surprisingly resolute and ruthless when it came to safeguarding his power. At a banquet to entertain his generals, Liu Xuan deliberately pulled out the sword of Liu Yan and examined at it. Just then, his trusted aide Shen Tujian presented Liu Xuan with a piece of jade. These were signs that Liu Xuan wanted to get rid of Liu Yan, but that he had not yet found the proper excuse to do so.

After the party was over, Fan Hong, the uncle of Liu Yan, said, "Liu Xuan's behaviour reminded me of the banquet at Hongmen when Xiang Yu's adviser, Fan Zeng, raised his jade as a sign for Xiang to kill Liu Bang. We must be more cautious."

Liu Ji, a general under Liu Yan, did not think much of the emperor, and so he said, "It was the two brothers of Liu Yan and Liu Xiu who raised the banner in fighting Wang Mang. Emperor Gengshi had nothing to do with it!"

When these words were passed on to the emperor, Liu Xuan decided his chance had come. So he had the big-mouthed Liu Ji arrested. Liu Yan went to see the emperor to appeal on behalf of Liu Ji, only to be labelled a supporter of Liu Ji. Liu Xuan would not let this opportunity slip away and so he had both Liu Yan and Liu Ji killed.

News of his brother's tragic death took Liu Xiu by surprise. Realizing that he did not have the strength to confront the emperor, Liu Xiu buried his indignation and went to apologize to the emperor for his brother's mistake. Openly, he refused to wear clothes of mourning for his brother and cut all his contacts with his brother's subordinates. He ate and laughed as usual to show no change of mood. It was with such restraint that he was able to fool Liu Xuan and stay alive.

Later, the emperor sent Liu Xiu to be stationed in Hebei, a move that revealed the emperor's lack of vision. This was just like releasing a tiger into the mountain. It buried the seed for his doom in the years to come.

4. Building his power base in Hebei

After Wang Mang's Xin Dynasty had been reduced to the two isolated cities of Luoyang and Chang'an, Wang scraped together a force to fight Liu Xiu. But as soon as the two forces engaged, Wang's army gave up and fled.

Though about to die, Wang did not want to give up his wealth. He sat in the front hall of the palace, with the imperial jade seal taken from his aunt dangling on his body and a dagger in his hand, guarding his treasures of gold and jade, and not providing any rewards for his defending soldiers.

Assisted by people from all walks of life who were against Wang Mang, the Han Army soon fought its way into Chang'an. Wang Mang was killed and his tongue, with which he had fooled so many people, was cut out and chopped into pieces.

Wang Mang's death made Emperor Gengshi feel somewhat secure. He decided that Wanxian was not large enough to be his capital and wanted to move to Chang'an. But most of his subordinates were from the east and wanted to move the capital to Luoyang, to which Liu Xuan agreed. Having gone through a fierce war, Luoyang was in complete shambles. The emperor gave the task of rebuilding the palace to Liu Xiu. During the day, Liu Xiu worked hard, laughing and talking as if he were in high spirits. When night came, however, he shut himself up in his home and cried. One day a trusted follower, Feng Yi, saw that Liu Xiu's pillow was wet and tried to persuade him to refrain from sorrow. Liu immediately told the man, "Don't say a word about this."

Since Liu Xiu disguised his emotions well, Liu Xuan gradually relaxed his guard against him. As someone was needed to guard Hebei, he decided to send Liu Xiu to accomplish this task, allowing him to take only a few aides and servants, instead of an army.

When Liu Xiu entered Yecheng (west of today's Linzhang, Hebei Province), a close friend from school days came to see him and said, "Emperor Gengshi is incapable and only knows how to enjoy luxury. All his close aides know is to amass wealth for themselves. They won't last long. Now that you've come to Hebei, you should make use of the opportunity to get to know gallant people, bring a peaceful life to the local population and begin your career of re-establishing the Western Han." His general Feng Yi also suggested to him, "You should do a few things to win people's support, such as abolishing the cruel regulations and laws of Wang Mang, righting the wrong verdicts, releasing the wrongly accused from prison and telling people the virtues of the Western Han." Liu accepted these suggestions and did as he was told after he took up his post in Hebei, much to the joy of the local people.

In governing Hebei, Liu Xiu ran into his first difficulty at Handan. While discussing ways of conquering the Red Brow Army with his men in Handan, a man called Liu Lin, a prince of the Western Han royal family, proposed that they break the river dike and flood the million-strong Red Brow Army east of the river.

But it was a time for Liu Xiu to pacify the people in Hebei and to win their support, and so he naturally turned down this suggestion. Liu Lin, dissatisfied, went to see Wang Lang.

Wang Lang was no ordinary man. He claimed to be the son of Emperor Cheng of the Western Han Dynasty and a singer. He said that Empress Zhao Feiyan had once wanted to have him killed, but luckily palace maids put another boy in his place so that he could escape and stay alive. With this story he had made up, Wang Lang deceived many people. Now he and Liu Lin banded together, with Wang being called the emperor and Liu Lin being his prime minister. They turned Handan into a little kingdom of their own.

Finding Handan a hostile place, Liu Xiu travelled north to Jixian County (southwest of present-day Beijing), only to find that the magistrate there had announced himself loyal to Wang Lang. The magistrate even said that "Whoever catches Liu Xiu will be rewarded by being made into a marquis with tributes from 100, 000 households." Liu Xiu detoured Jixian and went to Raoyang. Tired and hungry, he could not travel anymore. He pretended to be an envoy from Wang Lang and asked for a meal at a courier post. When the food was brought to the table, his followers gulped it down like hungry wolves, which naturally aroused the suspicion of the post officials who tried to sound them out by telling them, "A general from Handan has arrived on an inspection tour." This caused Liu Xiu and his party to turn white with fear. Liu Xiu got into his carriage and was ready to flee but, on second thought, he decided that it was impossible for his party to flee away safely. So he told the post officials, "Ask the people from Handan to come out and I'll see them." They waited a long time and nobody came out, so Liu Xiu and his party were able to finish their meal and leave.

They arrived at Xindu (northeast of present-day Jixian County, Hebei). The governor there was Ren Guang who came from the same hometown as Liu Xiu and had fought at his side in the battle of Kunyang. He welcomed Liu Xiu into the town where Liu Xiu made Ren Guang the grand general. Together they took several other counties and their army grew to several dozen thousand strong.

In the fifth month of AD 24, Liu Xiu led his army to attack Handan. Wang Lang tried to flee in the night but was captured. He was beheaded. Thus Liu Xiu finally had all of Hebei under his control.

While examining the archives kept by Wang Lang, it was discovered that a great many of the reports submitted by prefectural governors and county magistrates sang praises of Wang Lang and smeared Liu Xiu. Refusing to read them, Liu ordered they be burned in public. People asked him why he behaved this way. He smiled and said, "To burn them will allow those who find it hard to sleep (referring to those who wrote the reports) to sleep well." People admired his generosity and united around him.

In reorganizing his army, Liu Xiu adopted a completely new measure: letting the soldiers choose the commander they wanted to serve under. All the soldiers told him, "We want to follow the Big Tree General."

Liu Xiu had to ask, "Who is the Big Tree General?"

"Feng Yi," he was told.

During battles, Feng Yi always charged at the forefront, but when the battle was over and other officers vied with each other for merits and rewards, Feng Yi would quietly sit under a big tree, without saying anything about his own merits. People admired him for this and fondly gave him the nickname.

After Liu Xiu took Handan and wiped out Wang Lang, Emperor Liu Xuan's fear of him began to grow. He immediately sent an envoy to bring Liu Xiu back to the capital. Liu Xiu, however, did not want to leave the power base he had just managed to build up so he said, "Hebei is still unstable and it is not yet time for me to go back to Chang'an." With this, he openly showed his disloyalty towards Liu Xuan.

Firmly planted in Hebei, Liu Xiu turned his attack on the peasant rebels. Those he could pacify, he did. Those he could not, he suppressed. In the fall, he defeated a powerful peasant rebel force called the Bronze Horse Army at Guantao. After the battle, he met with the rebel army leaders and made several of them marquises. He saw that some of them were not taking their loss lying down, and so he announced, "Those who do not admit defeat can go back to your own forces and let us fight another battle to see who will be the winner. How about that?"

The Bronze Horse Army was moved by this and expressed their willingness to follow Liu Xiu from then on. Now Liu Xiu's army grew to be half a million in strength. Since he had won over the Bronze Horse Army, he became popularly known as the Bronze Horse Emperor.

Liu Xiu worked hard to win over the hearts of surrendered enemy generals and soldiers. For example, he would go among them, talk with them, ask questions, and laugh with them so that they felt that Liu Xiu treated them just as he did his old comrades-in-arms.

At the time, the Red Brow Army was still quite powerful. Recognizing that Liu Xuan, Emperor

Gengshi, was marching towards his doom, they found a cow tender called Liu Penzi and made him their emperor. Liu Penzi was said to be closely related with the royal family. This man who began tending cows at a very early age was really not at all interested in becoming emperor.

With the emperor they instated, the Red Brow Army began to march towards Chang'an to bring down Emperor Gengshi, who soon lost the war and handed the imperial seal to Liu Penzi, the cow tender now turned emperor. Troubled by lack of grain, the Red Brow Army marched towards the east and was wiped out by Liu Xiu in Henan. Fan Chong, the leader of the Red Brow Army, took along the newly-instated emperor to surrender to Liu Xiu. The imperial jade seal now became the possession of Liu Xiu. By this time, all the uprising peasant forces such as the Green Forest, Bronze Horse and Red Brow armies had been defeated by Liu Xiu, who enjoyed the final fruit of the national rebellion against Wang Mang.

In the sixth month of AD 25, Liu Xiu proclaimed himself emperor in Hao (north of present-day Baixiang, Hebei). Later he made Luoyang his capital.

5. The rule of gentleness

When Liu Xiu, now known as Emperor Guangwu of the Eastern Han, entertained his royal family members, several of the older women members could not help saying with admiration, "Wenshu (a name Liu Xiu used during his childhood) was a very careful and honest person even as a child. Never did I expect to see such a gentle child to grow up to be the emperor."

Liu Xiu chatted amiably with these ladies, telling them "I now use the same gentleness to run the country."

Yes, Liu Xiu was a person who best combined gentleness with resoluteness and always adopted the right strategy. He proved to be successful during the war years and now he adopted the same strategy in running the country. He first reduced taxation, liberated slaves, righted wrong verdicts and abolished cruel punishments and torture so as to win the hearts of the people. Later, he streamlined the government, demobilized large numbers of soldiers so as to reduce government spending and promote production. He was down to earth and diligent. As a result, production was quickly restored once the war was over. Historians describe his rule as a period of "revival and rejuvenation" and praise him as an outstanding emperor.

The following stories to illustrate their conclusions:

Liu Xiu was receptive to good advice. Once he came back late from a hunting trip and the east gate of the city wall was already shut. Zhi Yun, a minor official in charge of the gate, refused to open it, saying, "To shut the gate after nightfalls is a rule made by the emperor and it is not to be broken by anyone."

Liu Xiu moved near the gate so that Zhi Yun could clearly see that he was the emperor, in the hope of making him open the gate.

But Zhi Yun said, "It's so dark that I cannot see clearly. I won't open the door for you."

The emperor had to make a detour and entered the city from the central gate.

The next day, Zhi Yun wrote a petition for the emperor, reading, "Your Highness not only went out hunting, but came back very late. How do you find time to manage state affairs?"

The emperor decided there was something in what he said and so rewarded the man with a hundred bolts of cloth. The man who opened the door for him at the central gate was criticised.

Liu Xiu had a sister called Princess Hu Yang whose servant murdered someone. The servant hid in the princess' home. Unable to go in and catch the murderer in the princess' palace, Dong Xuan, the county magistrate, waited to capture the man during an outing of the princess' convoy. He had the man put to death in front of the princess.

Feeling that she had been publicly humiliated by the county magistrate, the princess reported the magistrate to the emperor. The emperor had the magistrate brought to the court to be whipped so as to pacify his sister.

Dong Xuan, the county magistrate, however argued, "Your Highness is the leader of the programme of rejuvenation, but you allow the princess to protect a killer. How can you rule the country well in this way?" So saying, he tried to commit suicide by throwing himself against a stone pillar.

The emperor told his aides to stop him, and said, "I'll let you go if you kowtow to the princess and make a self-criticism."

Dong Xuan refused. Palace guards tried to press his head down into a kowtowing position, but he stood upright, holding his head high.

Emperor Guangwu admired the man for his uprightness and had a dinner prepared for him after persuading the princess to leave. The county magistrate ate everything served to him and then turned the plates upside down on the table. Palace eunuchs dragged the man before the emperor, saying that by turning the plates over, he was expressing his contempt for the court. When asked why he did so by the emperor, Dong Xuan said, "When I ate the food bestowed on me by Your Highness, I knew I should eat with all my ability just as I do my work. By turning over the plates I have intented to say that I have eaten all the food granted to me."

Instead of criticising him, the emperor burst into laughter and gave him some money as reward. Dong did not keep the money for himself, but divided it among his subordinates in the county government.

Liu Xiu was always eager to enlist capable people. Yan Ziling, once a classmate of his, was very talented. The emperor had a picture of him drawn by painters according to his recollections. He then sent people carrying this portrait, to search for the man all over the country. At the time, Yan was living in seclusion and it took a great deal of effort before he was found fishing by a river.

The emperor had a house built for him and sent people to tend to his every need. When the emperor went to visit Yan personally, Yan turned his face to the wall, pretending not to know that the supreme ruler who had come to see him. The emperor walked up, touched his belly, and asked, "My old friend Yan Ziling, don't you want to help me?"

Yan cast a glance at the emperor and replied, "People have different aspirations and you should not force me to do what I don't want to do."

Still, when evening came, Emperor Guangwu took Yan back to the palace and shared his bed with him. Yan pretended to snore loudly and put his leg on top of the emperor's body. The next day, the emperor told him he was to be made the grand master of remonstrance. Yan then said to the emperor, "You should not force me to do things. Otherwise you're putting our friendship in jeopardy."

The emperor had to let him go. However, when stories circulated about how the emperor loved people of talent, many men offered their services and helped him build the country. After years of recovery and development, an unprecedented time of economic prosperity and social stability appeared in the Eastern Han.

IV   Three Generations of the Sima Family that Ran Two Dynasties

The founding of the Western Jin (265 – 316) put an end to the contention of the Three Kingdoms Period (220 – 280) and brought China a short period of reunification. Four emperors reigned during the Western Jin for a total period of fifty-two years.

Sima Yan (236 – 290), the founding emperor of the Western Jin, was a man of unsurpassed talent. From his grandfather, Sima Yi, to his uncle, Sima Shi, to his father, Sima Zhao, and to himself, the three generations of the Sima family all served as prime ministers for the State of Wei (220 – 265) and their merit and power were recognized all over the country. In the last month of 265, Sima Yan forced Cao Huan, or Emperor Yuan of Wei, to cede the throne to him with the reign title of Emperor Wu of Jin. He changed the name of the dynasty to Jin, which later became popularly known as the Western Jin. Four people in three generations of the Sima family ruled the two dynasties, first Wei and later Jin. Such a high degree concentration of talent and power within one family was rather rare in Chinese history.

1. Faking illness in preparation for power

Sima Yi (179 – 251), grandfather of Sima Yan, was a man of exceptional talent and boldness. When Cao Cao (155 – 220), the founder of the State of Wei, asked for his services, Sima Yi felt it would be too humiliating to serve Cao Cao, who came from a rather lowly background, so he chose to stay at home and pretended to be ill. Cao Cao thought highly of his talent, however, and had him captured so as to force him to accept the official post. Cao Pi (187 – 226), son of Cao Cao, also had great respect for Sima Yi.

The many merits he performed gradually elevated Sima Yi to a position of a major general and strategist at the centre of the state power of Wei. On his sick bed, Cao Pi entrusted his son Cao Rui, soon to become Emperor Ming of Wei, to Grand General Sima Yi. In assisting the young emperor, Sima Yi fought bravely and held in his hand the supreme military power. After the death of Emperor Ming, he assisted the eight-year-old ruler, Cao Fang, together with Cao Shuang, who was the son of the late grand general Cao Zhen. In contention for the supreme power of the State of Wei, an intense struggle then broke out between Sima Yi and Cao Shuang.

At first, Cao Shuang was respectful to the senior general, Sima Yi. Later, egged on by others,

Cao Shuang grew ambitious and became eager to expand his own forces. He petitioned the young emperor to reduce the political and military power held by Sima Yi and to make him serve only as the grand teacher for the young sovereign.

The astute Sima Yi pretended disinterest in the increasing growth of the power for Cao Shuang and stayed at home on the grounds of bad health. Secretly, he helped his son, Sima Shi, to take a firm grip of the command of the imperial garrison troops.

In the winter of 248, Li Sheng was appointed regional commander of Jingzhou. Cao Shuang sent him to bid farewell to Sima Yi and to try to find out whether or not he was faking illness. Sima Yi turned Cao Shuang's trick against him by pretending to be seriously sick. He came to greet Li Sheng with the help of two housemaids and with dishevelled hair. During their meeting, he asked for a bowl of porridge which, when brought to him, he did not accept with his hands, but stuck out his head to sip it from the bowl held by the maid. Soon porridge began to leak out of the corner of his mouth and onto his chest. In the conversation, what he said often followed no logic. Li Sheng reported to Cao Shuang that, "Mr. Sima is really critically ill." This false report put off Cao Shuang's worries and he grew more unscrupulous in seeking power.

When spring came the next year, together with his brother, Cao Shuang, who had not let down his guard against Sima Yi, they accompanied Emperor Cao Fang and the court ministers in going to offer sacrifices at the tomb of Emperor Gaoping, south of the capital. Sima Yi, until then still faking illness at home, seized the opportunity to launch a surprise coup. Clad in a military outfit and in high spirits, he led his two sons to shut the gates to the capital city of Luoyang and lift the suspension bridges over the moat, thus cutting off the Cao brothers' return to the city. He also released a decree he forged in the name of the empress dowager, listing crimes committed by Cao Shuang. Then he sent an envoy to negotiate with Cao Shuang, promising him that if he admitted his guilt, all that would happen to him was that he would be stripped of his official post.

Huan Fan, a confidant of Cao Shuang, insisted that he admit no defeat, but should instead take the emperor to Xuchang where he could issue a call in the name of the emperor, mobilizing the people to fight the Sima family and thus begin to fight their way back to the capital.

Cao Shuang, however, was a man lacking vision and bravery. He was rather hesitant whenever it was time to make a major decision. He shut himself in his room and thought hard throughout the night. Next morning, he threw his sword on the ground and said, "All Sima Yi wants is to take the power away from me. Let him do it and I'll return to my residence and enjoy a wealthy life."

These words enraged Huan Fan who could not

help saying to him, "Never did I expect that the resourceful and gallant grand general to have you two brothers as his sons. You're worse than beasts! We'll all suffer because of you."

Later events proved that Huan Fan was right. As soon as the Cao brothers returned to their home in Luoyang, Sima Yi sent several hundred people to surround their residence. He captured the two brothers and later killed them after accusing them of committing treason. From this event onward, the power of the State of Wei was in the hands of the Cao clan only in name. State affairs were in the control of the Sima family. Emperor Cao Fang had to listen to everything Sima Yi said. When Sima Yi was sick and stayed at home, the emperor had to personally visit him and ask for advice at his home.

In the eighth month of 251, Sima Yi died at the age of seventy-three. He was succeeded by his son, Sima Shi, whose job was to assist the emperor in running the country. More domineering in the court than his father had been, Sima Shi could demote or kill at will members of the Cao clan or officials on intimate terms with them. Emperor Cao Fang was indignant and secretly conferred with his trusted aides on how to strip Sima Shi of his military power. Sima Shi, however, noticing what was going on, acted first, forcing the emperor's mother to issue a decree instructing Emperor Cao Fang to abdicate. Once a mighty emperor, Cao Fang now had to leave the city in an ox-drawn cart, crying as he bid goodbye to his former ministers and generals. Cao Mao, the grandson of Cao Pi, was made the new emperor. At the age of fourteen, all he could be was a puppet controlled by the Sima clan.

Sima Shi's rude and unreasonable behaviour aroused discontent among court officials. In 253, General Mu Qiujian and Wen Qin, regional commander of Yangzhou, joined their forces in a revolt against Sima Shi.

At that time, Sima Shi was resting at home after undertaking an operation to remove a tumour from his eye. News of revolt forced him out of bed. He personally led his army to the battlefront to fight the rebel army. As a result, his eye disease worsened as his eyeball dropped out of its socket.

Sima Shi won the battle, but he knew his final days had come. He called his brother, Sima Zhao, over and told him, "You should succeed me as the grand general and keep the military power firmly in your hands. You should never delegate major decisions and power to any others, or you might be inviting death to our entire clan."

As soon as he finished these words, he died after a loud cry.

2. Killing of the emperor

After Sima Shi's death, his brother, Sima Zhao, became the grand general, firmly keeping the military power in the hands of the Sima family.

He even outshone his father and brother once he took control of the real power of the State of Wei. One example was his success in putting down a rebellion led by Zhuge Dan in 257.

One day of the fifth month in 260, Emperor Cao Mao made known his displeasure at the fact that three men of the Sima family had controlled the court of the State of Wei for so long. He told three senior officials, indignantly, "Sima Zhao's ill intent is obvious. I will not sit tight and wait for him to tell me to abdicate. I want you to fight him now."

Wang Jing, the grand secretary, tried to persuade the emperor to do otherwise, saying, "The Sima family has been in power for a long time. They have built a strong power base and Your Highness should not act hastily. Besides, the imperial guards are rather weak and it will be difficult for them to win such a battle."

Still, Cao Mao brought out an imperial decree he had already written. He threw it on the floor and said, "I have made up my mind. I am not afraid of death. Besides, we may not have to die."

Wang Shen and Wang Ye, the other two senior officials, secretly told this all to Sima Zhao.

On that very same day, Emperor Cao Mao got into his carriage and went with several hundred guards to fight Sima Zhao.

Sima Zhao was well prepared and was waiting for the arrival of the emperor with a strong army of his own led by General Jia Chong. The two sides arranged themselves in battle formation at the front of Sima Zhao's residence. Waving his sword, the emperor shouted in a loud voice. "I'm here to capture Sima Zhao. Whoever dares to stop my advance will be killed along with the members of three generations of his family." The soldiers guarding Sima's residence were afraid and began to pull back. Some even laid down their weapons. Jia Chong, however, roared at his troops, "Mr. Sima has fed you and paid you for this day. If he loses, we will also be murdered."

At that moment, Cheng Ji, an officer in Sima Zhao's guard, stepped forward and asked, "Do you want the emperor captured alive or killed?"

"Kill him!" Jia Chong told the officer.

So Cheng Ji walked up to the emperor and stabbed his knife into his chest. The emperor dropped from the carriage and died instantly.

Learning that his subordinate had killed the emperor, Sima Zhao realized this was an extraordinary event. He immediately called court officials for a conference, at which he said hypocritically, "This was really unexpected. How should we deal with it?"

Chen Tai, a veteran official, answered, "We must kill Jia Chong by way of acknowledging his mistake in murdering the emperor."

Sima Zhao did not agree. He decided to make Cheng Ji the scapegoat. Cheng Ji, however, would not accept the verdict. With both shoulders bare, he climbed onto the roof and cried out, "I'm being wronged. It was Sima Zhao who told me to kill the emperor." As he continued to shout, many people gathered to look at him.

An order was issued to shoot him to death with arrows.

Sima Zhao had hoped to kill Cheng Ji and thus pacify public opinion, but Cheng Ji's words revealed the truth of the event. Astute as he was, Sima Zhao did not dare to take the throne himself. A month later, he made Cao Huan, the fifteen-year-old grandson of Cao Cao, the new emperor.

3. Unifying the country

Having murdered Emperor Cao Mao, Sima Zhao now had the entire state under his control. So he launched a massive offensive against the State of Shu.

At that time, three states, Wei (220 - 265), Shu which was also known as Han (221 - 263) and Wu (222 - 280) divided China into three separate parts. In order to unify the country, Wei had to conquer Shu and Wu.

In 263, General Deng Ai of Wei led his troops into Chengdu, capital of Shu, by taking a small mountain path. As they neared Chengdu, Liu Shan, the incapable ruler of Shu, didn't even think of putting up any resistance. He had his servants bind

his hands behind him and surrendered to the attacking army, taking along with him hundreds of civil and military officials.

Liu Shan was brought to Luoyang, capital of the State of Wei, and was demoted to the position of Duke of Anle. To win over the hearts of the people of Shu and maintain stability there, Sima Zhao held a grand banquet to entertain the former officials of Shu. During the dinner, the band played the music of Shu, which moved the surrendered officials to tears. Liu Shan alone among the guests was laughing foolishly.

After the dinner, Sima Zhao asked Liu Shan, "Are you still homesick and thinking of Shu?"

Laughing, Liu Shan told him, "I enjoy it so much here, I no longer think of Shu."

Xi Zheng, a former Shu official, tried to talk to Liu Shan, saying, "Your answer just now was not quite appropriate. Next time you're asked similar questions, you should cry and say, because my ancestors are all buried in Shu, how can I not miss Shu?"

Later, when Sima Zhao again asked Liu about whether he missed home or not, Liu replied in the way he had been told, but he failed to produce any tears.

Sima Zhao asked him, "How come your answer sounds something like what Xi Zheng said?"

Liu Shan believed that Sima Zhao could almost foretell things and so he admitted, "It was indeed

Xi Zheng who told me to answer in this way."

Sima Zhao and his officials burst into mocking laughter, but Liu Shan did not understand what they were laughing about.

After conquering Shu, Sima Zhao was crowned Prince of Jin with an enfeoffment of twelve prefectures. Later, he had flags made like those used by the emperor and he even enjoyed the same music and dance rituals as the emperor did. Sima Zhao, who was just a stone's throw away from the throne, died in the eighth month of 265. It would be his son who would eventually ascend the throne.

Sima Zhao was succeeded by his son Sima Yan (236 – 290). On the 17th day of the last month of 265 by the lunar calendar, Sima Yan held a grand ceremony at which he compelled Emperor Cao Huan to "abdicate and hand over the crown" to him, by following the precedence of the way Cao Pi forced Emperor Xian of Han to give up the throne. First, a ceremony was held in the suburbs of Luoyang to pray to heaven. Emperor Cao Huan announced that "he was willingly" offering the throne to a wise minister, while he would abdicate and live in seclusion. As soon as the ceremony was over, he was struck with such remorse that he cried his heart out. Sima Yan, however, pretended to refuse the offer three times before he finally agreed to it. He took the imperial seal into his hands, the symbol of state power, and changed the dynastic title to Jin. Thanks to the merits of his grandfather and father, he finally realized the goal of becoming the emperor.

Only the State of Wu still stood independently. Sima Yan, now known as Emperor Wu of Jin, busily made preparations to conquer Wu and thus unify the country.

Sun Hao was the spoiled and debauched emperor of Wu. In a state with a population of just 2. 3 million, he had over 5,000 concubines in his palace. Arrogant and rude, he did not allow his subordinates to look at him face to face. When they made a report to him, they had to hold their heads low. Over a period of more than a decade, he had more than forty loyal ministers and generals killed, arousing much hatred inside and outside the court.

In the winter of 279, Sima Yan sent out a force of 200,000 men under the command of General Du Yu to attack the State of Wu at six different places. Wherever the Jin army marched, Wu troops surrendered. As Liu Shan of Shu did, Sun Hao also had his hands bound behind him in order to beg for the acceptance of his surrender, taking with him a coffin and hundreds of court officials. General Wang Jun of Jin had his hands unbound, the coffin burned and accepted his surrender. As a result, confrontations and splits in the last one hundred years of the Eastern Han Dynasty and the sixty-one year situation of three states existing in rivalry came to an end. Once again China was a unified country.

Sima Yan adopted many reform measures after

thus unifying China. He encouraged farming and rewarded farmers, built irrigation networks, practised frugality, reduced punishment and promoted talented people. These measures brought about social stability and economic recovery so as to make the period known among historians as "the prosperity of the Taikang era" (Taikang being the reign title of Sima Yan).

4. Debauched emperor; extravagant officials

Even before he conquered the State of Wu, Sima Yan gave an order to "bring to the palace beautiful girls from honest and minor officials' families." He even made an absurd rule that before his selection of these beautiful girls ended, no woman was allowed to marry. At one time in 274, some 5,000 girls were brought to the palace. At that time, however, Sima Yan was pretty diligent with his court duties and people did not treat his selection of so many girls too seriously. After he conquered Wu, however, he thought that now that peace had been restored it was time for him to enjoy life, a rather debauched one. In 281, he brought all the 5,000 concubines that Sun Hao, the Emperor of Wu, had kept in his residence into his own palace. How could he decide which beauty he would sleep with every particular night? He found a way. Every evening, he would sit on a little carriage pulled by sheep and where the sheep stopped, he would go into the room and sleep with the occupant there. To attract the emperor, the concubines devised their own method. They knew sheep loved to eat bamboo and lick at whatever was salty. So they competed with each other by planting bamboo and leaving salt in front of their rooms to attract the sheep to that room first, and so the emperor would get off and come in.

As the emperor lived in luxury and pleasure all day long, his court officials followed suit. Luxury and pleasure seeking became the fashion of the day.

Shi Chong became wealthy by looting merchants who passed by when he served as the regional commander of Jingzhou. He had a villa called the Golden Valley Garden built in Heyang (present-day Mengxian County, Henan) which became known far and wide for its sumptuousness and splendour. Wang Kai, a court official, unscrupulously extorted and plundered so much wealth that he grew rich almost instantly, simply because he was the uncle of Sima Yan. When Shi Chong and Wang Kai competed with each other in amassing wealth, the emperor secretly aided his uncle.

When Wang Kai washed his wok with sugar, Shi Chong burned wax instead of firewood. When Wang Kai used purple silk some twenty kilometres long as his carpet whenever he took an outing, Shi Chong outdid him by using twenty-five kilometres of brocade.

Wang Kai was given a piece of coral by the emperor that was two feet long. He took it to show off in front of Shi Chong. But Shi took the piece of coral and smashed it with iron. Then he told his servant to bring out the corals he possessed. Those exceeded three or four feet in length and numbered six or seven. Pointing at them, Shi said to Wang, "Your decorative coral which I just smashed is not worth pitying. Take one of these."

Shi Chong had a girl musician called Green Pearl. She was particularly good at playing the flute for the pleasure of her master. Sun Xiu, a confidant of the Prince of Zhao, or Sima Lun, asked to be given Green Pearl to the resolute rejection of Shi Chong. Sun Xiu thus accused him of treason and sent soldiers to arrest him.

Shi Chong said to Green Pearl, "I've offended Sun Xiu because of you. Today is the end of me."

With tears in her eyes, Green Pearl answered her master. "I won't let Sun Xiu have it his way. I'll die as a way of thanking you for your love." With that, she jumped out of the window of the building.

Shi Chong was arrested and sentenced to death. Before being killed, he sighed, "I know that what you are really after is my wealth!" Indeed his ill-obtained wealth brought his own doom.

He Zeng, the prime minister, spent ten thousand strings of cash for his daily food and still complained that there was nothing to eat. His son, He Shao, outdid him by doubling the amount of money he spent on food.

Wang Ji, the son-in-law of Emperor Sima Yan, had weakness for horses. At the time, land was very costly in Luoyang, but he still bought a large piece of land for his horses. The low walls around his stud-farm were built of copper coins. So people referred to the farm as "Gold Valley." One day, he offered a family dinner for Sima Yan. All the delicious food was placed in transparent glass containers. The emperor found one particular dish quite tasty and so he asked how it was cooked. Wang Ji told his father-in-law, "It was a small pig raised with human milk and then stewed in human milk. That's why it's so delicious." The emperor concluded that extravagant as he could be, he was outdone by his son-in-law. So he put down his chopsticks and departed.

5. An idiot in the imperial seat

In picking his successor, Emperor Sima Yan made the fatal mistake by naming his retarded son as the crown prince. He was Sima Zhong, who was then only nine years old.

Quite a few court ministers believed that the crown prince was so ignorant that he could not shoulder the tasks of being an emperor, but his emperor father would not listen to their opinions.

Once when the ministers were having a dinner with the emperor, Wei Guan, the grand secretary, pretended that he was drunk and said in a muffled voice, "Your Highness, there is something I want to tell you."

The emperor told him to speak out, but Wei Guan managed to hold the words back before he revealed what he had in mind. Instead, he touched the emperor's throne with his hand and sighed, "What a great throne! What a pity!"

The emperor understood what he meant, but said deliberately, "You're indeed drunk." After that, Wei Guan never mentioned the topic again.

In reality, Sima Yan was aware that this son of his did not have the IQ to be an emperor, but Empress Yang insisted, "It is not virtuous to fail to make the eldest son the crown prince." Besides, the emperor believed that, though his son was somewhat retarded, the prince's son was clever and there was hope for the future. Once when the palace caught fire, Sima Yan ascended the city wall tower to suvey the situation. Suddenly a tiny hand pulled at his shirt rim. He looked down and saw his five-year-old grandson, Sima Yu, who said to the grandpa emperor, "It's getting dark and you should be more cautious for any emergencies. Just don't let yourself be unnecessarily exposed." If he was still wondering whether he should make another son the crown prince, the emperor, now deeply impressed by the grandson, gave up such thoughts.

What remained to be done was to find his son a virtuous and capable wife to assist him. After much observation, he decided that Wei Guan's daughter would be the choice. Empress Yang, however, insisted that Jia Chong's daughter should be the wife because the empress had accepted bribes from Mrs. Jia Chong, whose maiden name was Guo.

Sima Yan tried to reason with her. "Mr. Wei's daughter has five capabilities but Mr. Jia's daughter has none. The Weis are virtuous and have a large family. His daughter has a fair complexion and is tall and beautiful, but Mr. Jia's daughter is short and dark and their family is known to have an inclination for jealousy. Besides their family is small, with only few sons."

Finding it hard to convince the emperor of her decision, Empress Yang asked a few ministers to help her persuade the emperor. They told him that, "Mr. Jia's daughter is unusually beautiful and talented. She has the virtues of an empress." In the end, Sima Yan agreed to make Jia's daughter his son's wife. At first it was to be the second daughter, Jia Wu, who was the candidate. But she was too young and too short, and so she could not support the costumes worn for important ceremonies. So Jia Nanfeng, the eldest daughter, became the bride.

Jia Nanfeng had inherited all the shortcomings of her parents. She was short and rather dark complexioned, apart from being extremely jealous in nature. She was, however, a calculating and cunning person. Three years older than the prince, she managed to hold him under her control. The prince loved her and feared her at the same time.

Jia Nanfeng's jealousy came from her mother, Guo Huai, who was the second wife of Jia Chong. Jia's first wife, Lady Li, was exiled to the border region after her father was convicted as a criminal and killed. Later, Sima Yan pardoned Lady Li and asked Jia Chong to bring Lady Li back home and reinstate her as his first wife. When this happened, the second wife, Guo Huai, made a great fuss and Jia Chong had to put Lady Li into a separate house. He did not even dare to visit her in her isolated dwelling. Guo Huai had given birth to two children. When the first child was three years old, he stretched out his little arms one day, asking his father to hold him in his arms. Just as he was taking the child from the wet nurse, Guo Huai saw them. She suspected that her husband and the wet nurse were having an illicit relationship and so beat the nurse to death. Now without the wet nurse to breast feed him, the child cried, fell ill and soon died. Later another wet nurse was holding the second child in her arms when Jia Chong, the father of the child, fondly touched his child's head with his hand. His wife, Guo Huai, saw this and again suspected that her husband was having an illicit relationship with this wet nurse. So she also beat this wet nurse to death. Without the care of a wet nurse, the second child died as well.

After Jia Nanfeng became the wife of the

crown prince, she personally killed several women that her husband, Sima Zhong, loved, out of extreme jealousy. One concubine was already pregnant with Sima Zhong's child, when Jia Nanfeng had her, along with her unborn baby, poked to death with a halberd. When Emperor Sima Yan learned of the outrageous wrongdoing of his daughter-in-law, he flew into a rage and wanted to annul her marriage to the crown prince. Jia Chong's supporters all went to speak on behalf of him and begged the emperor to be lenient. Their efforts paid off and Jia Nanfeng was able to maintain her position in the royal family.

To further test his son's ability, Sima Yan had some documents sent to his eldest son and asked him to decide how to deal with the issues raised in them. Jia Nanfeng, the wife of the crown prince, was worried that her husband would not pass this test. So she found someone to write down solutions and then asked her husband to copy them. Sima Yan did not know this and happily showed the solutions offered by his crown prince to Wei Guan, who felt rather uneasy since he was the one who had touched the throne and remarked, "What a great throne. What a pity!" Jia Chong secretly told his daughter, Jia Nanfeng, "That old slave Wei Guan once nearly overturned the position of the crown prince." Jia Nanfeng took this to heart and gritted her teeth in hatred towards Wei Guan.

6. An ugly woman and a vicious empress

In 290, Emperor Sima Yan died and his throne was then occupied by the thirty-two-year-old crown prince Sima Zhong, who took the reign title of Emperor Hui. Jia Nanfeng was elevated to the position of the empress at the age of thirty-five.

Sima Zhong, the new emperor, was still as foolish as he had always been. All day long, he found pleasure in eating, drinking and playing. Once he took a group of guards to tour the Hualin Garden where frogs were heard singing. Sima Zhong asked his subordinates: "Are the frogs singing for the court or for private individuals?"

His question took those who accompanied him by surprise. They wanted to burst out laughing, but did not dare to do so. Someone made a clever answer by saying, "Those in the official land are singing for the court while those in private plots are singing for individuals."

The reply satisfied the emperor who kept nodding foolishly.

One year there was a severe famine and petitions for help poured into the court from all over the country. After listening to the report, the foolish emperor thought for a while and then said, "Since they have no rice to eat, why don't they eat meat porridge? I don't eat rice for breakfast. All I have is a bowl of meat porridge." The officials waiting for a decision from the sovereign ruler didn't know whether to laugh or cry after hearing such a remark from the emperor.

Foolish as he was, the emperor was at the mercy of his family and court officials.

Before he died, Sima Yan, afraid that his idiot son could not handle state affairs and therefore could not stay on the throne for long, asked Yang Jun, his father-in-law, and uncle Sima Liang, then Prince of Runan (fourth son of Emperor Sima Yan's grandfather Sima Yi), to assist Sima Zhong in handling official duties. Yang Jun was a careerist. He drew up support, monopolized decision-making at the court and tried to muscle Sima Liang out of the way to such a degree that the latter didn't dare to come into the palace. Yang Jun also knew that the wife of the emperor was not an easy person to deal with. So he acted quickly by declaring Sima Yu, the son of Emperor Sima Zhong and Xie Mei, the crown prince. Empress Jia Nanfeng realized that her husband was incompetent, but she was capable. She wanted to take the power into her own hands, instead of leaving things in the hand of Yang Jun, who was not related by blood to the royal family. So she mobilized members of the Sima clan and those of her maternal family for a showdown with Yang Jun.

In the third month of 291, Empress Jia secretly summoned Sima Wei (the fifth son of Sima Yan) to court and ordered him, in the name of the emperor, to get rid of Yang Jun, saying that Yang was trying to launch a coup. One dark evening, Yang Jun was told that military forces were being redeployed at court. He hurriedly conferred with some court officials.

"If anything happens" General Zhu Zhen said, "it is Empress Jia who is behind it. You'd better burn Yunlong Gate, open Wanchun Gate and take the emperor along to fight your way into the rear palace and have those vicious people killed."

Yang Jun, however, replied, "It took a great deal of money and much effort to have the Yunlong Gate built. How can we now destroy it by setting fire to it?"

Just as Yang Jun was trying to decide what to do, palace soldiers surrounded his residence. They shot arrows into it. Yang Jun immediately took shelter in a horse shed, but he was pulled out by the soldiers and killed with a halberd.

After Yang Jun's death, the court ministers unanimously chose Sima Liang and Wei Guan, two senior officials, to assist the emperor. Thus Empress Jia was unable to realize her plan to take the power in her own hands. So she acted again, making the emperor issue a decree sending Sima Wei to attack and kill Sima Liang and Wei Guan. After this was done, she denied that the emperor had ever issued any such decree, thus making Sima Wei appear to be a criminal who killed two senior court ministers on his own initiative.

Someone tried to persuade Sima Wei to kill the empress, after he had killed the two senior ministers, and thus make himself the emperor. But before he could fully understand the significance of what was involved, the empress acted. As Sima Wei was being taken to the execution ground, he pulled out the emperor's decree and yelled, "I acted according to orders. Why am I convicted as a criminal? I'm being wronged and framed!"

With one stone Empress Jia had killed three birds, removing from the political scene Sima Liang and Wei Guan, who dared to contradict her, and getting rid of Sima Wei of whom she felt jealous. Now she had a firm grip on the state power. Immediately she appointed trusted aides to important posts and ran the court the way she liked. This gave rise to a saying: "The fake empress (her name. Jia, in Chinese, was a homonym for the word fake) has become the real emperor."

As she succeeded on the political front, she began to feel even more strongly that her idiot husband could not satisfy her womanly needs. Her first target was Cheng Ju, the imperial doctor. Under the pretext of not feeling well, she often called Cheng Ju to her palace. Cheng Ju alone, however, could not meet all the needs of the empress, who was at the prime of her youthfulness. Secretly she sent people to look for handsome young men, most of whom served her for one night and then were secretly murdered so as to shut their mouths. Only a tiny minority of young men, who could really exite her sexually, were able to survive.

According to one story, a handsome young man, clad in exceptionally luxurious clothes, was seen walking in the streets of Luoyang one day. He caught the attention of many young women who kept stealing glances at him. The county magistrate decided that such a young man could not afford to buy such expensive clothes and so he must have stolen them from someone. So he had the young man brought to the court for questioning. The young man told the magistrate the truth. "One day as I was walking idly in the street," he said, "when an old woman suddenly came up to me and asked if I was married. I told her I was not. Then she told me that someone in her family was sick and a young man was needed to help expel the evil spirit in her house so that the patient could be cured. She helped me climb into a big chest on a cart that was immediately pulled away. After going several kilometres, I was let out. I was surprised by the dazzlingly magnificent palace around me. It was like I was in heaven. Then I was told to take a bath, given beautiful clothes and fed a delicious meal. When evening came, a woman of about thirty-five or thirty-six years of age came out. She had a rather dark complexion and was rather short. She pulled me into her bedroom and told me to take off my clothes and sleep with her. I did so for several days and enjoyed it very much. Before I was told to leave, she gave me this robe and told me that whenever I missed her, I should put on this robe and someone would come to pick me up." Those questioning the young man realized that the route he took, the house he entered, and the age, complexion and size of the woman all indicated that it was Empress Jia. So they immediately released the young man so as not to bring any trouble on themselves.

Since she had not given birth to any son of her own, the empress was very resentful that Sima Yu had been made the crown prince. She stuffed some silk under her jacket and pretended that she was pregnant. When her sister gave birth to a son, the empress brought the baby to her palace and raised it as her own child, giving the boy the name Sima Weizu. From then on she began to plan how to replace Sima Yu with her adopted son as the crown prince.

Sima Yu, despite the fact that he was bright and was deeply loved by his grandfather, did not behave well when he grew up. The empress told eunuchs to teach him only how to seek all kinds of pleasure. The crown prince's mother, Xie Mei, was the daughter of a butcher and was very good at weighing things with her bare hands. The prince learned this skill from his mother and could easily tell the exact weight of anything he held. A market was opened inside the palace so that the prince could seek pleasure by selling pork and wine. His good reputation thus began to fade.

One day the empress lied that the emperor was sick and wanted to see the crown prince. The empress told a palace servant, Chen Wu, to bring the crown prince a lot of wine so as to make him drunk. Taking advantage of the prince's drunkenness, they made him copy the following words: "His Highness should make a quick decision about himself, or I will put an end to him. . . . " Before the prince could take another look of what he was told to copy, the writing had already been taken away from him and shown to the emperor. The empress advised the emperor to tell his son, the crown prince, to kill himself. Two senior ministers, however, strongly urged the emperor not to give such an order, and so the emperor finally decided to strip the crown prince of his noble position and put him under house arrest at Xuchang.

After he was removed as the crown prince, Sima Yu feared that the empress might place poison in his food. So he often cooked for himself. The empress told Sun Lü, a eunuch, to offer the prince poison as medicine. Sima Yu refused to take the medicine and hid himself in the toilet. The eunuch followed him into the toilet and beat him to death with a wooden club used to grind medicine. The prince thus died at the age of twenty-three.

As Jia Nanfeng, the empress, had persecuted her mother-in-law, the parents of her mother-in-law and the crown prince to death, she had aroused great indignation among court officials. Ten days after the death of the crown prince, the commander of the capital garrison, Sima Lun, or the Prince of Zhao (the ninth son of Sima Yi), rose in rebellion. It was the fourth month of the year 300. The mother of Prince of Liu, whose name was Sima Jiong, was the daughter of Lady Li, the first wife of Jia Chong. Empress Jia Nanfeng and her mother Guo Huai, who was the second wife of Jia Chong, treated Lady Li as their arch enemy. So Sima Jiong took the lead among his soldiers and charged into the palace. Jia Nanfeng was greatly scared and asked, "Why did you come into the palace?"

Sima Jiong gave a crisp answer. "To arrest the empress at the order of the emperor!"

The empress then asked him, "Who started all this?"

"Prince of Zhao, Sima Lun!" she was told.

Only then did she utter a helpless sigh. "To tie up a dog," she said, "one should tie its neck. But what I did was like tying up the dog's tail. No wonder I am in such a situation."

Finally, Sima Lun issued an imperial decree to force the ugly empress to commit suicide by drinking poisoned wine. Thus, in the end, she had to take her own life.

The man who masterminded the court struggle for the supreme power from behind the scenes was Sima Lun, known as the Prince of Zhao. He first instigated Empress Jia Nanfeng to persecute the crown prince to death, and then he poisoned the empress. All of this he did with careful planning and faultless execution. Six months later, he kicked out the idiot emperor and he himself ascended the throne. His action induced resentment among dukes and princes all over the country. They rose in revolt one after another and a chaotic war ensued. This fight within the imperial family went on for sixteen years and has come to be known as "The Rebellion of Eight Princes." The idiot emperor was treated much like a basketball, being passed back and forth among the warring factions. He was first reinstated and then forced to abdicate. Finally he fell into the hands of the Prince of Donghai, whose name was Sima Yue, who fed the idiot emperor some poisoned cakes. After the emperor ate them, he fell ill and died at the age of forty-eight. The short-lived Western Jin Dynasty that Sima Yan had taken such pains to establish came to an end after only fifty-two years.

V　Emperor Wen of the Sui Dynasty and His Brutal Son

Yang Jian (541 – 604), the founder of the Sui Dynasty(581 – 618), came from a prominent family in Huayin County, Shaanxi. His daughter married Emperor Xuan of the Northern Zhou (557 – 581), one of the short-lived kingdoms that divided China at the time. Making use of the power he had, Yang Jian annulled Emperor Jing of the Northern Zhou in the second month of 581, enthroning himself as Emperor Wen, and named his kingdom Sui. During the next thirty-eight years, five emperors ruled the Sui Dynasty.

Short-lived as it was, the Sui put an end to the division and splits in China that had continued for more than two hundred years, unified the country for the third time since the days of the First Emperor of Qin, and prepared conditions for the rise and prosperity of the powerful Tang Dynasty that succeeded the Sui.

Emperor Yang of Sui, or Yang Guang (569 – 618), the second emperor of Sui, was an infamous tyrant.

1. A difficult path to the throne

Yang Jian took the first step towards official-dom at the age of fourteen. At sixteen he had already been promoted to the position of a calvary general. An official called Lai He loved to do palm reading for others. He once said to Yang Jian, "Your eyes are like morning stars, radiating with a special glow. You have an exceptionally noble look and eventually will be the ruler of the world."

When this was heard, the imperial family of the Northern Zhou was greatly disturbed. Someone suggested at that time that Yang Jian be killed.

During the reign of Emperor Wu of Zhou, the court was controlled by Yu Wenhu who tried several times to assassinate Yang Jian. Once during a hunting trip, when Yang Jian was in hot pursuit of a fox, Yu Wenhu tried to shoot an arrow at Yang, but the arrow was deflected by a general with his bow. Otherwise there would not have been an emperor called Emperor Wen of Sui.

As Yang's fame and reputation grew at court, the royal family began to step up their slander of him. One day, Yu Wenxian, known as the Prince of Qi, said to the emperor, "Yang Jian has an unusual look and every time I see him I feel uneasy. I hope you will act soon to have him removed." When this was passed on to Yang Jian, he grew worried.

Yu Wenzhao, Prince of Zhao, one day invited

Yang Jian for a dinner and Yang came with over thirty bodyguards. The Prince of Zhao only allowed two of these bodyguards to enter the banquet hall on the pretext that the hall was not large enough for more. The Prince of Zhao had already planned with his two sons to find an opportunity to kill Yang Jian during the dinner. The feast began amidst loud music. After three rounds of drinks, the Prince of Zhao's two sons came in with watermelons. The prince took out his sword and cut the watermelons. Then he held a piece of watermelon on the point of his sword and offered it to Yang Jian. He knew that if he pushed the watermelon forward, it would be the end of Yang's life. One of Yang's bodyguards, Yuan Zhou, stood closely next to Yang and put his hand on his own sword while looking menacingly at the Prince of Zhao. The prince realized that he could not escape from death if he killed Yang, so he withdrew his sword. Later the prince pretended that he wanted to vomit and asked to be excused. Yuan Zhou knew that what the prince really had in mind was to go out and bring in more troops. So he blocked his way. Just then the Prince of Teng was reported to have arrived. Yuan Zhou took the opportunity to whisper to Yang Jian, "We'd better go now." Yang could hear the sound of armour clashing behind the house and realized the danger. With the protection of Yuan Zhou, Yang quickly left the place. Later on, the prince felt remorseful at his slowness in taking action and was so angry with himself that he kept hitting the table hard until blood oozed from his fingers.

Emperor Xuan was also very suspicious of Yang. Once he had four of his favourite concubines dressed up to stand on both sides of him and he then summoned Yang to the court. The emperor told his guards, "If Yang shows any dissatisfaction, kill him." When Yang came into the court, the emperor played with the beauties, but Yang maintained his composure, giving the emperor no chance to criticize him.

Emperor Xuan lived an excessively licentious life and died at the age of twenty-two. He was succeeded by his nine-year-old son, Yu Wenyan, with the reign title of Emperor Jing. Liu Fang and Zheng Yi, two important ministers of the court, were trusted friends of Yang Jian. Making use of their power for publicizing major news about political and military affairs, they made up a decree from Emperor Jing to summon Yang to help the emperor run the court. Members of the royal family were of course unhappy with the arrangement. Yu Wenzan, the younger brother of Emperor Jing, had long wanted to be emperor himself. So once his brother died, he moved into the palace and sat next to Yang Jian when the court was in session. To foil him, Liu Fang came up with the idea of sending several beautiful women to Yu Wenzan to occupy his time and divert his attention from the court. He also said to Yu, "Emperor Xuan has just died and there is political instability. You're better off if you stay in your residence for the time being and come to the court later on." Yu Wenzan did not see through this trick and returned home with several beautiful women tailing along.

Fearing princes all over the country might rise in revolt against him, Yang Jian summoned them to the capital under the pretext that a princess was being married to a man in a distant place. He then put all the princes under his control. Someone did, however, rise in revolt. This was Chi Jiong, the commander-in-chief of Xiangzhou (southwest of today's Linzhang County, Hebei), but soon he was crushed. So on the twenty-fourth day of the second month of 581, Yang Jian declared himself emperor at a grand ceremony held in Linguang Hall in the imperial palace in Chang'an. He changed the name of the dynasty from Zhou into Sui.

2. Unifying China

In order to put an end to the separation of the north and south of the country, Yang Jian, now Emperor Wen of Sui, called a conference of top military aides to discuss the strategy for taking the southern dynasty, which was called Chen. Someone argued for building boats and training navy so as to break through the natural barrier of the Yangtze River. As a result, Yang Su was put in charge of overseeing the building of several thousand warships.

The largest one had five stories with the capacity for carrying eight hundred soldiers, while the smallest ones carried only twenty soldiers. When the navy was ready, Emperor Wen of Sui issued a statement to Chen Shubao, Emperor of the Chen Dynasty, listing twenty crimes he had committed. Over 300,000 copies of this declaration of war were disseminated in the south.

In the tenth month of 588, Yang named his sons, Yang Guang and Yang Jun, along with Yang Su, a royal family member, generals to command eight columns of a total of 518,000 men who would roll mightily towards Chen.

At Liutou Beach, Yang Su received a report that not far from this position was Langwei Beach which was guarded by Qi Xin, a Chen Dynasty general. He was told that the place was dangerous and hard either to take or to pass through.

Yang Su decided not to launch a strong attack on Langwei Beach during the daytime, fearing that he might reveal the strength of his army. Instead, he drew up plan for a surprise attack on Langwei Beach at night. Under his command, tens of thousands of soldiers carried in a thousand small boats moved quietly near to the enemy position. Yang Su also dispatched some soldiers to feign an attack from the south of the bank so as to divert the enemy's attention, and he sent the main force of his army to wage a surprise attack at the enemy's rear barracks in the north. It was a battle that ended in a great victory, lasting from midnight until dawn.

When news of battle reached the Chen court, Emperor Chen Shubao, the last emperor of Chen, summoned his generals and ministers to court. Most of them wanted to concentrate their forces for a decisive battle, but Kong Fan, the adopted brother of Lady Kong, said, "I don't believe the Sui troops will be able to cross the natural barrier of the Yangtze River!" Chen Shubao was a muddle-headed ruler and easily believed Kong Fan, saying, "We Chens are predestined to be rulers. Did not the State of Qi, which attacked us three times and the forces of the State of Zhou who attacked twice, all fail? What is there to fear from the Sui army this time?" So he and his concubines went on with their pleasure-making in the living quarters of the palace.

During the Spring Festival of 589, the Sui army launched their general attack in three columns. Only then did Chen Shubao realize the seriousness of the situation. He issued a decree saying he would personally lead the force of counterattack, but there were few soldiers left in the capital. He had to put together a force that included monks and nuns.

Finding that the Sui army was about to take Jiankang (now Nanjing), capital of Chen, General Xiao Moke suggested that all the forces be brought together to attack the forward armies of Sui before they could build a firm foothold. The only thing that Emperor Chen Shubao could do now, however, was cry. He was no longer in any position to make decisions.

Within several days, the Sui army roared into the Chen capital. Before he had time to open a jug of wine, Sui soldiers had charged into the living quarters of the palace. Chen Shubao, the emperor, jumped out of bed and ran towards a big well. A dozen palace servants ran after him and caught him before he could jump into the well to drown himself. They tried to persuade him not to kill himself, but he eventually shrugged them off and jumped into the well. When the Sui soldiers arrived, they shouted into the well and received no response. Then they threatened him. "If you don't answer, we are going to throw stones into the well!" Then a plea for mercy was heard from within the well. The soldiers dropped a rope so that the man in the well could come up. When they pulled on the rope, they found it extraordinarily heavy. After they brought the emperor up, they discovered there were also two of his most favourite concubines with him, Zhang Lihua and Lady Kong. It turned out that Chen Shubao knew that the well was rather shallow and had arranged for the two concubines to hide in the well by slipping down a rope before he jumped in himself. Looking at the three drenched people, the Sui soldiers could not help laughing.

In just a little over a month, the Sui army had across a territory with more than thirty prefectures. Chen Shubao, as a captive, was allowed to live the life of a third ranking official. All day long, he drank to kill his indignation and remorse. Several years later, he died.

Having conquered the Chen Dynasty, the Sui put an end to the separation of north and south and reunified China, laying the foundations for the rise of the great empire of Tang that was soon to emerge.

3. Advocating diligence and frugality

As Emperor Wen of the newly-founded Sui Dynasty, the new ruler was rather understanding about the life and hardships of the ordinary people. Whenever he came across people who wanted to present a petition during his inspection trips, the emperor would stop his carriage and listen to the complaint or report. One year, the Guanzhong region was hit by a drought and the people there had nothing but husks to eat. The emperor condemned himself for his inability to fight natural disasters, cut his own food ration, and stopped eating any meat and drinking any wine. He was kept busy making arrangements for the transportation of relief grain to the disaster-stricken area. Whenever furniture in the palace was broken, he would have it repaired and continue to use it. People living in the palace seldom made new clothes as they all wore mended ones. The emperor's advocacy of diligence and frugality had such a strong impact on the nation that nobles and rich people also wore coarse homespun cotton clothes instead of silk. And they did not wear expensive jewelry.

The Sui Dynasty, with a history of less than thirty years, was as short-lived as the Qin Dynasty. It did, however, occupy an important position in Chinese history. In drawing up the political system, Yang Jian, the emperor, took measures in favour of strengthening the centralized power and safeguarding state unity. He established a powerful central government of three ministries and six departments. The three ministries were the Ministry of the Chief Secretary (charged with drafting political decrees and making political decisions), the Ministry of Review (responsible for reviewing political decrees) and the Ministry of Administration. The last had six departments responsible for appointing and removing officials, administering rites, maintaining the grain supply, military affairs, judiciary affairs and civil engineering. As for local administration, the original three levels were incorporated into two levels: prefectures and counties. He abolished the more than three-hundred-year-old system for promoting officials under the control of hereditary noble families, and introduced a new system according to which, for the first time in history, candidates for official positions had to take examinations. This new method of promotion allowed middle and small landlords the opportunity to take part in political affairs and expanded the power base of the emperor. This political system was followed by all the succeeding dynasties.

In economic affairs, a system of equal land distribution was implemented whereby all people, including princes, officials and ordinary people, were subject to a restriction on the acreage of land they could own, so that all people had land to farm. This mobilized people's enthusiasm for farming and guaranteed a rise of grain production. In 592, the finance officials reported to the emperor that "The government granaries and warehouses have all been so filled with grain and cloth that even the corridors and under the eaves have become temporary warehouses." The emperor ordered more warehouses to be built. Then he was told that the new granaries and warehouses were filled with grain and cloth. This time, the emperor decided to exempt people from that year's taxation. According to records, the grain and cloth in the warehouses would last the court for fifty to sixty years. Indeed, the same storage lasted for twenty years after the Tang Dynasty replaced the Sui Dynasty.

4. The disaster of replacing the crown prince

Once Yang Jian became the emperor, he made his eldest son Yang Yong the crown prince. Yang Yong had been an eager learner from an early age and he was straightforward and honest to the liking of the emperor and empress. Though only fifteen years of age, the crown prince often joined the court ministers in discussing state affairs as a way of training himself.

But while the emperor advocated diligence and frugality, the crown prince loved luxury. A friend of the crown prince presented him with a suit of expensive armour. When the emperor learned of this, he gave his son a dressing down. Yang Yong, the crown prince, however, soon forgot his father's admonition. Once the court officials went to the crown prince's palace to celebrate his birthday. The prince changed into official garments, had drums beaten and formally accepted the congratulations and respect of the officials. The emperor had to issue a decree after this event that said: "Although my eldest son is the crown prince, he is still my subject and is not to accept congratulations from court officials." These events gradually wore thin the emperor's love and trust for the crown prince.

The empress was strongly opposed to people who forgot about their first wives once they had married concubines, and her son, Yang Yong, turned his love from his first wife to his concubine. One day the empress tried to persuade the crown prince, saying, "Your wife, Lady Yuan, is a kind person and you should care for her more than you do. You should not divert your passion to other palace ladies." Coincidentally, Lady Yuan died of a severe illness several days after this conversation and the empress suspected that she had been assassinated by her son. From that time on, the empress grew disdainful of the crown prince.

The second son, Yang Guang, had his eye on the throne and so he did everything to curry favour with his parents. Knowing that his brother had fallen out of favour because of his pursuit for luxury, the second son pretended to love a frugal life by dressing humbly. He also knew that his mother, the empress, did not approve her sons taking in many concubines, so he lived together with his wife, pretending that he was not at all interested in other women. When the emperor and empress occasionally came to his palace, he would hide his concubines and only let old and ugly palace maids be about. He even deliberately broke the strings of his fiddle and let dust gather on it. Seeing all this, the emperor and empress were quite happy, believing their second son was not interested in music and beauties. At the same time, Yang Guang collabourated with Yang Su, one of his father's trusted aides, so that Yang Su would often speak ill of the crown prince in front of the emperor and empress. In the tenth month of 600, Emperor Wen removed Yang Yong as the crown prince and put Yang Guang, instead, as first in line to the throne, against the objections of the court officials. Further, he ordered that the eldest son should be watched by the new crown prince, which made the eldest son's life more difficult. The younger brother put his elder brother under house arrest so that the latter could not get near their father. The eldest son asked many times to be allowed to personally appeal to the emperor, but he was totally ignored. He had to climb up on a tree and shout aloud in order for the emperor to hear him. Yang Guang used this incident to suggest that the former crown prince had gone mad. From then on, Yang Yong never saw his father again.

Yang Guang, now having become the crown prince, was eager to become emperor, but his father was in good health, which really worried him. Then in the seventh month of 604, his father fell ill to his great delight. Not knowing exactly what preparations he should start making for his ascent of the throne, he secretly sent a letter to Yang Su who wrote down an itemized list of things the prince needed to do. Yang Guang was attending to his father and so he temporarily lived in his father's palace. So the letter by Yang Su had to be taken to the emperor's palace in order for it to reach Yang Guang. Somehow the messenger delivered the letter into the hands of the ailing emperor, whose anger rose after he read it. At that point the emperor's favourite concubine, Lady Chen, rushed in, disheveled. Seeing her terrified look, the emperor asked her what had happened. Lady Chen said, with tears running down her cheeks, "The crown prince has been very rude to me!" In fact, the prince had long coveted Lady Chen's beauty. Taking the opportunity when the woman was changing her clothes, the prince embraced her from behind. Startled, she roared at the prince, "I'm your mother! How can you act like this to me?" Yang Guang said, brazenly, "You're no more than a step-mother! Not my mother by birth!" Lady Chen managed to free herself from his grasp and ran into the emperor's chamber. Having heard her story, the emperor was so enraged that he shouted, "That rascal! How can he shoulder up the tasks of running the country? My wife's advice to make him the crown prince has landed me into great deal of trouble." Then he asked for Liu Shu and Yuan Yan, two ministers, to come to his place and told them, "Ask my son to come here!" When Liu Shu was about to go and ask Yang Guang to come, the emperor reminded him, "I want to see Yang Yong!" Yang Su heard this and hurriedly told the news to Yang Guang who decided to charge into the palace with soldiers and besiege the emperor's Benevolence and Longevity Palace. He dismissed all the emperor's servants. Then he had a secret meeting with Zhang Heng who entered the emperor's chamber. The emperor was choking with phlegm and Lady Chen and Lady Cai were worried about what to do to help the emperor spit it out. Zhang Heng said rudely to the two empresses, "His Majesty is so ill, why don't you ask ministers to come in and hear the reading of his will? All the ministers are now waiting outside and you women should stay away from here." Under his threat the two ladies had to leave. Then Zhang Heng stabbed the emperor, whose blood splashed on a screen near the bed. The emperor gave a wild and loud cry of pain that could be heard a long way from the palace. On the very day that the emperor died, the crown prince sent Lady Chen a gold box. At first the woman thought it was poison she would have to take and so she did not dare to open it. The messenger, however, urged her to open the box. It turned out to contain jewelry symbolizing love. That very night, the crown prince raped his step-mother.

On the third day of the seventh month in 604, Yang Guang took the throne to become known as Emperor Yang of Sui.

5. A licentious and tyrannical ruler

During his lifetime, Emperor Wen once remarked to his ministers, with self-congratulation, "In the past, rulers had too many wives and concubines, and the children by different women always vied with each other as to who would be the next ruler. All my five sons were born of the same woman and are true brothers. In my house, there will be no infighting." Later events proved his prediction entirely wrong. His second son, Yang Guang, who won the favour of his parents through playing tricks, not only killed his father but also killed three of his brothers: Yang Yong, Yang Xiu and Yang Qiong. He proved to be the most licentious, ruthless and squandering emperor in Chinese history.

Soon after he took the throne, Emperor Yang

decided to move the capital from Chang'an east to Luoyang. This meant a massive-scale project that cost the labour of two million people every month. In order to make the new capital big, he forced more than 10,000 households of merchants and rich people to move into Luoyang. To build the palace, he had people collect rare timber and stones from the south. A single log brought to the palace from deep in the forests of the south cost the efforts of over two thousand labourers. From the south of China to the Central Plains, it was a common sight to see bodies of labourers who had been worked to death lying on the ground. According to archaeological studies, the original site of the ancient capital city of Luoyang was west of present-day Luoyang. It had a circumference of more than twenty-five kilometers. Traces of the original city gates and waterways can still be seen today.

Just three days after he issued the order to build the east capital, the emperor ordered the Grand Canal to be dug. The project did not mean the digging of an entirely new waterway, but one to link up the natural rivers. Still it is not difficult to imagine what a massive project it must have been over 1,300 years ago to link the Haihe, Yellow, Huaihe, Yangtze and Qiantang river systems between Beijing in the north and Hangzhou in the south with primitive tools and means of digging. The digging and dredging of the Grand Canal undoubtedly facilitated south-north economic exchanges, but what Yang

Guang had in mind was to make his own trips to the south much easier.

When the canal opened for service, the emperor took a trip south from Luoyang. His boat, called the Dragon Boat, was about 15 metres tall and 70 metres long. His wife's boat was equally luxurious, except that it was slightly smaller. Trailing behind were nine other boats called collectively the Water Palace. Further behind were large boats for the concubines, royal family members, court officials, monks and nuns. The number of boat pullers alone was more than 80,000.

If the boats containing guards were also included, the fleet stretched out to over a hundred kilometres. Wherever he went, prefectures and counties within a radius of 250 kilometres had to provide tribute in the form of food, fruits and local delicacies. What the emperor and his retinue could not consume was buried. From Yongqiu (today's Qixian County, Henan) to the Huaihe River bank, there were 129 places where the water was not deep enough for this armada, much to the displeasure of the emperor. The result was that the unhappy emperor buried 50,000 men alive.

In 608, the emperor again enlisted over a million men and women labourers to open up the Yongji Canal that joined the Yellow River in the south with Beijing in the north. The fact that he had to draft women labourers suggests that there were no longer enough men labourers.

In 610, Yang Guang, the emperor, invited many chieftains of ethnic minorities to Luoyang to watch artistic performances. His music band employed 18,000 people, whose performance could be heard dozens of kilometres away. The night was lit with so many lanterns that it was as bright as the day. The performances went on throughout the night because he wanted to impress people with a scene of peace and joy. The event lasted for two weeks. It is said that this half-month of merry-making later gave people the idea of celebrating the lantern festival on the fifteenth day of the first month.

Since the chiefs of ethnic minorities and foreign merchants wanted to come and do business, the emperor had all the stores redecorated and many large tents put up and filled with treasure goods. Even small businessmen were told to dress in luxurious clothes. When foreign businessmen passed any of the restaurants, they were invited in and treated meals free of charge. The emperor had the trees on both sides of the streets wrapped up in silk. He did all this because he wanted to show people that the Sui empire was wealthy and generous.

Emperor Yang was not content to just rule China. He began to conquer neighbouring countries as well. In 611, he started preparations to invade Korea by raising an army of 1,138,000 men with a supporting force of drafted labourers of two million. He also had wealthy families pay for the war horses and weapons. He enlisted labourers to build three hundred ships. Working all day long while standing in water, many of them suffered from water rot in their legs. Many died during the process. On the road, discarded carriages and corpses exuding a rotten smell were a common sight. In the first month of 612, the emperor issued the order to attack. He had thought that the country he was invading was small and would be easy to take. He did not realize that the people he was attacking were united and put up a tenacious defence. The emperor's forward army of 300,000 men had an initial victory and then suffered defeat. Only 2,700 escaped death.

The emperor then launched three more offensives against Korea, and his defeat grew more serious with each attack. People throughout the country began to revolt against his tyrannical rule. In 617, local officials and army officers joined the rebels or became local rulers independent from the central court. The most powerful of these separate local rulers was Li Yuan, who later founded the Tang Dynasty.

By 618, the Sui empire was practically lying in pieces. Only two cities, Luoyang and Jiangdu (present-day Yangzhou in Jiangsu), were still loyal to the emperor, who kept consulting fortune tellers and drinking to drown his worries.

He knew his days were numbered, so he had a jar of poisoned wine prepared and said to his concubines, "If the enemy attacks the palace, you should drink this wine first and then I'll do the same."

As the peasant rebellions were about to topple the Sui Dynasty, the garrison troops revolted on the third day of the third month in 618. The soldiers charged into the palace and Emperor Yang escaped by changing into civilian clothes. Guided by palace maids, the revolting officers rushed to the West Pavilion and found the emperor crying there together with his empress. The concubines had already fled and the poisoned wine could not be found. After listing his crimes, the officers decided to have the emperor killed. The emperor took off his belt and said, "I have my own way of death." An officer took the belt and tied it around his neck. Emperor Yang of Sui died at the age of fifty.

VI   Father and Son, Co-founders of the Great Tang Dynasty

The Tang Dynasty (618 – 907), a powerful empire with a prosperous economy and splendid culture, marked one of the most glorious historical stages in Chinese history.

The empire was founded together by a father, Li Yuan (566 – 635), and his son, Li Shimin (599 – 649), and it was ruled by a total of twenty emperors over a period of 290 years. During this time, a woman emperor, Wu Zetian, named her reign Zhou instead of Tang and ruled for sixteen years from 690 to 705.

1. Rise in revolt

When Li Yuan was serving as the local military commander in Taiyuan in 617, the Sui court was on the brink of falling apart under attacks from peasant uprisings. Though he held a powerful military post, Li Yuan had no aspirations for great endeavours. Instead, he was more interested in women, so much so that he even had the boldness to play around with palace maids in the auxiliary royal palace of emperor in Jinyang (present-day Taiyuan). His second son, Li Shimin, however, was a man of bravery and talent. The noble positions in his family were hereditary and in order to prepare for accepting their positions and to be commanders, he and his brothers were trained from an early age. They were well versed in military theory as well as in such fighting arts as horse riding and archery. Among the brothers, Li Shimin proved the most outstanding. The arrows he used were larger than those used by others and they were so powerful that they could pierce through door boards. From childhood, Li privately cemented strong bonds with men of gallantry and prepared to build a strong force with himself at the command. With the Sui empire about to topple, he secretly pledged to take power and to become the ruler some day.

Liu Wenjing, the county magistrate of Jinyang, had a firm belief in Li Shimin, positive that he was a man who would do great things. The two thus became trusted friends. Liu was a relative of Li Mi, and he was thrown into prison because Li Mi was a member of the rebel force. Li Shimin hurried to visit him in prison.

Liu at that time told Li, "Heaven is now under great disorder and I'm afraid there will be no man like Emperor Liu Bang of Han who can bring peace and order to the whole country." Liu said this purposely to arouse Li's aspirations.

As expected, Li Shimin replied, excitedly, "Brother Liu, how can you be so sure that there is no man who can do the same today? I came here precisely because I wanted to discuss with you this matter of most importance."

Liu offered his opinion, saying: "As there are uprisings everywhere, it is now the best time to win the power of the nation. This country of ours is full of outstanding men and, with a call from you, you're sure to be able to raise an army of over 100,000. Together with the dozens of thousands of soldiers under your father's command, you can fight your way into Chang'an and, in less than six months, you will have the whole country under your control."

Upon returning home, Li Shimin located a man who had the same physical features as Liu Wenjing and offered him a handsome sum of money as payment for him to stay in prison in place of Liu so that Liu could get out of jail and help Li realize this grand aim.

How to convince his father to join in a revolt was something Li Shimin found difficult to achieve. But then the Tujues, a northern tribal minority, launched a southward invasion. Li Yuan, the father, led his troops in a counterattack but suffered a series of defeats. Li Yuan worried that the Sui court would hold him responsible for being unable to stop the enemy invasion.

Li Shimin saw his opportunity in this situation and tried to convince his father to start an uprising against Sui right away. His suggestion surprised Li

Yuan, who roared at his son, "How can you have such an idea? I'll have you reported and arrested!"

"I'm even not afraid of death," the son said calmly, "let alone of your reporting."

The father, of course, never reported the son, but simply reminded him not to say such things again.

That night Li Yuan was unable to fall asleep. Li Shimin and Liu Wenjing also had a sleepless night because they were drawing up their plans.

The next day, Li Shimin tried again to reason with his father, saying, "Can you really fight off the rebels, Father? Besides, Emperor Yang is a highly suspicious man. If you achieve success and are meritorious, you will still be in danger."

This was true. Though the emperor and Li Yuan were cousins, the ruler did not trust Li Yuan. He sent Li two deputy commanders——Wang Wei and Gao Junya——whose real job was to watch him.

Li Yuan now sighed, saying to his son, "There is some truth in what you say. From now on, you can have full responsibility for the fate of the family."

Coming out of his father's chamber, Li Shimin ran into Pei Ji, an old friend of his father. Pei was a supervisor in the auxiliary palace and had smuggled out palace girls for Li Yuan's pleasure. To provide the emperor's women for other men was a crime for which one would be put to death. Li Shimin now asked Pei to urge his father to start the revolt. When Pei met with Li Yuan he pretended to be greatly worried and said to him, "It's too bad. There has been a leak about my sending you girls from the emperor's palace. People are talking about it throughout the city." Li Yuan, terrified to hear this, asked in agitation, "What shall I do?" Pei showed him the way out: revolt against Sui. With this, Li Yuan finally agreed to the uprising.

Under the pretext of suppressing the rebellious Liu Wuzhou, Li Yuan drafted soldiers and relocated his troops. Wang Wei and Gao Junya urged Li Yuan to attack Liu Wuzhou, but Li Yuan kept putting this off with the excuse that more training of the troops was necessary. Wang and Gao then discovered signs of revolt and were greatly alarmed. After discussing this between themselves, they decided to use the excuse of the spring drought to request that Li Yuan go to pray for rain at the temple, where they had laid an ambush to kill him so that they could take over the military command. This was learned by Liu Shilong who quickly passed it on to Li Yuan. That very night, Li Yuan told his son, Li Shimin, to prepare an ambush outside the town and he sent Liu Hongji out with troops to set fire and to disguise themselves as the Tujues attacking the town. The next morning, Li Yuan sent for Wang Wei and Gao Junya, with this message: "Last night the Tujues attacked again and I want to consult on the matter with you two." Not suspecting anything, the two deputy commanders came. Just then someone arrived with a secret report. Wang Wei stretched out his hand to take it, but the man refused to give it to him, saying, "This report shows that Wang Wei and Gao Junya banded together with the Tujues to attack the city." Li Yuan feigned great surprise, saying, "Is this true?" Wang Wei knelt down and pleaded, "This is a pure slander. Please don't be fooled by it." Gao Junya simply swore angrily. Li Yuan then said, "It is hard to tell whether this report is true or not. For the time being, you two will have to bear the suffering." He ordered that they be arrested. Generals loyal to the two refused to accept the verdict, but they were suppressed by Li Shimin's army hiding in ambush. Several days later, the Tujues did come with another attack. Li Yuan took the opportunity to say, "They were really brought over by Wang Wei and Gao Junya!" And the people, both the military and civilians, believed him. Next, he had the two deputy commonders beheaded. Then he put up a poster announcing that he was launching an uprising. This took place in the sixth month of 617, and Li Shimin was then only eighteen years old.

2. Taking Chang'an

Learning that Li Yuan was moving towards Guanzhong, the officials of the Sui Dynasty in Chang'an hurriedly sent generals Song Laosheng and

Qu Tutong, each leading a crack force, to block Li's advance. Li Yuan and Song Laosheng clashed in Huoyi (today's Huoxian County, Shanxi). It had been raining there for several days and Li's army had just run out of grain. It was then reported that the northern Tujues had joined forces with Liu Wuzhou and were about to attack Taiyuan. Li was terrified by this news and decided to pull his army quickly back to defend Taiyuan.

His son, Li Shimin, hurried to Li Yuan's camp that night with the intention of persuading Li Yuan not to pull back to Taiyuan. The guards, however, would not let him in, saying, "The Grand General is asleep. Come again tomorrow if you have things to discuss."

Frustrated, Li Shimin stomped his feet and cried aloud which surprised Li Yuan. So the father called his son into the camp.

Li Shimin said: "At this critical moment, if our army advances, we are sure to win. But if we retreat, the enemy will pursue us and it will be the end of us. That's why I am so saddened by your decision to go back to Taiyuan!"

His father found his logic reasonable and gave up the plan of retreat.

It was the eighth month (which began sometime between late August and mid-September). Once the rain stopped, the land was cast in great sunshine. Li's army launched a major offensive against the Sui army defending Huoyi. The defending

155

general, Song Laosheng, was a gallant man and hot-tempered. He was greatly enraged by the swearing and shouting of Li Yuan's troops challenging outside the city wall. He ordered that the city gate be opened and he then charged out at the head of his army. Li Shimin had a bugle sounded and led his forces to attack Song Laosheng from the side. Li Yuan and his soldiers also charged at the enemy. For a while the whole place echoed with the sound of attack. When Song Laosheng and his troops realized that they should pull back into the city, the gates had already been closed on them. He feigned that he had been wounded and fell off his horse, intending to cross the moat and flee. But he was captured by a general under the command of Li Yuan, and was killed right on the spot.

The Lis' armies took Huoyi, were reinforced with new draftees, and pushed southward to Hedong. Here the defending general, Qu Tutong, was known for maintaining strong discipline in his army and therefore his forces were highly combatant. Realizing that Li Yuan and his troops were in high spirits because of their recent victory, he decided to stay in the city and shut Li and his army outside. Li Shimin then suggested that the two armies should not tangle with Qu Tutong but march forward to Chang'an.

Pei Ji thought otherwise, saying, "Qu commands a force of dozens of thousands of men. If we fail to take Chang'an, he will use his troops to block our retreat. Then what will happen if we are being attacked from both the front and the rear?"

Li Shimin replied, firmly, "We are determined to take Chang'an once we start our march westward. I will never think of making a retreat."

So he led his forces westward, marching victoriously along the way. Li Yuan also took his army westward along the southern bank of the Weishui River, and the two armies gradually met to form a seige on Chang'an. Along the way, they opened up government granaries to help the poor and took smaller forces of rebellion into their ranks. In a matter of just a few months, the Lis' two armies grew to 200,000 strong. Wei Wensheng, the minister of justice, who was the commanding officer at Chang'an, was terrified by the mighty marching forces of the Lis. Within a few days he died. Without a commander, the defending troops fell apart and Chang'an was taken by the Lis.

Qu Tutong was shattered by news of the fall of Chang'an. Realizing that it was meaningless to continue to defend a solitary city, he surrendered. When he later learned that the strategy of directly attacking Chang'an came from the young general Li Shimin, he showed his admiration by saying, "He is undoubtedly an unusual person to have developed such tactics." He so respected Li Shimin that he became a gallant general under him.

After Li Yuan took Chang'an, he abolished all the ruthless policies of the Sui court. Out of political considerations, he decided to temporarily let Yang You, the grandson of Emperor Yang of Sui, serve as the new emperor. In the third month of 618, Emperor Yang was killed by his subordinates at Jiangdu, signalling the fall of Sui. Li Yuan decided there was no longer any need of keeping Yang You as the emperor and so, two months later, he forced Yang You to abdicate. Li Yuan proclaimed himself emperor and named his newly-established empire Tang. Li Yuan himself came to be known as Emperor Gaozu of Tang.

3. The Xuanwumen Incident

After Li Yuan became emperor, he made his eldest son, Li Jiancheng, the crown prince. His second son, Li Shimin, became the prince of Qin, and his fourth son, Li Yuanji, became the prince of Qi. His third son, Li Yuanba, died at an early age. A bloody fight later took place at Xuanwumen, as the brothers competed for the throne.

Li Shimin spent most of his time comanding his army in battles on behalf of the emperor, performing meritorious deeds, and surrounding himself with a host of talented people in the process. When it came to military affairs, he had the assistance of Yuchi Jingde, Qin Shubao, Xu Shixun and Li Jing among others. In civilian and cultural affairs, he had the aid of eighteen learned men represented by Fang Xuanling and Du Ruhui. With Li Shimin at the core, a powerful group that combined both military and civilian talents took shape.

As the crown prince, Li Jiancheng had a legitimate right to succeed the throne. He maintained close relationships with two favourite concubines of his father, the emperor, and had the support of a large number of the royal family members and relatives. The garrison troops of the palace were also under his control. Still Li Jiancheng was afraid of Li Shimin, who was so meritorious and commanded so much respect. He was afraid that his brother might take over his position. Several times he made plans to get rid of Li Shimin.

One evening, Li Jiancheng asked his brother to come to his palace for a drink. He had poison put into the wine. Unaware of the plot, Li Shimin drank the wine and was gripped by fierce pain in his stomach. Fortunately his uncle was there and helped him back to his own palace where Li continued to vomit blood. He escaped death thanks to the timely intervention of the doctor.

In order to get rid of Li Shimin as quickly as possible, Li Jiancheng and his youngest brother, Li Yuanji, then decided to sow discord among the military aides of Li Shimin. Li Jiancheng secretly had a cart loaded with gold and treasures taken to General Yuchi Jingde along with a letter of respect, hoping that the general would change sides. The general, however, reported the incident to Li Shimin. Failing in this attempt to buy over the general, Li

Jiancheng sent an assassin to kill him. However Yuchi Jingde was a man known far and wide for his extreme gallantry; he simply opened the door wide to allow the assassin to come in. How could any assassin be so bold as to march into an open house to kill the general? After failing with this attempt, the crown prince began to work on the advisers of Li Shimin. The prince told his youngest brother, "Among the advisers at the house of Prince of Qin, Du Ruhui and Fang Xuanling have the greatest influence." So the two brothers banded together to speak ill of these two advisers in front of the emperor, in the hope of driving them out of Li Shimin's camp.

Earlier, Zhangsun Wuji, brother of the wife of Li Shimin, and Li's adviser, Fang Xuanling, had discovered the plot of the crown prince and Prince of Qi to kill Li Shimin. The two of them went secretly to confer with Du Ruhui, another adviser. When the northern Tujues came invading again and had Wucheng (in present-day Wuyuan County, Inner Mongolia) surrounded, the crown prince saw this as an opportunity to strip his brother of his military power. He recommended to the emperor that his younger brother be appointed the commander for a counterattack against the invaders. The younger brother said that he wanted to take with him generals Yuchi Jingde, Cheng Yaojin and Qin Shubao from Li Shimin's ranks. It was clear he was trying to take forces away from Li Shimin's command. Li Jiancheng and Li Yuanji also discussed plans to assassinate Li Shimin, when he came to see the soldiers leaving for the front, and to bury General Yuchi Jingde alive. Fortunately their conversation was overheard by a night watchman who quickly reported it to Li Shimin so that the latter was able to narrowly escape death.

During his discussions with Zhangsun Wuji and Yuchi Jingde about how to deal with the impending danger, Li Shimin came to the conclusion that he must act first. So he exposed the plot of Li Jiancheng and Li Yuanji to Emperor Gaozu, their father. He also told the emperor that his two brothers maintained illicit relations with the emperor's two most favoured concubines, Zhang Jieyu and Yin Defei. This revelation hit hard on the emperor and, enraged, he sent out an order that the three brothers come to court next morning to confront each other.

The next morning, Li Shimin and his soldiers laid an ambush at Xuanwumen, a gate leading to the palace of the emperor. The garrison commander was originally from the ranks of Li Jiancheng, but had changed sides after accepting money from Li Shimin. When the emperor's concubines realized that something was amiss, they immediately informed Li Jiancheng. Li, however, believed that Xuanwumen was guarded by his own troops and that he had the assistance inside the palace of Zhang and Yin, the two concubines, so he came to court with Li Yuanji without bringing any of his own troops with him. When the two arrived at the Linhe Hall, they felt the atmosphere was not right and began to turn their horses around to go back. But it was already too late. Just then Li Shimin shouted a loud question at them: "Your Excellencies, the Crown Prince and Prince of Qi, why don't you go to court instead of turning back?" Li Yuanji, the youngest brother, took out his arrows and shot three of them at Li Shimin, but missed his target. With one arrow, however, Li Shimin toppled Li Jiancheng from the horse, who was killed. Li Yuanji then tried to flee west but was met head–on by Yuchi Jingde and was forced off his horse by the arrows shot at him. He sneaked into the bushes. Li Shimin came chasing him but was knocked off his horse by tree branches. Li Yuanji took that opportunity and jumped on Li Shimin, sitting straddle on him and clutching at his throat. In this moment of life and death, Yuchi Jingde rushed over and killed Li Yuanji with a single arrow, thus freeing Li Shimin. The event has come to be known in history as the Xuanwumen Incident.

When Emperor Gaozu learned of the death of the crown prince, Li Jiancheng, and his youngest son, Li Yuanji, he was overwhelmed with sorrow, but he had to accept the reality of the situation. He made Li Shimin the crown prince on the seventh day of the sixth month of 626. Three months later, Li Shimin forced his father to step down and he took the throne, naming his reign period Zhen'guan.

4. Eager for suggestions

Learning from the lessons of Emperor Yang of Sui, Li Shimin, now emperor of Tang, introduced a relatively enlightened political rule. One of the first policies he implemented was to let people speak out, and he eagerly listened to the opinions and suggestions of all his subjects. After that he would decide whether to accept each suggestion or not.

One day he asked Wei Zheng, the chief appraisal officer for the emperor, whose job was to pass on suggestions to the supreme ruler, what an emperor must do in order to be well informed and correctly handle state affairs.

Wei Zheng replied, "Listen to both sides and you'll be enlightened; listen to just one side and you'll be benighted."

Wei Zheng himself was, in fact, most outstanding in putting forward suggestions. He often argued with the emperor and persisted in what he believed to be the truth, even when it enraged the emperor.

Once Li Shimin signed a decree stipulating that all tall young men, even those under eighteen, might be drafted into the army. Wei Zheng withheld the edict to Li's great indignation. The emperor repudiated Wei for having the audacity to withhold his decree. Wei responded coldly, "I have heard that if you empty a lake in order to catch all

the fish, there will be no more fish. Now Your Highness has ordered young men under eighteen to serve in the military. It is an action taken without enough consideration of the possible consequences. Besides, you have issued decrees earlier stipulating that only people aged eighteen or above are to be drafted. Will not the change of your edicts in this regard lead to a loss of faith in the government on the part of the common people?"

Li had no answer to this question. A moment later he admitted his mistake and decided to withdraw this decree.

One day Li Shimin was playing with an eagle that not only looked beautiful but could also help hunt game. While he was enjoying this amusement with the bird, Wei Zheng arrived. Afraid of being criticized by Wei for his pursuit of such pleasures, Li Shimin hurriedly hid the bird under his robe. Wei pretended not to have seen this, but deliberately prolonged his dealings with the business matters. By the time Wei was ready to leave, the bird had been choked to death.

Another occasion, when Li Simin was returning to his living quarters after attending court, he said angrily, "I've got to find a way to kill that country pumpkin!"

Empress Zhangsun heard the remark and asked him who he wanted to kill.

Li Shimin answered, "Who else can there be? It's that old fool Wei Zheng. He kept arguing with me in court and that really makes me mad."

The empress departed and then came back wearing the formal clothing used for appearances in court. She solemnly congratulated Li Shimin, saying, "Because the ruler is enlightened, his subjects dare to speak out. The fact that Wei Zheng dared to talk back to you today simply verifies that you're an enlightened ruler." Li Shimin found her logic reasonable and his anger disappeared.

The Zhen'guan period under Li Shimin was one of peace and prosperity, and praise for Li Shimin spread far and wide. Wei Zheng was the only one who kept a cool head, analysing things and pointing out whatever shortcomings there were to the rulings of Li Shimin. Li had the reminders offered by Wei written down and pasted on a screen so that he could always look at them. He said to Wei, sincerely, "I want to overcome whatever shortcomings I have. Otherwise, how can I face you!"

Li Shimin was greatly saddened by Wei's death. Standing in the tower watching Wei's bier being taken away, he was in tears. He said with a heavy heart, "If a man mirrors himself with a copper plate, he can straighten out his clothes. If he mirrors himself with history, he will know what makes him a success or a failure. If he mirrors himself with other people, he will discover his shortcomings and correct them. With Wei Zheng's death, I have lost a mirror."

In the early part of his reign, Li Shimin avoided making many mistakes, simply because he was able to listen to all sorts of opinions.

5. Assigning the right people to right jobs

When he first ascended the throne, Li Shimin was only twenty-seven years old and ambitious to do a good job. Thus he was eager to enlist the service of talented people. He opened a literary hall to train people to be capable of running the country. He asked Feng Deyi, a court minister, to recommend talented people, but Feng told him, "I want to very much, but today's world has no real talent."

Li immediately criticized Feng Deyi, saying, "To enlist the services of men is just like making use of a utensil. You use them for what they are good at. In ancient times there were periods of peace and prosperity. Do you mean to tell me that the talent that made that possible was borrowed from other historical periods? It is you who cannot recognize the talented people and insist that there is no talent."

Wei Zheng, whom Li Shimin so respected, was originally a minor officer in a peasant rebellion force. Later he became an adviser to crown prince Li Jiancheng. During the brothers' contention for the throne, Wei several times tried to convince the crown prince to get rid of Li Shimin as soon as possible. After the Xuanwumen Incident, Li Shimin asked Wei Zheng, "Why did you try to sow discord among us brothers?" Wei answered frankly, "At the time I was advising the crown prince. Naturally I was obligated to serve him and help him with his plans. Unfortunately the crown prince did not follow my suggestions, otherwise he wouldn't have suffered what happened to him." When other people heard this dialogue, they were all worried for Wei, thinking that Li Shimin would certainly kill him. Unexpectedly, Li Shimin not only showed no anger, he praised Wei for being straightforward, bold and talented. He made Wei Zheng the officer specially charged with making suggestions to the emperor.

Yuchi Jingde, Li Shimin's most trusted military officer, was originally a gallant general in an army under the command of Liu Wuzhou. After Liu's defeat, Yuchi Jingde and Xun Xiang, another general, surrendered to Li Shimin. Later Xun Xiang changed sides and was again captured by Li's troops. People suggested that Yuchi Jingde should be put to death together with Xun Xiang to prevent further dire consequences.

But Li Shimin knew Yuchi Jingde well and spoke on his behalf. He also presented Yuchi with many expensive gifts. This really moved him. Later, when crown prince Li Jiancheng tried to bribe Yuchi with a handsome sum of money and then threatened to assassinate him, Yuchi remained loyal to Li Shimin. All his life thereafter, he followed Li as a reliable general. During the Xuanwumen Incident, he performed meritorious deeds that helped secure Li's position as the new emperor.

In 629, Li Shimin solicited suggestions from all officials. General Chang He put forward twenty suggestions that were all to the point. Admiring these suggestions, Li Shimin questioned Chang He as to whether he personally wrote them. Chang told him the truth that they were written by a permanent guest of his called Ma Zhou. Ma was a poor scholar from a lowly family background, but Li summoned him that very afternoon. Ma Zhou was slow in coming to court and so the emperor sent out people four times to hurry him up. After talking with him, the emperor was convinced that Ma Zhou was a man who could really be entrusted with managing state affairs. So he made him chief supervisor and later the prime minister. Unfortunately, Ma died at the age of forty-eight and Li Shimin's heart was broken by his early death. Li decided that Ma should be buried in the royal family's mausoleum in order to show that, in death, a man who served the emperor so well would remain with the ruler.

In enlisting the services of people, Li Shimin opposed to the principle of seniority and promoting only relatives. In 627, Li Shimin issued rewards according to people's merit and people such as Fang Xuanling, Zhangsun Wuji and Du Ruhui were awarded first prizes. Li Shentong, the emperor's uncle, was not happy about this, saying, "I was the first to follow you in the rebellion and have fought with you for many years, but I am given a lower grade reward than some men who were only good at writing, persons such as Fang Xuanling and Du Ruhui. This is not fair!"

Li Shimin replied, "It is true that you were the first to respond to my call for rebellion, but later you lost many battles. Fang Xuanling and Du Ruhui, however, devised strategies that ensured our victory, so their merits are greater than yours, my uncle. You're a close relative of mine and I trust you, but I cannot issue rewards on the basis of how closely we're related." These words calmed down Li Shentong.

To recognize their deeds, Li Shimin had the portraits of twenty-four meritorious officials, including Zhangsun Wuji, Du Ruhui, Wei Zheng and Fang Xuanling, painted on the Lingyan Pavilion. He personally wrote eulogies to each of them.

6. Rule by understanding people

Li Shimin, as Emperor Taizong of the Tang Dynasty, personally experienced how the powerful empire of Sui was shattered and overthrown by peasant uprisings. After he became emperor, he therefore carefully administered state affairs so as to avoid rebellions breaking out among the populace.

When the Guanzhong and Guandong areas suffered from floods and droughts for three years running, compelling the people there to sell their children in desparation, Li Shimin ordered that the granaries be opened to distribute food among the disaster-stricken people, in fear that the natural disasters might lead to unrest. In some prefectures and counties, the authorities even delivered grain to the homes of people. Li also ordered the distribution of money and goods from government warehouses so that the people could buy back the children they had sold. Li said to his officials, "To sponge on the people for our own pleasure is like cutting meat from one's own body for food; you may have something to eat, but you're finished." He also said, "When I make speeches at court, I have to think them over carefully, because I'm afraid of saying things that might be against the interest of the people. This is why I do not dare to speak often."

He was very strict with education for his children. At meal time, he said to the crown prince, Li Zhi, "If you understand how hard it is to cultivate crops, you will always have things to eat." While they were riding horses, the emperor said to him, "You should pay attention to the proper use of a horse and not overwork it. Then you will have horses to ride." While riding in a boat, he said something that was highly thought provoking: "The water can carry a boat, but it can also overturn a boat. The people are like water and the ruler is like the boat." Such thoughts made it possible for him to reduce taxes and implement lenient judicial punishments so that the people could enjoy their lives.

During his reign, he introduced a system of dividing the land equally among farmers according to the number of people in each household. He also made sure that people did not miss the farming season by allowing prisoners to return to work on their land during that season. This brought about a relatively stable social order and an increasingly prosperous economy, making China the most powerful feudal nation in the world at the time.

After he joined the revolt in Taiyuan, he helped his father conquer all the enemies and unify the country. After becoming emperor, he extensively enlisted the services of capable people, eagerly listening to and accepting workable suggestions. He worked hard to develop production, laying a good foundation for the three-hundred-year-rule of the Tang Dynasty. His deeds, vision and insight as a politician, his ideas and strategies in running the country all received favourable comments from people over the centuries, who have listed him as one of the most outstanding emperors in feudal China.

VII   Wu Zetian, the First and Only Woman Emperor

Wu Zetian (624 - 705), a native of Wenshui, Shanxi, became a concubine at age fourteen of Li Shimin, known as Emperor Taizong of Tang. After the emperor's death, she became the concubine of Li Zhi, Emperor Gaozong, the son of Emperor Taizong. Later she rose to become the empress, and eventually she proclaimed herself the sovereign ruler. Among the more than four hundred emperors in Chinese history, she was the only woman. Though she sat on the throne for only sixteen years, she in effect ruled the country for more than half a century.

1. Entering the imperial palace for the first time

The father of Wu Zetian, a man named Wu Shihuo, was a rich timber merchant. While serving as a regional commander during the Sui Dynasty, Li Yuan often stayed at Wu's house when he travelled near the place. When he waged his revolt, Li Yuan also received funding from Mr. Wu. And after the establishment of the Tang Dynasty, Wu Shihuo was given important posts, including those of minister of works and prefect of Lizhou. It was in such a prominent family that Wu Zetian was raised and pampered.

A cousin of Wu Zetian's mother was a concubine of Emperor Taizong and she often praised her niece, Wu Zetian, and extolled her beauty to the emperor. So the emperor had Wu Zetian, now fourteen years old, brought into the palace as a low ranking concubine. Young as she was, she quickly won the favour of the emperor because of her wit and eloquence. Emperor Taizong loved horses and kept many of them in the palace. One of these horses was so strong-willed that nobody could tame it. One day the emperor took his concubines to see the horse and teased the women with the question, "Which one of you can tame it?"

The young Wu Zetian stepped forward and volunteered to do so. Looking at the delicate and petite lady, the emperor asked her how she would do it. Wu Zetian told him, "All I need are three things: an iron whip, an iron hammer and a dagger. If it is naughty, I will slash it with the iron whip. If it still does not become agreeable, I'll hit it on the head with the iron hammer. And if that fails to tame it, I'll stab the dagger into its throat."

The emperor was aghast at this answer from such a beautiful and delicate young lady. It led him to think that if she dared to use an iron whip and an iron hammer in dealing with a horse, she might well use the same in dealing with her subordinates once she achieved power. From then on, the emperor began to be on guard against her. Until the emperor's death, she remained in her low rank, receiving no promotion in status.

Wu was well aware that it was not easy to change the mind of a mature man. Thus, when other concubines tried hard to curry favour with the emperor, she directed her attention to the crown prince. If she could win the favour of the crown prince, who would eventually succeed to his father's throne and become the emperor, there was hope for her.

When she was initially brought into the palace, she had been the companion of the emperor, but a few days afterwards, the emperor left her in the cold. Li Zhi, the crown prince, was four years younger than Wu Zetian. However, he was captivated by her beauty. It happened that the emperor was once suffering from a sore on his back and the crown prince came to his father's palace to attend to him. During that time he stayed in his father's place, which provided an opportunity for him and Wu Zetian to be together more often. Gradually they started flirting with each other. Wu Zetian secretly congratulated herself: the seed of passion now sowed would bring a harvest in times to come.

2. Entering the imperial palace
for the second time

When Wu Zetian was twenty-six years old, Emperor Taizong died. According to rules of that time, once an emperor died, those concubines who had given birth to children for the emperor could continue to live in the palace, while those who had not must leave. Wu Zetian had no children and disappointingly she had to become a nun at the Ganye Temple.

The dull life of the temple was unbearable for Wu. All day long she had to find companionship in the carved wooden or clay statues of Buddha, had to light incense, and had to kowtow and recite monotonous scriptures again and again. Wu quickly grew weary of spending her prime life amidst the sound of morning bells and evening drums at the temple.

Dramatic changes may occur at some point in one's life and this certainly applied to Wu. One day, Li Zhi, now Emperor Gaozong, came to the Ganye Temple to offer sacrifices to his father. Among the many nuns, the emperor spotted Wu Zetian who had shaved her head and was in a nun's robe. The old flame of romance was immediately rekindled. Wu noticed the eyes of the emperor. But she realized that she looked like as an ordinary nun and was so overwhelmed by a sorrow for herself that tears began to run down her cheeks. With people around, neither of them could openly express what was in their hearts. They looked at each other quietly as the emperor departed.

News of this encounter was heard by Empress Wang, who at the time was competing with Lady Xiao for the emperor's favour. She had, in fact, been racking her brains to find a way to pull the emperor out of the arms of Lady Xiao. Without giving the matter careful thought, Empress Wang decided to use Wu Zetian to ward off Lady Xiao. She sent people to tell Wu Zetian to let her hair grow and urged the emperor to bring Wu back to the palace. She thought in this way she would make the emperor happy and win back his love. Her suggestion was exactly what the emperor wanted. As soon as Wu recovered some of her hair, he eagerly had her head covered with a scarf and brought her back to the palace. That very night, the two old lovers shared the same bed and, like fish in water, had a night of sleepless joy.

Coming back to the palace, Wu was no longer the fourteen-year-old she had been. After more than a decade of palace life and the mechanical and desolate days at the Ganye Temple, she emerged a mature woman. She used all her skills to keep the emperor tightly to her. The emperor, who had fallen in love with Wu when he was still the crown prince and who now enjoyed the whole-hearted devotion of the woman he loved, felt even more inseparable from her, entirely leaving Empress Wang and Lady Xiao in the cold. The empress, who only now regretted her previous decision, banded together with her original rival, Lady Xiao, to smear Wu Zetian. By then, the emperor was submerged by the unsurpassed pleasures brought to him by Wu Zetian and no longer wanted to listen to anything against Wu. Knowing that Empress Wang and Lady Xiao had formed a united front against her, Wu Zetian spared no measures in counterattacking the two rivals in love. Ordinarily Empress Wang was a woman who liked to put on airs to the dislike of those working in the palace. Wu Zetian, on the other hand, won over the palace maids and eunuchs by spending money on them and by giving them gifts. She often divided among them the gifts given to her by the emperor, such as jewellery, silk and brocade. She gave more gifts to those who praised her so as to show her generosity and easy-going temperament. Gradually a small clique formed around her. Whatever happened in the palace, particularly actions of Empress Wang and Lady Xiao, were quickly reported to her. She added her own opinions to the report and relayed them to the emperor.

Soon Wu Zetian gave birth to a baby girl. Empress Wang, who loved children, had never been able to have a child of her own, so she came to congratulate Wu. Wu Zetian deliberately evaded her when the empress arrived. The empress took the baby into her arms, teased her and then put her back on the bed. After she left, Wu came out of hiding and pinched her own baby to death. Then she covered the baby up with a quilt. As soon as the emperor arrived back from court, Wu put on a broad smile and greeted him as he eagerly went to see his little princess. He removed the quilt only to discover that the baby was already dead. Wu pretended to be greatly surprised and shaken by this and gave out a loud cry.

The emperor was enraged and asked, "How did this happen?"

Wu Zetian hurriedly answered, "She was fine when I left her there not long ago."

The maids reported to the emperor that Empress Wang had been there, and that she was the only one who touched the baby.

"Then it must be her who killed my little girl!" the emperor concluded, gritting his teeth.

From that moment on, the emperor decided to strip the empress of her position and replace her with Wu Zetian as empress.

3. As empress

Wu Zetian, a descendant of a merchant, had the lowest social position among the nobles. Besides she had been a concubine of the late Emperor Taizong. The fact that Emperor Gaozong had taken his father's concubine as his own was already a subject for criticism, so the emperor's plan to make Wu the empress was not going to be easy to achieve. What the emperor feared was opposition from the senior ministers and generals who had helped found the Tang Dynasty.

One day, Emperor Gaozong and Wu Zetian went to the residence of Zhangsun Wuji, a senior official who helped establish the Tang Dynasty, with the intention of persuading him. They took with them ten cartloads of gold, silver and silk as gifts, and they promised official positions to his three sons. During the dinner, the emperor said to the host, "Empress Wang has not born any children and I intend to remove her as empress."

Zhangsun Wuji fully understood the intention of the emperor, but he did not bend his will to offer his endorsement. He simply changed the subject. The emperor had to return to the palace without obtaining his support.

As there are people who are upright and outspoken, there are also people who are simply opportunists. Li Yifu, a court official, had for a long time been on bad terms with Zhangsun Wuji and was about to be demoted to Bizhou (present-day Tongjiang County, Sichuan). To protect his position and prepare for promotion in future, he sent a petition to Emperor Gaozong suggesting that he make Wu Zetian the empress. Nicknamed "Li, the Cat," Li Yifu always smiled broadly when he talked with people. Deep in his heart, however, he was a vicious person. Those not to be his liking suffered from his frame-ups. So he was also known as the "Smiling Knife." His life story gave rise to the Chinese proverb: *xiao li cang dao*, meaning with murderous intent behind one's smiles.

To curry favour with the emperor and Wu Zetian, Xu Jingzong, another minister, spread the word that "Even old peasants want to replace their wives with new women once they have had a good harvest, let alone the Son of Heaven." Gradually a small clique of people was formed who supported Wu in her bid to become the empress.

One day in the ninth month of 655, the emperor asked senior ministers Zhangsun Wuji, Chu Suiliang, Li Ji and Yu Zhining to go into the inner chamber for a discussion, after he dismissed the morning session of the court. Chu Suiliang said to the other three, "This must be the issue of stripping the position of the empress that the emperor wants to discuss with us. I am prepared to try to persuade him out of that even at the expense of my own life." Li Ji went home with the excuse that he was not feeling well as soon as he sensed the intensity of the situation.

When the meeting began, the emperor said directly to the other three, "The empress has not given birth to any children, but Wu Zetian has. I intend to make Wu Zetian the new empress. What do you think?"

Chu Suiliang replied immediately, "The empress came out of a noble family background and was hand-picked to be your empress by the late emperor. Before he died, the late emperor held my hand and said that he entrusted the young couple to me. Today his words still resound loud and clear in my ear. You were there when he said this to me. The empress has committed no mistakes, so how can she be stripped of her position like this?"

The emperor turned sullen. Having already gone this far in his persuasion, Chu Suiliang decided that he might as well continue. "Besides," he said, "Wu Zetian was a concubine of your father, the late emperor. How can you hide this from the public?"

So saying, he placed the note board (what ministers used for taking notes when attending court sessions) on the staircase, untied the towel on his head and kept kowtowing until his head began to bleed. The emperor was extremely annoyed to hear his minister suggesting that he had taken his father's concubine and to see the minister resigning by turning in the note board. He told the eunuchs to drag Chu Suiliang out of the inner chamber.

Just then a woman jumped out from behind a curtain in the side chamber. Gritting her teeth, she said, "That old fellow should be killed right away!" It turned out that Wu Zetian had been listening to the discussion between the emperor and his senior ministers from the side chamber.

Zhangsun Wuji tried to stop this from happening, saying, "Chu Suiliang was an official entrusted

182

by the late emperor and should not be punished even lightly. Your Highness, please think twice before you punish him." The discussion broke up in discord.

Li Ji, who had evaded the inner chamber discussion on the issue of replacing the empress, went one day to see the emperor. When the sovereign ruler mentioned the issue of replacing the empress, Li Ji said, "This is your personal affair, why do you bother listening to what others have to say?"

This helped the emperor to finally make up his mind. Several days later, he demoted Chu Suiliang as governor of Tanzhou (today's Changsha, Hunan). Then he issued a decree stripping Empress Wang and Lady Xiao of their positions and shutting them up in the back palace. He made Wu Zetian the new empress.

4. The woman ruler from behind the scenes

Once having been made the empress, Wu Zetian changed her behaviour from ingratiating herself with the emperor on everything and turned into a much tougher person. She had such a strong and insatiable hunger for power that she could not be satisfied by just being made the empress.

Taking the opportunity of her going home to visit her parents, the emperor went to the prison to see former Empress Wang and Lady Xiao. The cell was securely locked and there was only a small hole in the door through which food was delivered. The emperor shouted into the hole, "Empress Wang and Lady Xiao, where are you?"

He heard a faint reply: "We have already been made prisoners. Please Your Highness don't address us with our honorary titles. If you still cherish our past, please let us out."

The emperor promised he would meet their request. Upon her return from home, Wu Zetian learned about this. She sent people to slash the two imprisoned ladies one hundred times each. Then she had their hands and feet chopped off and their bodies thrown into liquor vats. Within just a few days, they were dead. Before her death, Lady Xiao burst into a repudiation of Wu Zetian: "You vicious Wu Zetian have subjected me to untold suffering. In our reincarnation, I'll become a cat and you'll be a rat. Then I will tear open your throat!" Ever after that, Wu Zetian would not allow any cats to be kept as pets in the palace.

It was not until after the two women died that Wu Zetian informed the emperor of that fact. He was taken by supprise. This incident was her warning to the emperor, reminding him not to ignore her presence.

At the same time, Wu began to take actions against those ministers who had opposed her becoming the emperor. Chu Suiliang soon died of depression as a result of his demotion. Then Zhangsun Wuji, who had helped in the founding of the Tang

Dynasty, was accused of plotting a revolt. He was exiled to Yangzhou and then to Qianzhou (today's Guizhou) where Wu dispatched her trusted aide to order Zhangsun Wuji to commit suicide. By then, all the ministers who had helped the previous Tang emperors to establish the empire had either been persecuted to death or had died of natural causes. Without the assistance of able and loyal ministers, Emperor Gaozong saw his influence gradually diminish.

Not long after, the emperor fell ill as a result of his promiscuous life. He felt dizzy all day long and left Wu Zetian to deal with court affairs. Empress Wu Zetian was bright and clever and had a good memory. She also had great political skill. Ever hungry for power, she was naturally happy to accept the new task. At first she would always consult the emperor, but gradually she began to leave him in the dark. Though a weak person by temperament, the emperor was not yet muddle-headed. Thus he began to grow weary of the empress. When a eunuch reported to the emperor that the empress had invited a man of witchcraft to her living quarters and all day long he read spells and practised witchcraft together with the empress, the emperor could no longer put up with her. He called trusted ministers and eunuchs to his side to tell them how dissatisfied he was with the empress.

His dissatisfaction was what Shangguan Yi had been waiting for. So he said to the emperor, "It's easy, Your Highness. You're the emperor and you can simply issue a decree and strip her of her position."

The emperor agreed with the advice and had Shangguan Yi draft the edict. He would remove Wu Zetian just as he had once done to Empress Wang. They, however, were too simple-minded. Empress Wu was not the Empress Wang of the past! The eunuchs serving the emperor had all been bribed by the empress and acted as her informants. Before the ink of the decree Shangguan Yi had drafted was dry, Empress Wu rushed in. She angrily interrogated the emperor, "What is it you want to do?"

The emperor was so terrified to see the anger in Wu Zetian that he did not know what to do. His determination a moment before totally evaporated. Instead, he evaded responsibility by saying, "I did not mean it. It was all Shangguan Yi's idea."

"If that's the case, show me the edict!" she said, stretching out her hand to take it.

The emperor had to show her the piece of paper bearing the decree. Wu Zetian tore it into pieces.

Several days later, the empress had her trusted official Xu Jingzong accuse Shangguan Yi of plotting to rebel, and thus had him killed along with his two sons. All women members in his family——including Shangguan Wan'er, the granddaughter of Shangguan Yi, who was still an infant——were made slaves in the palace. This baby girl grew to become a woman of outstanding talent. She even became the secretary of Wu Zetian, which is a topic for another story not to be dealt here.

After this incident, the emperor was further weakened. When the court was in session, a purple gauze curtain was hung behind the emperor and behind that curtain sat the empress. All major decisions had to be made by consulting the person sitting behind the curtain. At first when the ministers and generals saw the emperor but heard the voice of the empress speaking, they felt rather uneasy, but gradually they became accustomed to it. Wu Zetian was indeed a gifted politician who dealt with everything in great order. Since she was more capable than her emperor husband, the ministers could say nothing to oppose her. Whenever they submitted a petition or a report, they always addressed it to the "Two Sovereigns." To rule from behind a curtain was something that happened in several dynasties in China's history, but it was Wu Zetian who set the precedence.

5. Changing the crown princes three times

Emperor Gaozong had twelve children and the youngest six, four boys and two girls, were borne by Wu Zetian, which is an indication that Wu was able to monopolize the emperor's love and attention. Before Wu Zetian became empress, Emperor Gaozong had already made Li Zhong the crown prince. Now

that Wu Zetian was the empress, she compelled the emperor to abrogate his decision to make Li Zhong the crown prince and, instead, to make her eldest son, Li Hong, the new crown prince. That year Li Hong was only four years old.

Emperor Gaozong was very fond of Li Hong, who received a good education and was very courteous. When the emperor was away from the palace, he always entrusted Li Hong, the crown prince, to sit in for him for the court sessions. Many people in and out of the court also hoped that this crown prince would eventually succeed to the throne. This wish, however, was in contradiction with Wu Zetian's desire for running the country herself. What she wanted was a puppet emperor, not an emperor with insight who might be capable of running the country. So even though the crown prince was her own flesh and blood, she was determined to block his way to the throne. In 675, she learned that Emperor Gaozong was ready to vacate the throne in favour of the crown prince, Li Hong, and so she poisoned her own son to death. He was then aged twenty-four.

In the same year, Emperor Gaozong appointed the twenty-two-year-old Li Xian, the second son borne by Wu Zetian, as the new crown prince. Li Xian loved to read and wrote beautifully. He was fair and efficient in dealing with political issues. Like his brother, the previous crown prince, he did not go along with his mother on all issues, which irritated Wu Zetian. She thus made up her mind to remove her second son from the position of crown prince. Wu's thoughts were recognized by Ming Chongyan, a court official, who, in order to win the favour of the empress, petitioned that the empress' third son, Li Xian, should be made the crown prince. Empress Wu Zetian was delighted with the suggestion but the emperor did not grant the request. Empress Wu had to wait.

One evening, Ming Chongyan was assassinated and Wu Zetian suspected that it was the crown prince, Li Xian, who had arranged the assassination. She tortured Zhao Daosheng, a palace servant working for the crown prince, into confessing and then she sent people to search the crown prince's palace where they found out over three hundred weapons. Wu then accused her second son, the crown prince, of treason. Emperor Gaozong, however, thought otherwise. "The crown prince's residence is guarded by armed soldiers and therefore it is not extraordinary to find some weapons there," he said. Wu Zetian, however, had made up her mind to remove the crown prince so as to clear the way for her own ascendency to the throne. She shouted loudly, "He has committed a crime. I want to see him punished, even though he is my own son, because this is a matter of principle." In the end, the crown prince was removed, made an ordinary citizen and exiled to the remote Bazhou (present-day Bazhong, Sichuan). Overwhelmed by this development, Li Xian wrote this poem: Melons were planted; they should be harvested when ripe. The first harvest will make remaining melons grow better; the second harvest will make the vines less overladen; the third harvest will still find some melons; but the fourth harvest will only reveal fruitless vines. When the poem, which people passed around to allude to the empress' removing her own sons from the political centre, was heard by Wu, she sent people to Bazhong to force Li Xian to commit suicide. He died at the age of thirty-one. It was not until after Wu Zetian's death years later that the prince was cleared of this wrong accusation. The prince was given the posthumous title of Prince Zhanghuai. His tomb was discovered twenty years ago at the foot of Liangshan Hill in Qianxian County, Shaanxi. Known for its superb murals, the tomb site is now open to the public.

Wu Zetian's third son, Li Xian (a different character with the same sound as the character in the previous crown prince's name), was now the new crown prince. Three years later, in 683, his father, Emperor Gaozong, died. Li Xian took the throne with the reign title of Emperor Zhongzong. With a rather weak temperament, Emperor Zhongzong was afraid of his mother and soon all real political and military power fell into her hands.

Once, the emperor wanted to make his father-in-law, Wei Xuanzhen, the prime minister, which alarmed the emperor's mother. She kicked the emperor off the throne, demoted him to become prince of Luling, and exiled him to Junzhou (in today's Hubei). All this happened within two months after he became the emperor. A week later, Wu Zetian made her twenty-two-year-old fourth son, Li Dan, the emperor with the title of Emperor Ruizong. Though he was the emperor, Li Dan could never take over court affairs. Nor could he live in the emperor's palace. He remained in his old residence built for the crown prince and was an emperor only in name. Everything was now decided by Wu Zetian.

With a strong will and ruthless methods, Wu Zetian moved about between her husband and sons. Step by step she moved towards victory. Finally on the ninth day of the ninth month in 690, she herself ascended the throne, changing the name of the Tang empire to Zhou. The ninth day of the ninth month was the Double Ninth Festival, an occasion for people to go mountaineering, meet with friends, and enjoy great feasts. It was by no means accidental for Wu Zetian to choose this day to take the throne and become the only woman emperor in Chinese history.

6. Governing by her style

As the sovereign ruler, Wu Zetian first and foremost appointed a number of officials in charge of torture, who would help her suppress the opposition. A man called Yu Jiabao came with the suggestion that a bronze secret – letter box be designated and informants be rewarded. The letter box was made specially for collecting reports from informants. And the woman emperor personally met each informant. So long as he came with the information needed, the informant would be rewarded. Thus, the number of informants grew and cases piled up. The woman emperor appointed a number of judicial officials to look into the mounting number of cases. During this process, there were more than twenty widely-known officials who specialized in torture, including Lai Junchen, Zhou Xing and Suo Yuanli. Lai Junchen even compiled a book on how to frame up and persecute the accused. A great number of members of the Tang royal families and the opposition lost their lives during this wave of persecution under cruel torture.

Zhou Xing, as an official in charge of torture, had killed so many people that he was eventually accused of plotting a revolt by those who hated him. Wu Zetian had Lai Junchen deal with the case. Lai pretended that nothing unusual had happened and invited Zhou Xing to a dinner. While drinking and eating, Lai asked him, "I'm working on a case in which the accused does not admit guilt. What do you suggest I should do?"

Not knowing this was a ruse, Zhou Xing said, off-handedly, "It is pretty easy. Get a big vat and put the criminal into it. Then heat it over a fire and he is sure to confess!"

Lai admired his suggestion and said, "Great idea, and we might as well try it." He had a large vat brought in and placed it over a fire. Then he stood up, bowed to Zhou Xing, and said calmly, "The man I have been secretly instructed to question is none other than you. Now please get into the vat!" Zhou Xing started to shake with fear and kept kowtowing, admitting that he was guilty. This incident gave rise to the Chinese proverb of *qing jun ru weng*, which means "please step into the vat," suggesting that to deal with a man as he deals with others.

The random torturing and killing of the innocent aroused the indignation of the public. The cunning Wu Zetian then sensed that her aim of suppressing the opposition had been realized and so she turned against the officials of torture so as to quiet people's wrath. Lai Junchen, who had committed many sins, was sentenced to death and executed in 697. Those who hated him rushed to the execution ground, gouged out his eyes, took out his heart, and broke his bones. Having vented their anger and fear, the people congratulated each other by saying, "Tonight we can shut our eyes and have a quiet sleep."

Meanwhile, in order to cultivate and expand her own political power base, Wu Zetian enlisted many talents. She attached great importance to the examinations through which candidates for official posts were selected. She personally read the examination papers of the students and created a system of "interview examinations." She also added examinations for military prowess so that those with superb military skills could become officials. She allowed all officials, as well as ordinary people, to recommend themselves for various posts. And so long as they had some special expertise, they would be enlisted. Still she worried that talented people might be left out of her camp and so she sent scouts across the country to look for capable people. Under the pretext of writing books, she invited people with literary skills to the palace to work as advisers to the prime minister. In putting people into appropriate posts, Wu Zetian was not restricted by established rules and traditions. As a result, during her reign, she was helped by many persons with real talent. Some of the historically famous prime ministers who served her include Li Zhaode, Wei Yuanzhong, Di Renjie, Yao Chong, Song Jing and Zhang Jianzhi. Thus at a time when the palace was full of treacherous officials, men good at torturing others and male prostitutes, justice was maintained at high level in the decision-making process, and the state apparatus worked smoothly.

On one hand, Wu Zetian tirelessly recruited men of capability; on the other, she kept a strict control over the people around her. To use a person according to his skills rather than his family relationship was a major aspect of her way of governing. She was fond of her daughter, Princess Taiping, who looked very much like her and was full of strategies. Wu allowed her daughter to attend secret meetings, but never gave her a chance to make decisions. Princess Taiping thus became quite cautious and in fear of offending her mother emperor. After she took the throne, Wu Zetian made her nephews from her maternal family side princes, and Wu Chengsi, one of her nephews, was even appointed prime minister. Li Zhaode, one of the chief ministers, reminded Wu Zetian that, "Wu Chengsi holds too much power, and I'm afraid, this has created the danger of his eventually taking over the throne." Wu accepted the suggestion and removed Wu Chengsi from the post of prime minister. Naturally Wu Chengsi hated Li for this and often spoke ill of Li Zhaode in front of his aunt, Wu Zetian, who in return criticized her nephew. "Li Zhaode is a loyal official whom I can trust. He shares my burdens, and you're a far cry from him," she said.

Wu Zetian was first involved in political decision-making in her early thirties and remained at the political centre until she died, at the age of eighty-two. For half a century she gave full play to her intelligence, bravery and resoluteness, leaving the strong mark of her capability and influence on the political arena. During her reign, she encouraged and rewarded farming, enlisted the service of men with real skills, and kept strict control of her relatives and trusted aides, thus effectively ensuring social stability and economic and cultural progress.

7. Unwillingly returning power to her son

In 705, Wu Zetian fell seriously ill as she was getting old. Attending her in her living quarters, apart from the palace maids, were two male prostitutes——Zhang Yizhi and Zhang Changzong, who were brothers. In her later years, Wu became very suspicious of everyone except for these two brothers. She left major military and political affairs in their hands. Court officials were gravely worried, as the two brothers carried around their misconduct in the name of the woman emperor. And their worries were not groundless. If the emperor should die, they might simply fabricate a decree that would allow them to seize political power. The consequences would be unthinkable.

In mentioning the two Zhang brothers, it is impossible not to say something about Wu Zetian's craze for male prostitutes. She was originally brought to the palace to attend Emperor Taizong when she was fourteen years old, and she became a concubine for the late emperor's son, Emperor Gaozong, when she was twenty-six. When her second husband died, she was already sixty-one years old, but she retained her youthfulness. In order to make her happy, a princess introduced her boy-friend, Feng Xiaobao, to her. Feng was a veteran in love affairs and not a single woman who had had sex with him was unhappy. When Wu began to have sex with Feng Xiaobao, she found him really satisfactory. She had him change his name into Xue Huaiyi and pampered him to an unlimited degree. Later she asked the palace doctor, Shen Nanqiu, to prepare some stimulant to improve her sexual life and she ended up having sex with the doctor. Princess Taiping, Wu's daughter, recommended a twenty-year-old, handsome young man called Zhang Changzong to serve her mother. And Zhang Changzong introduced the woman emperor to his elder brother Zhang Yizhi. The two young men were most favoured by Wu Zetian and their wealth grew with each passing day. In feudal society, when a man became emperor he could have as many women as he wished. What was so strange about a woman emperor having a few male lovers? Of course, Wu was aware of the political ambitions of her male lovers. Xue Huaiyi became so arrogant that one day he walked into the living quarters where only the prime minister was admissible. He was seen by Su Liangsi, the prime minister, who had him slapped on the face dozens of times. Xue went to complain to Wu Zetian who reprimanded him, saying: "Did you think Nanya (name of the residence) was the place for you? You should have taken the north gate." To her, male prostitutes were there only to serve her in her bedroom. In her later years, she grew muddle-headed and more suspicious. As a result, she let the two Zhang brothers interfere in political affairs.

The two brothers, however, were not easy people to deal with. Besides, male prostitutes were always more active in political affairs than their female counterparts. The two of them made a great mess of the court, which resulted in Wu losing the respect she had commanded in the past.

In response to the situation, persons led by Zhang Jianzhi, the prime minister, began to take secret actions to restore power to the Li family and bring back the Tang Dynasty. Having drawn to his side the general guarding the palace gate, he took Li Xian, the crown prince, along to charge into the palace right up to the living quarters of Wu Zetian, known as the Fairy Heralding Palace, with five hundred palace garrison guards, in the first month of 705. They captured the two Zhang brothers and killed them on the spot.

Wu Zetian heard the noise outside and struggled to see what was going on. Zhang Jianzhi and his party then walked in. Zhang petitioned as follows: "Zhang Changzong and Zhang Yizhi have been plotting to take over the power of the country. We acted with instructions from the crown prince to have them executed. We were afraid that our plan would leak out so we didn't come to report to Your Majesty earlier. We are here to apologize."

The ailing Wu Zetian had no way to revert this and so she helplessly nodded her head. Several days later, Wu was compelled to leave the throne to crown prince Li Xian. She also had to give up her title as emperor and had to be content to be the empress dowager. The name of the dynasty was changed from Zhou back to Tang.

In the eleventh month of 705, at the age of eighty-two, Wu Zetian finally breathed her last.

Her body was buried together with Emperor Gaozong in Qianling, west of Chang'an. According to her will, a wordless tombstone was planted in front of her tomb site and the tombstone has been standing there to this day for more than 1,900 years. She knew people would have different opinions of her. And so, instead of writing her epitaph, she let people in later generations make their own judgements.

VIII　Zhao Kuangyin Ascends the Throne by Launching a Coup

During the 10th century, the then most powerful empire in the world——the Tang Dynasty——met its demise. After that, China entered a period of warlords fighting one another, a period known as the Five Dynasties and Ten States (907 – 979). For decades these warlords contended with each other, resulting in killing thousands and the emergence of five different dynasties. Many fertile lands now became wastelands inhabited by wild hares. People who suffered tremendously from the civil wars longed for national unity and social stability. During this historical time, Zhao Kuangyin (927 – 976), a descendant of a general's family, stood out and finally established a new dynasty called the Song, after waging a coup. Also known as the Northern Song, his empire brought the divided China into unification once again.

The Northern Song (960 – 1126) was ruled successively by ten emperors for a period of 167 years. In 1127, the empire was overrun by the Kin, another empire founded in the north by an ethnic minority group. In the fifth month of that same year, Zhao Gou (1107 – 87) re-established the Song in the south. The empire he founded came to be known as the Southern Song. It had nine emperors and existed for 153 years.

1. Born in the age of turmoil

On the sixteenth of the second month of 927, a baby boy was born into a military officer's family in the Jiama Barracks of Luoyang, the ancient capital. The boy, named Zhao Kuangyin, was to eventually become the founding emperor of the Song Dynasty. Due to his prominent life, people later said that when he was born, he radiated golden rays and an aromatic smell permeated the room the whole night. Thus they gave him the nickname, the "Fragrant Boy."

His family background and the continuous wars of the time helped the boy develop a strong interest in archery and other weapons. From early childhood he trained constantly. Once, when he rode a galloping horse through the city gate, his head banged on the lintel of the gate and he fell off the horse. Those who saw this were worried for him, but he simply stood up, ran after the horse and jumped on it as if nothing had happened.

At the age of twenty-one, the handsome Zhao Kuangyin left home to look for ways of developing his career. He went first to Fuzhou (in present-day Hubei) and asked to see Wang Yanchao, a former subordinate of his father. Seeing the sorry condition

Zhao was in, Wang packed him off with some money. This story was remembered at a dinner after Zhao became the emperor, when Zhao said to Wang Yanchao, now a general, "When I went to join you, why didn't you accept me?" Wang quickly kowtowed and used this excuse: "I was just a minor officer at the time. How could I take on such a great man as you? If I had taken you and made you an ordinary soldier in my army, how could there have been this day?" Zhao laughed the matter off when he heard this answer.

Later Zhao went to join Dong Zongben, another subordinate of his father, who did not find him disagreeable, but Dong's son would not have the young man. Young and inspiring as he was, Zhao could not bear the coldness of Dong's son and left without even bidding goodbye.

Where should he go? Zhao, at the end of his resources, had to beg for food from monks. At one temple, an old monk predicted that this young man would become a person of greatness. So the monk gave him some money and told him to keep walking to the north and he would be sure to run into good luck.

Zhao came across many fortune tellers at Gaoxin Temple, Guide (in present-day Henan) and had one of them predict his future. He was told that he had a future of unlimited development, which was like a shot of stimulant to the depressed Zhao. He wrote a poem to express his excitement: The rising sun casts its sparkling rays, tinging the mountains red. It rises to the sky, chasing away all the stars and the crescent moon. His determination of doing something great was made clear in this poem. He continued to travel north and came to Yedu, where he joined the ranks of Guo Wei, garrison commander of the Later Han (947 – 950), a small state.

To consolidate his grip on power, Emperor Yin of the Later Han first had a number of powerful ministers murdered, and then he directed his attack on Guo Wei, who held the military power. Guo was thus compelled to rise to fight the emperor. He marched towards Bianliang (now known as Kaifeng), capital of the Later Han. The emperor was killed by his bodyguards and Guo Wei asked the emperor's mother to preside over the court. Meanwhile he prepared to make Liu Bin, nephew of the late Emperor Yin, the new emperor.

Just then news came that the Liao troops in the north had invaded. Guo had to take the garrison troops to fight the invading army. On the way, officers and men kept saying, "We have defeated the forces led by the emperor and taken the capital. Everyone of us has committed a crime against the emperor. Now there is a new emperor and we won't be able to escape being punished." So they decided to wage a coup. As they were in a hurry, they simply tore a piece of yellow cloth from a flag, draped it on Guo and declared him the emperor. Guo then decided to turn back to the capital where he replaced the Later Han Dynasty and declared the founding of the Later Zhou in the first month of 951. He, of course, was the emperor of the newly founded dynasty.

During the mutiny, Zhao Kuangyin worked the hardest, winning the trust of Guo, who promoted Zhao to be a garrison officer.

In 955, Guo Wei died and his ruling position was inherited by his adopted son, Chai Rong, known as Emperor Shizong of Zhou. The new emperor had the ambition of unifying the whole country and so he particularly depended on Zhao, who was both gallant and intelligent. Zhao also did everything to curry favour with the emperor. Once, Zhao's father, Zhao Hongyin, led his troops past Chuzhou City during the night. Zhao Kuangyin, who was the garrison commander of the city, refused to open the gate for his own father. He said, as he stood on the city wall tower, "Though we are father and son, the opening of the city gate is ruled by specific regulations and I won't open it until day breaks." On another occasion, someone tried to bribe Zhao with three thousand taels of silver. Zhao turned the whole amount over to Emperor Shizong, winning more trust from the sovereign ruler. Later the emperor entrusted him with recruiting more soldiers so as to build up the royal garrison force. He also gave the command of this crack force to Zhao. From that moment on, Zhao had the supreme military power of the Later Zhou firmly in his hands.

When Emperor Shizong died of illness, his son, Chai Zongxun, at the age of seven took the throne. With such a child as the sovereign ruler, the country was thrown into instability. Rumours started to spread from the capital. It was a time of great turbulence. Whoever had the military power had the strength to ascend the throne. A military coup organized by army officers was already quietly in the making.

2. Taking the throne

As garrison commander, Zhao Kuangyin not only firmly held the military power in his hands, he also managed to convince a number of major military leaders to become his close allies. Using the method of cementing relationships through becoming sworn brothers, he made pacts with Shi Shouxin and Wang Shenqi, thus greatly expanding his forces. More importantly, he cemented his friendship with Zhao Pu, an outstandingly resourceful man, who later proved indispensable to Zhao's career.

During the Spring Festival of 960, while the court of the Later Zhou was celebrating the holiday, it received a fake report fabricated by Zhao's close allies saying that the Northern Han (951 – 979) and Liao, a northern minority state, had launched a joint attack on the Later Zhou border.

The news threw the court into confusion. Prime Minister Fan Zhi decided to send Zhao Kuangyin with the garrison troops to the border to help ward off the enemy.

Zhao was beside himself with joy to receive such an order. In just two days he marched off with his troops. Going with him were two of his most trusted aides. One was Zhao Kuangyi, his brother, and the other was the resourceful Zhao Pu. When they came to the post station at Chenqiao, twenty kilometres from the capital, darkness fell and Zhao gave the order to rest. The soldiers were tired and soon all felt asleep. The officers gathered for a discussion. A trusted aide of Zhao Kuangyin said, "Our emperor is very young and knows nothing about our going to the front to fight and die. General Zhao loves his soldiers like his own children. Perhaps we should first make him our emperor and then march north to fight." Many responded positively to this suggestion. Just then Zhao Kuangyi and Zhao Pu came in and the officers attending the discussion reported to them that, "We have decided to support General Zhao as our new emperor!" Zhao Kuangyi, who had been the mastermind of all this from behind the scenes was quite happy with the development, but for the time being he pretended to try to stop it, though in reality he was being more inciting: "An emperor must have the support of the people. Only when all people are united as one, can there be eternal prosperity and wealth." All those present expressed the desire to work closely together, and they then went to see Zhao Kuangyin. Zhao, however, pretended to be asleep in the post station by snoring thunderously. Deep in his heart, he was eager to hear the result of the discussions and anticipated the arrival of the great historic moment.

When the officers heard him snoring, they did not go in to wake him up, but went about making preparations for a mutiny. Zhao Pu, meanwhile, sent the news to Shi Shouxin and Wang Shenqi, who were guarding the capital.

As day broke, a group of fully armed soldiers went towards the rear hall of the post station. The leader of the group carried a yellow robe. The guards at the door let them in and they instructed Zhao to sit on a large chair where they helped him put on the yellow robe. Since the official outfit of an emperor was always yellow, this was the symbol of the power of the emperor.

Zhao Kuangyin pretended to be surprised. "How can I accept this?" he asked.

The officers and men said, "If you don't agree, it means we are rebels against you, in which case we will have to fight you first."

Zhao Kuangyi, his brother, came forward and said, "It is the common wish of the officers and men. Brother, please give your consent."

At that point all the officers and men knelt and shouted: "Long live our great emperor!"

"You want to live a life of wealth and prosperity, so you make me the emperor," Zhao said. "If I give orders will you listen?"

"Of course," they replied in unison, "we will carry out all your orders."

So Zhao made them agree on three things, saying, "When we reach the capital, we must first protect the empress dowager and the young emperor of the Later Zhou; second, no court ministers should be dealt with rudely; third, no one should take anything from the state warehouse or from the common people."

Zhao now led his army towards the capital. All the way there, the army maintained strict discipline without harming anyone. Since Shi Shouxin and Wang Shenqi were in the city as agents working from within, Zhao and his troops easily entered the capital. By then the officers and soldiers had already captured the prime ministers Fan Zhi and Wang Pu, and now they brought them to Zhao Kuangyin who apologized to them, saying, "I have had the trust of the emperor of the Later Zhou, but I have had to do this under the pressure of my subordinates. I really feel ashamed!" So saying, he began to take off the yellow robe he was wearing. Fan Zhi wanted to say something, but an officer holding a sword shouted loudly, "General Zhao is the emperor today. Whoever does not accept this will be killed." Seeing that the situation was irreversible, Wang Pu knelt down and shouted long live the emperor. Fan Zhi then had to do the same.

On the fifth day of the Chinese New Year, Zhao Kuangyin officially ascended the throne and changed the name of the empire to Song, historically known as the Northern Song. As founding emperor of this dynasty, Zhao had the reign title of Emperor Taizu of Song.

Before this time, when emperors discussed state affairs with their ministers, they all sat together and tea was served. After Zhao became the emperor, whenever the prime minister made a report, Zhao deliberately said, "My eyesight is bad, please give me the report." As soon as the prime minister stood up and came forward, the emperor motioned to a servant to remove the chair of the prime minister. Thus prime ministers had to make their reports while standing. This change in the court ritual was a reflection of the upgraded power of the emperor. Emperor Taizu, however, was not content with this change only. Next he would centralize military power.

3. Reducing the power of army generals

Within six months after Emperor Taizu took the throne, two local military commanders led revolts against his rule. The emperor had to personally go into the battlefield and, with much difficulty, put them down. After that, he began to look for ways to consolidate his power. One day he asked his trusted minister, Zhao Pu, "What is the reason for the frequent change of emperors and protracted war that has gone on for decades following the demise of the Tang Dynasty?"

Zhao Pu replied, "It's very simple: the tail is bigger than the head. Local power is too strong and makes the emperor weak. When an emergency rises, the emperor had no means of controlling the situation, and the result is the changing of emperors. If you can centralize military power and thus cut the tail, there will be peace."

Emperor Taizu liked Zhao Pu's idea of reducing local and grassroots power in favour of strengthening centralized power.

Later, Zhao Pu suggested to the emperor: "The garrison commanders Shi Shouxin and Wang Shenqi are now too powerful. They should be removed from their posts of commanding the garrison troops."

"You're being over sensitive," the emperor replied, "they are my old friends and will not do anything to oppose me."

Zhao Pu, however, pushed his point. "I'm not worried that they will betray you. From my observations, I find them rather lacking in the ability to lead the army. But if their subordinates start to make trouble and compel one of them to become the emperor, he would have to agree."

This reminder drove the point home to the emperor, who said with a start, "Thank you for reminding me."

While serving under Guo Wei, garrison commander of the Later Zhou, Zhao Kuangyin had taken an active part in helping Guo to assume the supreme power of the Later Zhou by tearing a piece of yellow cloth from a flag, draping it over Guo, and making Guo the emperor. Within less than ten years, he himself had become the emperor in much the same fashion. He clearly understood the truth that the establishment and overthrow of a dynasty depended on the military officers. He could see that his ten sworn brothers and senior generals now posed potential danger to his throne. At any time they could easily take away the yellow robe and crown that they had put on him. With this thought, he made up his mind to bring into his own hands the power of leading the military.

One day in the seventh month of 961, he threw a party and invited the generals of the capital, such as Shi Shouxin. After everybody had a little too much to drink, the emperor spoke, in a worried tone. He said, "Without your support, I could not have become the emperor. But I find being the emperor is not an easy job. Often I cannot sleep well!"

Shi Shouxin and others were surprised at this, and asked him, "What is it that makes Your Highness unable to sleep well?"

Emperor Taizu looked around at the generals and said, "Who does not want to be an emperor?"

This statement terrified the generals, who hurried to respond, "How can Your Highness have such an idea? We now have peace and you're the ruler, who can harbour the ambition of becoming the emperor himself?"

The emperor had to make his point clear to them. "You don't have the ambition, but how can you be sure that none of your subordinates have such ideas? If they put the yellow robe on any of you, you will have to go along with them and become the emperor."

The generals all knelt and kept saying, "We are too dumb and have never thought of this possibility before. Now please, Your Highness, tell us what to do."

Emperor Taizu relaxed his tone. He said, "Life flies by. Everyone wants to have enough money to enjoy a wealthy life. At the same time, they want enough wealth for their children to enjoy a rich life. What I have been thinking is that you should give up your military power, go and serve as local officials, buy a lot of land and property for your posterity. Meanwhile you can have a pleasant life with girls singing and dancing for you at every meal. We can become relatives with our children marrying each other, and there will be no suspicions between us. We will all have a life of wealth and pleasure. Wouldn't that be wonderful?"

No matter what they thought privately, they all kowtowed to the emperor to thank him for pointing out a way for them.

The next day Shi Shouxin and other generals all

petitioned to hand over their commands with the excuse of being in poor health. The emperor granted their requests, gave them money and other gifts, and appointed them to local official posts.

Now the military power of the capital was in the hands of the emperor himself, but regional commanders still held great power, which worried the emperor.

In the tenth month of 969, the emperor gave another party in his palace garden, one for the regional military commanders such as Wang Yanchao. The emperor simply repeated the same process as he said slowly, "You're all generals who have performed meritorious deeds for the country. You've been stationed away from the capital and kept busy. I really feel sorry for this situation."

Wang Yanchao and others, who were all aware of the story about the dinner for capital military generals fully understood what the emperor was driving at. They knelt down and said, "We really haven't done much and do not deserve the glory we are given. Now we are getting old. Please, Your Highness, allow us to retire." Quickly the emperor agreed to their requests. There were, however, a few generals who did not understand the situation and kept praising themselves for their performance. The emperor was tired of listening to their bragging, and said simply, "What you have said about yourselves all happened in the past. It is not worth mentioning any more." The next day, the emperor announced the removal of these generals from their posts as regional commanders and packed them off to minor official positions without any real power.

With this done, all the military power, from the central level to the regional level, was now firmly in the grip of the emperor himself.

4. Making the plan for unification on a snowy evening

With his position as the emperor fully secured, Emperor Taizu now began preparations for his grand aim of unifying China.

The period of the Five Dynasties and Ten States in the wake of the fall of the Tang Dynasty was an era of great disorder. When Zhao Kuangyin became Emperor Taizu of Song, there were still five states remaining: the Northern Han, the Southern Tang, the Later Shu, the Southern Han and the Wuyue. The emperor racked his brains for a solution as to where to begin in his cause of conquering them.

It snowed heavily one evening and Zhao Pu, the prime minister, was sitting by the fire in his home. Just then he heard knocking on his door, and he felt it was strange for someone to come and visit him on such a snowy evening. He opened the door and found a man standing there in a cape. The visitor turned out to be the emperor. Once inside, the emperor told the prime minister, "I've also asked my brother, Zhao Kuangyi, to come. He'll be here in a moment."

Soon Zhao Kuangyi arrived and a meeting of the three as the core of the rule of the Song Dynasty took place in Zhao Pu's house. They sat around the fire, drinking and eating as they discussed the grand cause of China's unification.

The emperor said, "I've been thinking of something lately and could not sleep. That's why I've come to discuss it with you." He relayed to them his plan of taking the small state in the north, the Northern Han, as the first stage in bringing the entire country under the banner of Song.

Zhao Pu, an ever resourceful man, thought for a while and then concluded, "This plan may not work. The Northern Han is our protective screen in the northwest against the northern state Liao, which is a minority state with a very powerful military force. If we take the Northern Han, we come face to face with Liao's threat. Besides, the Northern Han is a dependency of Liao. Once we start to march on the Northern Han, Liao will immediately come to its rescue and we may fail in our plan. A better alternative would be to take the states in the south first and then come back to deal with the Northern Han. I think we would stand for a better chance of success that way."

Emperor Taizu was happy to hear this and said with a big smile: "That is exactly what I think. I was just now only testing you."

The plan for taking the southern states first, as

the first step of unifying China, was finalized on that snowy evening.

The Song first conquered the Later Shu and then the Southern Han. Its next target was the Southern Tang. Covering a territory south of the Yangtze River, the Southern Tang was a land of plenty and fertile soil. Its last ruler, Li Yu was originally a noted poet who was also well versed in music, painting and calligraphy. The only thing he was bad at was running his country. Every year he sent a great amount of gold, silver and other treasures as tribute to the Song Dynasty in order to obtain support from Emperor Taizu for sustaining his rule of the Southern Tang. Having witnessed the conquering of one small state after another by the Song Dynasty, he grew worried and sent a letter to Emperor Taizu, expressing his willingness of abolishing the name of his state, Southern Tang, and to just be called "ruler of a southern state." How could a letter suing for peace on such humiliating terms stop Emperor Taizu's determination to take the whole China?

In the ninth month of 974, Emperor Taizu dispatched two generals, Cao Bin and Pan Mei, to march south and attack the Southern Tang both on the land and along the river.

Cao Bin took the navy to sail along the river and soon occupied Chizhou (today's Guichi in Anhui) and then stationed his troops at Caishiji (today's Ma'anshan City, Anhui). Pan Mei and his infantry came to the northern bank of the Yangtze River. Someone suggested that a floating bridge be built with bamboo rafts and large boats. Pan Mei adopted this idea and had people start working to build such a bridge. When the news reached the capital of Southern Tang, Jinling (present-day Nanjing, Jiangsu), the ruler asked his ministers for advice as to what to do. The ministers, who had been drinking, did not make careful review of the situation, but said off-handedly, "We've never heard of building a floating bridge for crossing the river."

The ruler of the Southern Tang also laughed, saying, "That's right. I believe that what they are doing is a silly childish game."

Three days later, the floating bridge was ready and Pan Mei led his troops across the river towards the city of Jinling. The officers and men of the Southern Tang were terrified and surrendered along the way. The Song army, 100,000 strong, rolled on to Jinling, which was soon about to fall.

The decrepit and muddle-headed Li Yu was still chanting scriptures with monks in the palace. When he finally ascended the city wall to examine the situation, he was terrified by seeing the Song army flags fluttering in the wind and the Song troops standing menacingly with their sharp weapons in hand. He immediately sent Xu Xuan, a senior minister, to see Emperor Taizu of Song.

Xu Xuan said to the Song emperor, "My lord regards you as a son does to his father and has always been filial. Why do you still send troops to attack us?"

The emperor shot back his own question, saying, "To borrow your allusion of a father and his son, do you think the father and son should be divided into two families?"

Xu Xuan could not answer this and went back to report to Li Yu. Without any workable plan, Li Yu sent Xu Xuan back again to see the Song emperor to beg for peace.

Envoy Xu Xuan begged time and again that Emperor Taizu not to attack his capital, Jinling. But by then the emperor had run out of patience. He shouted with his eyes wide open and his hand on his sword, "Stop saying anything more. Li Yu has committed no crime, but how can I allow others to snore next to my bed?"

It was not until Xu Xuan had failed entirely to beg for peace that Li Yu began to mobilize a force of 150,000 men to come and rescue Jinling. Half way to Jinling, this troop was attacked from both sides by the Song army and was totally crushed.

Cao Bin gave the order to attack Jinling. Li Yu first wanted to burn himself to death, but did not have the courage to do so. Finally he took his ministers to surrender to Cao Bin. Later when Li Yu was brought to the Song capital, Emperor Taizu treated him rather generously, but Li himself was overwhelmed by sadness after he became a captive. So he wrote a poem in which he expressed the sadness for losing his country. It is said that when Zhao Kuangyi, the brother of Emperor Taizu, succeeded his brother to become the second emperor with the reign title of Emperor Taizong, he read Li's poem and became worried. He thus had Li poisoned to death.

With the Southern Tang crushed, the only state in the south that still stood independent was Wuyue. Emperor Taizu did not continue to march towards Wuyue, but adopted the method combining a stick with a carrot. He summoned the king of Wuyue, Qian Chu, to the Song capital. The king came with his wife, all the way worrying about their lives. During the meeting, Emperor Taizu gave him a yellow parcel and told Qian to go back. Qian opened the parcel and saw it contained nothing but petitions written by Song generals and ministers asking that Qian be attacked. The parcel made Qian both grateful and scared of Emperor Taizu. The small state of Wuyue was thus something already in Emperor Taizu's pocket and to take it was only a matter of formality.

5. Promoting cultural development and enlisting the service of the talented

Emperor Taizu came out of a military background and spent most of his life on the battlefield. The Five Dynasties were a time ruled by men of force. Like many other military men, the emperor extolled military prowess and despised men of letters. And now as emperor, he still retained the habits of a warrior.

One day he was in the back garden intently trying to shoot sparrows with a catapult. A subordinate came to see him. Realizing that the man came on ordinary administrative business, the emperor became unhappy. The subordinate tried to reason with him, saying, "The matter I've brought is at least more important than shooting a sparrow."

This enraged the emperor who picked up an axe and knocked the man's two front teeth out. The official picked up his teeth and put them into his pocket. The emperor then asked him, "Since you picked up the teeth, do you want to report on me?"

"As a subordinate," the official replied evenly, "I cannot report on the emperor, but the matter will be recorded by historians."

This reply fell heavily on the emperor. It meant a warning to Emperor Taizu that, even as an emperor, he should be careful with his behaviour. Immediately, he apologized to the man and presented him with many expensive gifts.

Thanks to a self-review of his own actions and the persuasion of ministers, the emperor finally came to realize this truth: "Political power may be won on horseback, but it should not be maintained on horseback." This realization accelerated the process by which the emperor turned from being a military man into a politician.

Once troubled by a difficult issue, the emperor consulted Prime Minister Zhao Pu, who also could not solve it. The emperor then turned to men with great cultural learning and the question was solved. So the emperor said to Zhao Pu, "The prime minister should be a man of cultural learning." The emperor loved to read, and also encouraged his military generals to read. He enlisted a large number of men of letters and departed from the situation in which the governing body was entirely formed by military officers. As a result, he fundamentally changed the attitude of placing military prowess above cultural learning.

The emperor also attached great importance to the official examination system. People could all take part in the official selection examinations regardless of their family background and social position. He personally read examination papers and sometimes appointed poor people with real talent to serve the country.

These measures brought great progress in culture, science, technology and education and, in turn, ushered in a glorious new era for feudal culture in China, after the period of stagnation during the warring years of the Five Dynasties.

His emphasis on developing agriculture, building irrigation networks and reducing the corvee system also promoted economic development and social prosperity.

6. The unsolved, age-old mystery

It snowed heavily during the night of the twentieth day of the tenth month of 976. Zhao Kuangyin, or Emperor Taizu of the Song, who had just turned fifty years of age suddenly died. The man who succeeded him was not his eldest son, Zhao Defang, but his brother Zhao Kuangyi. How did the emperor suddenly die? Why was he not succeeded by his son? These were mysteries that have not been answered for more than a thousand years.

Official history books and records of the Song Dynasty make no mention of this and it is only unofficial writings that offer varied interpretations.

The *Unofficial Records of Xiangshan*, written by monk Wenying who moved actively within the world of the royal family, dealt with the question at length. His book says that in the second month of 976, Emperor Taizu suddenly ran into the monk who years earlier had predicted that Zhao Kuangyin would rise to be a man of great prominence. The emperor asked, "Where have you been all these years? I have long wanted to ask you something?" The monk responded by asking the emperor what question he had. "Tell me how many more years I can live," Emperor Taizu replied.

The monk made some calculations and then said, "If the twentieth day of the tenth month this year turns out to be a fine day, you will live another twelve years. If it turns out to be a day of snow, it may be your last. If, however, you can overcome the emergency accident during the snow, you will be out of danger."

The emperor kept the monk's words at heart. On the evening of the twentieth day of the tenth month, the emperor went out to study the sky. All he saw were sparkling stars and so he was happy that it was a fine day. Suddenly something unexpected happened. With a gust of northerly wind, snow flakes began to descend. The emperor was taken aback and hurried to his living quarters. He summoned his brother, Zhao Kuangyi, to help him through this danger. When Zhao Kuangyi arrived, all the aides and servants were told to leave. From the shadows by candle light, the servants saw the two brothers begin to drink together while chatting. Then they saw the shadow of the emperor get up from his chair with something in his hand and point it at his brother. The brother, Zhao Kuangyi, leaped from his seat to dodge it. Then they heard the emperor scream these words: "Well done! Well done!" Next they heard the fall of an axe to the ground. This was soon followed by the sound of heavy snoring. Someone suggested they go in and see if the two brothers were drunk. However, Wang Ji'en, a eunuch, stopped them saying "Without the emperor's consent, no one is allowed to go in." At dawn, Zhao Kuangyi came out of the chamber and announced the death of the emperor. He said that in his will the emperor had passed the throne to him.

Ever since, that snowy night has became a thousand-year-long mystery of Chinese history.

The next day, after the death of Emperor Taizu, his brother Zhao Kuangyi put on the yellow robe and became the second emperor of Song with the reign title of Emperor Taizong of Song.

According to another story, after the death of Emperor Taizu, his wife asked the eunuch Wang Ji'en to summon her son, Zhao Defang, to the palace to get him ready to take the throne. Wang Ji'en brought Zhao Kuangyi into the palace instead. The empress was terrified to find that the man who came to see her was not his son. She said to Zhao Kuangyi, "Now the life and well-being of my son and myself are in your hands."

No matter which story is correct, the fact is that Zhao Kuangyi succeeded to the throne by a plot.

Unofficial history tends to explain the emperor's sudden death this way: eunuch Wang Ji'en was a trusted aide of Zhao Kuangyi and the killing of Emperor Taizu that evening had been planned beforehand. So when someone suggested that they go in and take a look, the eunuch stopped them. Even the prophet monk was a partner to this plot. He knew something about meteorology and took part in planning the killing that night. While drinking with his brother, Emperor Taizu told him what the monk had said and made arrangements in case he should die. Zhao Kuangyi caught him off guard and put poison in his wine. The emperor realized that he had fallen victim to the plot of his most trusted brother after he had drunk the wine, so he tried to beat his brother with an axe, while screaming at him sarcastically: "Well done!"

Hearsay is not enough to solve the case and records about the death of Emperor Taizu remain with these words: "The axe fell in candle light; mystery shrouded the death."

IX   Kublai Khan, Founder of the Yuan Dynasty

In the early 13th century, the Mongolians, an ethnic minority, began to rise in northern China. They consisted of two component groups, hunters in the forest region and herdsmen on the grasslands. Being the dominant group, the latter lived a nomadic life of "white canopy and black carts, moving about following water and grass." In 1206, Genghis Khan (1162 – 1227), the leader of the Mongolian tribe, established the Mongolian kingdom. Later he and his successors began a long period of fighting across the continents of Asia and Europe.

In 1234, Ogdai (1186 – 1241), the second Mongol ruler, defeated the Kin empire that was established in 1115. In 1260, Kublai Khan (1215 – 1294) became the fifth Mongol ruler. He adopted the administrative and legal systems of the Han Chinese in the Central Plains and shifted his political centre southward. In 1271, he established the Yuan Dynasty and made Yanjing (now Beijing) its capital.

The founding of the Yuan Dynasty put an end to the division of the country that had existed during the Northern Song and Southern Song period, and once again China was unified.

The Yuan Dynasty with Kublai Khan as the founder had a succession of ten emperors for a period of ninety-eight years.

1. Grandfather Genghis Khan

Genghis Khan (1162 – 1227) was the reign title of Temujin, son of a Mongol tribal chief. The Mongolians had the custom of marrying young, so in 1171, when Temujin was only nine years old, his father took him to another tribe to look for a future wife for him. The tribal leader there agreed to marry his ten-year-old daughter to Temujin. In keeping with the local custom of engagement, Temujin had to stay temporarily in his father-in-law's place, while his father went home alone. On his way, he met Tartars who were having a feast on the grassland and so the father joined them. He had forgotten that years before his tribe and the Tartars were enemies, but the Tartars hadn't, and they put poison in the food they gave him. By the time he arrived home, the poison in his stomach made things so painful that he soon died.

After he died, another tribe, the Taichiwu, came and took away his people. Temujin's mother and her four children had to live by picking wild fruits and fishing. The extreme hardship of his early life turned Temujin into a man of bravery, tenacity, coolness and brutality.

As Temujin matured, he became quite expert at

horseback archery. People in the Taichiwu tribe who had looted Temujin's tribe after his father's death were afraid that Temujin might rebuild his tribe's strength again. So they launched a surprise attack and captured Temujin. They put wooden shackles on him and paraded him publicly. When night fell, Temujin caught the guard by surprise and hit him hard with his shackles. He then fled, joined his mother and brothers, and moved to settle by a tributary to Herlen River.

When he came of age, he formally married his bride. His mother-in-law presented him with a coat made of marten fur. He, in turn, presented the coat to Wang Khan, leader of Kele tribe, and became the fostered son of Wang Khan.

Not long afterwards, three tribes came to attack Temujin and his tribe. They captured his wife and took her away. With the support of Wang Khan, Temujin was able to defeat the enemy and rescue his wife, achieving a major victory. After that, Temujin was made the Mongol Khan and he commanded a crack force. Whenever his willow-wood bow rang, his army would assemble and was able to take whatever castle it attacked.

In 1199, Wang Khan called Temujin and his army to attack the enemy. Temujin and his force fought all the way to Ulungur Lake in Xinjiang. On their way back, Wang Khan was attacked again by enemy troops. Temujin took the lead in beating back the enemy and won a series of victories. Seeing that Temujin was becoming increasingly strong, Wang Khan grew concerned. So he decided to get rid of Temujin when the latter came for a party. News of this plan leaked out and Temujin decided to depart from Wang Khan. They even fought a battle with each other, with Temujin losing it since his forces were too small to battle Wang Khan's. Taking along only nineteen close comrades-in-arms, Temujin resettled on the bank of the Banzhuni River. When there was no food, they slaughtered wild horses to tide them over.

In 1203, Temujin reorganized his forces and, taking advantage of Wang Khan having a party, attacked him in a surprise move. They caught Wang Khan off-guard and killed him as he was trying to flee.

Zhamuhe, a good friend of Temujin since their youth, commanded an army much stronger than that under the command of Temujin. Seeing Temujin's influence growing quickly, Zhamuhe began to be envious of Temujin, although ostensibly they were still on good terms. Once, Zhamuhe's brother tried to take away horses raised by Temujin's subordinates and was killed while doing it. According to the custom of Mongolians, it was no crime to kill the horse thief, but Zhamuhe used the incident to organize an attack on Temujin with an army of 30,000 divided into thirteen routes. Temujin also organized an army of equal numbers in an equal number of routes to fight the incoming at-

231

tackers. It was not a good tactics to fight the attackers this way, which indicated that Temujin still lacked practical experience in warfare. Naturally, the battle ended with Temujin losing. The victorious Zhamuhe, however, did something most foolish. He used seventy big pots to boil the captives in, thus losing the support of the people. Many of those in his army ran to fight under Temujin, who used all ways possible to win the hearts of new comers. The original loser of this battle, Temujin, eventually stood to benefit from his defeat.

From then on, Temujin conquered one tribe after another and eventually unified the Mongolian highlands.

In the spring of 1206, Temujin, now forty-five years old, called a meeting at the source of the Onon River. A shaman said that he had seen the heavenly god who had promised to give the earth to the management of Temujin and his descendants. Temujin then ascended the throne of the Great Khan and took the reign title of Genghis Khan. "Genghis" in Mongolian means "sea" while "khan" means sovereign ruler. Genghis Khan established the Mongol state with its capital at Horin.

Genghis Khan drew up a government combining both the military and political systems into one, with the administrative division separated into bodies of 10,000, 1,000, 100 and 10 households. Leaders of these bodies were both military commanders and administrators at the same time. He also built a crack force of 10,000 men whose job was to defend him in peaceful times and fight with him during times of war.

In 1207, the second year of Genghis Khan's reign, Emperor Zhangzong of Kin, a neighbouring state within the boundaries of China, died and was succeeded by Wanyan Yongji, formerly Prince of Wei. The Kin state sent an envoy with an imperial edict. According to past practice, Genghis Khan was expected to kneel to accept the edict from the new emperor, because before he unified the Mongol tribes, they were conquered by the Kin. The rulers of Kin implemented a policy of dividing the Mongol tribes and often instigated them into fighting among themselves. It was during one of these outbursts of infighting that an ancestor of Genghis Khan was captured by a rival tribe and sent to the Kin troops. He was nailed onto a wooden pillar until he died. Every three years, the Kin emperor would send troops to kill some of the Mongols in the name of "reducing the population." As a result, there was deep hatred between the Mongols and the Kin. Now how could Genghis Khan, young and aggressive, kneel for the new emperor of the Kin?

Genghis Khan asked the envoy, "Who is the new emperor of the Kin?"

"Prince of Wei, Wanyan Yongji," replied the envoy.

Hearing this reply, Genghis Khan spat in the direction of the Kin and said, in a scornful tone, "I thought the new emperor was an immortal. Instead, it is that coward Wanyan Yongji!" So saying, he got on his horse and sped away, leaving the envoy in the cold.

In 1211, Genghis Khan led his aides to a tall mountain by the Herlen River and swore to heaven that they would conquer the Kin. Soon the iron hooves of the Mongol cavalry overran Wushabao, a stronghold guarded by Kin troops. Next they attacked the Yehuling Mountain, inflicting heavy casualties on the crack force of the Kin. In 1213, the Mongol army broke through the defence line set up by the Kin along the Great Wall, taking in succession such towns as Xuanhua, Bao'an and Huailai and placing their army outside the Juyongguan Pass, gateway to Zhongdu (now Beijing). During the attack on Juyongguan, the advance troops of the Mongols feigned a retreat after making a strong attack. Not suspecting this was a ruse, the Kin troops went in hot pursuit. Just then the crack force led by Genghis Khan rolled towards the Kin army, engulfing the soldiers like flood. Genghis Khan pressed on through the Juyongguan Pass all the way into the North China Plain. In the spring of 1214, Genghis Khan had his troops stationed outside the Kin capital. The Kin ruler tried to sue for peace by marrying the princess to the Mongol leader and presenting the latter with a great amount of gold and silk. Then, once the Mongol army retreated, the Kin moved its capital south to Bianliang (present-day Kaifeng in

Henan). This enraged Genghis Khan who returned to attack Zhongdu, the Kin capital, saying that the Kin had broken the peace treaty. In 1215, Zhongdu fell into the hands of Genghis Khan and the Mongol army killed and looted in the city for a whole month. Genghis Khan took a great deal of wealth from the capital as well as the services of an outstanding talent, Yelu Chucai, originally an adviser to the Kin emperor and who later proved highly influential in drafting and implementing Mongol policies. Eventually he became a great statesman of the Mongol empire.

By then, Genghis Khan was already engaged in his western expedition which was to sweep across Central Asia and Eastern Europe. Thus he did not fight the Kin with his entire might and they were able to maintain their territory.

In 1226, Genghis Khan launched an attack on the Xia (1038–1227). Weak and with a small military force, the Xia immediately sued for peace. Genghis Khan was by then seriously ill and accepted the Xia's request for peace on condition that the Xia hand over its city. On the twelfth day of the seventh month, Genghis Khan died in the barracks in what is today's Qinshui County, at the foot of the Liupan Mountains in Gansu. In his will he ordered that no news of his death be released, so that when the Xia rulers came out of the city on the appointed day, the Mongols could take the opportunity to have them all killed. As planned, three days later, the

Xia ruler came to surrender with his subordinates. They were all killed and the Xia thus perished.

In order to keep Genghis Khan's death a secret, the officers and soldiers killed anybody who happened to see them when they took his bier back home. After Genghis Khan was buried, his tomb site was overgrown with woods, making the site hard to recognize. According to the *History of the Yuan Dynasty*, people only knew that he was buried in Qinian Valley, but no one knew the exact place. His descendants took the eight white felt tents that Genghis Khan had used during his lifetime as symbols for his mausoleum. Since the Mongols were a tribal people moving about on horseback, the eight white tents, known as the Eight White Chambers, were also moved from place to place.

Genghis Khan did not unify China, but he laid a solid foundation for his grandson Kublai Khan to achieve that goal and to become the founding emperor of the Yuan Dynasty. Particularly noteworthy was the fact that Genghis Khan eagerly drew on the services of talented people from among those he conquered, thus gradually making the Mongol nobles adapt to the needs of ruling the Central Plains. Without this, his posterity would have found it hard to maintain their rule by only relying on military force.

2. Marching south to take the Song

After his death, Genghis Khan was succeeded by his third son, Ogdai, who, carrying out his father's behest, asked for a route from the Southern Song court in order to lay seige to Bianjing (today's Kaifeng), capital of the Kin. The Kin was established by the Nüzhens, a northeast Chinese minority whose homes were originally in the region between the Changbai Mountains and the Heilong River. Emperor Taizong of the Kin launched two attacks on the Song in 1125 and 1126. In 1127, the Kin took the capital of the Northern Song at today's Kaifeng and captured emperors Huizong and Qinzong of the Song. With Zhao Gou as Emperor Gaozong, the Song tenaciously defended south China as its territory. Now the Mongols wanted to travel past the Song land to attack their arch enemy, the Kin, Emperor Lizong of the Southern Song gladly agreed. Emperor Aizong of the Kin sent a letter to the Song emperor, reasoning that: "Once Kin is overrun by the Mongols, your Southern Song will be the next target. Please think twice about letting them pass through your land." Emperor Lizong of the Song paid no attention to this warning and continued to collabourate with the Mongols in fighting the Kin. At the end of his resources, Emperor Aizong of the Kin committed suicide and his empire fell in 1234 under the joint attack of the Song and the Mongols.

Once the Kin had perished, the Southern Song was eager to recover Kaifeng and other places in Henan. Ogdai, the Mongol ruler, launched an offensive against the Southern Song with the accusation that the latter had broken their agreement. From then on, a long period of war between the two powers raged. Ogdai had a fatal weakness: uncontrollable drinking. Often he would become drunk, which weakened his health. His brother, Chahedai, appointed someone specially to help him control his drinking. Unable to resist his brother, Ogdai changed his small cups into big ones and drank more without exceeding the number of cups he had agreed would be his limit. The man appointed to control his drinking often gave him more than he should in order to curry favour with Ogdai. In the eleventh month of 1241, Ogdai drank until midnight at a feast given by a minister after his return from a hunting trip. He died early the next morning.

Ogdai was succeeded by his son Guyuk (1206 – 48) who died during a western expedition three years after he took over the leadership. Mangu (1208 – 59), nephew of Ogdai, then became the new Mongol ruler. In 1258, he dispatched an army to march on the Southern Song by three routes. He, himself, led the route of attack on Sichuan; his brother, Kublai, attacked Hubei and another route took aim at Hunan. Their final destination, however, was Lin'an (today's Hangzhou), capital of the

Southern Song.

At Hezhou in Sichuan, Mangu met with strong resistance from the defending troops. He besieged the city for five months without being able to take it. Instead, Mangu was killed during a battle.

While Kublai was marching towards Ezhou, Hubei, news of Mangu's death arrived. Someone suggested he should return home and seek the leadership before proceeding towards Ezhou, but Kublai refused to turn back without winning a victory. His troops then laid a tight seige on Ezhou.

Emergency reports poured into Lin'an, greatly shaking the Song court. Emperor Lizong ordered all armies to rush to help raise the seige on Ezhou and appointed the new prime minister, Jia Sidao, to supervise the battle.

Jia was an incompetent and dissolute man who had won the post simply because his sister was a favourite concubine of Emperor Lizong. All day long, he wallowed in drinking and singing by the side of the West Lake in the company of girls. Now being sent to the front, he was terrified. Without consulting anyone, he sent a trusted aide into the Mongol camp to sue for peace with the willingness to be subjects of the Mongols and offering annual tributes of silver and silk. Kublai, who was launching a tenacious offensive, was not about to stop. But just then he received a secret letter from his wife saying that his brother, Alibug had stepped up his efforts to become the khan with support of some noble families. Kublai had to sign the secret agreement of peace with Jia Sidao, who agreed to cede all the territory north of the Yangtze River to the Mongols and pay 200,000 taels of silver and 200,000 bolts of silk every year. Now Kublai marched towards home so as to contend for the position of khan.

Emperor Lizong was kept in the dark about the secret peace pact and believed Jia, who returned bragging about his beating back the Mongols. The emperor even rewarded Jia by promoting him and raising his remuneration.

3. Establishing the Yuan Dynasty

The death of Mangu on the battlefield without arrangement for succession left his brothers with an excuse to fight for the position of khan.

Kublai and his brother, Alibug, had equal advantage in winning the throne. Alibug had the support of the mother of the former khan and the sons of Mangu. As he was stationed in the capital, Horin, he was the legitimate organizer of a conference of nobles for selecting the future khan. Kublai, however, was good at winning the support of the princes and he commanded a powerful army. Besides he was well versed in warfare.

Taking action first, Kublai, on his return to the north, held a meeting of nobles who supported him for selecting the khan. They declared him the new

khan on the first day of the third month of 1260 at Kaiping (northwest of today's Duolun in Inner Mongolia).

Soon, in the capacity of the caretaker officer in the capital, Alibug also called a conference of nobles and declared himself the khan in the fourth month of the same year. For four years after that, the two brothers engaged in struggles to become the heir to the throne. In the ninth month of 1260, the two opposing armies had a fierce battle in which Kublai emerged as winner. Then he marched on towards Horin, the capital. Knowing he was no match to Kublai, Alibug pulled out of Horin. The next year Alibug sent an army to attack by surprise Kublai's troops stationed in the capital. Alibug's troops then quickly marched south. Kublai sent his army in hot pursuit, inflicting another defeat to his brother's forces. Alibug finally had to surrender to Kublai and the fighting between the two brothers for the throne of the khan came to an end.

In 1271, Kublai gave up the name of Mongol and adopted the name of Yuan for his reign. He issued an edict in which he announced that the Yuan was the inheritor of the previous Chinese dynasties. A year later, he moved his capital to Dadu (today's Beijing).

By then Beijing had become a city of ancient culture that had lasted for over 3,000 years. During the Qin Dynasty, it was known as Jicheng. During the Tang Dynasty, it was named Youzhou. The

Liao Dynasty called it Nanjing and then Yanjing. When the Kin set up its ruling headquarters there, the city's name was changed to Zhongdu. But it was in Kublai's time that the city really became the national capital.

Kublai delegated the job of building this capital to Liu Bingzhong, previously a young monk with a great cultural background. Liu became Kublai's aide and performed many meritorious deeds for the latter in the ensuring years.

The construction of the magnificent capital took a decade. The city had a circumference of 28.6 kilometres with eleven gates. It is said that the odd number of eleven, instead of any even number for the gates, came from the story about a young hero in Chinese mythology——Nezha——who was described as having three heads, six arms and two feet.

Now that he had become the khan, Kublai remembered his previous agreement with Jia Sidao, the renegade Southern Song Dynasty prime minister. He sent an envoy, Hao Jing, to discuss the implementation of the peace treaty. When Hao Jing arrived at Zhenzhou (today's Yizheng, Jiangsu), he sent his assistant to Lin'an to inform Jia Sidao of his visit. Fearing that his fraud would be exposed, Jia secretly sent people to have Hao Jing arrested in Zhenzhou. When news of this development reached Kublai, he flew into a rage. As he was still somewhat engaged in fighting off his brother in their contention for the throne, he could not tackle the issue immediately. Jia, therefore, was able to serve as prime minister of another decade and more. By that time, Emperor Lizong had already died and the crown prince was now the emperor with the title of Emperor Duzong. The ever cunning Jia Sidao pretended he wanted to retire because of old age, but at the same time had people spread the rumour that an attack from the Mongols was imminent. This greatly alarmed the new emperor, who tried hard to persuade Jia to stay on in his job and to fight the Mongols. This ruse worked and Jia was even more overbearing than before. To make him happy, the emperor had a special luxurious villa built for Jia on Geling by the West Lake. All day long Jia stayed there enjoying drink and women, and ministers who had something to report had to visit him at this villa.

In 1268, Kublai sent General Ashu to attack the Southern Song. In order to cross the Yangtze River, the Yuan troops had to take Xiangyang, a major town in the middle reaches of the river. The town was besieged for five years and Jia kept this a secret from the emperor.

One day Emperor Duzong said to Jia, "I hear that Xiangyang had been besieged by the Yuan troops for several years. Is this true?"

Jia answered shamelessly, "Well, I haven't heard such a thing."

"A palace maid told me this," the emperor

said.

When the court session was dismissed, Jia found out which of the maids that had leaked the news and had her murdered.

Though Xiangyang was in great danger, Jia continued his pleasure-seeking at his Geling villa. One day, when officials came with an emergency report, they found him pruning on the ground teasing crickets with his maidservants.

When Xiangyang finally fell into the Yuan hands, Jia put all the blame onto the commander of the town and stripped him of his post.

Kublai decided to ride on this victory and dispatched Generals Bo Yan and Ashu to press on along both land and the waterway.

Before they began their march, Kublai said to Bo Yan, "I have heard that when the Northern Song general, Cao Bin, took the south, he did not kill people and thus without antagonizing the local population. You should do the same." Because Kublai wanted to be the ruler of all China, he naturally didn't want to see the south reduced into a killing field covered with dead bodies.

When the Yuan troops were deployed outside Lin'an, the Southern Song court repeatedly tried to sue for peace, expressing willingness to pay tribute and to be content to be called as nephews or even grandsons of the Yuan, and if nephew was not acceptable, to just be subjects in return for a small territory of their own. Hewever, the Yuan refused this pleading of the Song. The peace negotiations broke up and in the first month of 1276, Zhao Xian, the young emperor of the Southern Song, had to present the imperial seal as a sign of surrender.

After the fall of the Southern Song, resistance to the Yuan continued. Officials such as Zhang Shijie, Lu Xiufu and Wen Tianxiang helped the eight-year-old Zhao Bing to become the new emperor and set up the new regime in Yashan (on an island in the present-day South China Sea near Xinhui City, Guangdong) where they struggled on against extreme difficulties. Under attacks from both sides waged by the Yuan troops, Zhang Shijie, leading a force carried on dozens of boats, tried to make a breakthrough. They ran into a heavy storm and the boats were overturned with the officers and men drowned. Seeing they had no way out, Lu Xiufu carried the young emperor on his back and jumped into the sea. Soldiers seeing the emperor and prime minister drowning themselves followed suit. It is said that more than 100,000 corpses floated on the sea. Wen Tianxiang was captured and brought to Dadu where he refused to surrender.

Later, Kublai Khan personally tried to persuade Wen to surrender. Kublai said, "If you surrender, I will make you the prime minister of the Yuan."

Wen Tianxiang replied, "I have been prime minister of the Southern Song and will not serve two dynasties in my lifetime. All I want is to die sooner."

The next day, over 10,000 people gathered at the execution ground to bid farewell to their beloved prime minister. Wen remained calm, saying, "Tell me the direction of south."

People pointed it out for him. Wen then bowed towards the south to express his firm loyalty to the Southern Song and then said to the executioner, "Do it. I have done what I need to do." Wen died in the last month of 1282 at the age of forty-seven.

4. Adopting the Han Chinese system

The Han Chinese system refers here to the basic state policies that the landlord ruling class in China had implemented for more than a thousand years in politics, economics and culture.

Kublai's mother had been attracted by and pretty well converted to the Han Chinese culture. Influenced by his mother, Kublai avidly studied Han culture from a young age and loved to hear about experiences and performances of the previous emperors. When he was twenty-seven, he invited monk Hai Yun, a master of Zen culture in Beijing, to teach him. Also with monk Hai Yun was a young monk called Zi Cong who, also known as Liu Bingzhong, became a chief adviser to Kublai in later years. Zi Cong was a highly learned man, well informed about the major events in the world, and thus won the appreciation of Kublai. Later, Kublai engaged

Wang E, who took the first place in an imperial examination during the Kin Dynasty, to lecture on Confucian classics and ways of running the country. Deeply interested in these lectures, Kublai said to Wang E, "Though I cannot do it right away, I am determined to carry out in the future what you have taught me now." Kublai recruited men of talent, including more than twenty scholars of Confucianism, to advise him, helping him become increasingly mature politically.

In 1251, his brother Mangu became the khan, who appointed Kublai to oversee the administrative and military affairs of the Central Plains, a region south of the Mongolian desert inhabited by Han Chinese. Kublai went south to Huanzhou (in present-day Inner Mongolia). Here he enlisted a large number of advisers on Han affairs, with Liu Bingzhong at the core. These scholars became the architects of Kublai's strategy of "pacifying the people and effectively running the country."

After he took the throne, Kublai worked hard to strengthen the centralization of power. At the central level, he established a Secretariat to be in charge of all administrative affairs of the country. Under this Secretariat were six ministries to handle administrative affairs, namely: ministries of personnel, revenue, rites, war, justice and works. A Censorate was established to supervise other governing bodies, and a Council of Military Affairs was also set up. So in the Yuan Dynasty the three branches of the state power——administration, supervision and the military were operating separately. Kublai Khan himself was above all three, thus keeping the supreme power firmly in his own hands.

In the economic field, he attached great importance to agriculture, reduced taxation and the corvee system, strictly forbade the development of animal husbandry at the expense of farm-crop production, or the turning of farmland into grazing grounds. He ordered Mongol soldiers to farm together with the Han farmers. To facilitate the flow of materials between the north and the south, Kublai organized the dredging and repairing of the Grand Canal so that ships from Hangzhou in the south could sail more than a thousand kilometres to the Jishuitan docks in Beijing. To promote the development of trade and commerce, he set up seven trading departments in coastal cities. Quanzhou in Fujian, for example, became the largest port in China at that time and was known as a world trading centre.

Across China, he had more than 1,400 post stations established. These institutions provided accommodations and food for travelling merchants and officials, in addition to providing protection for them. These stations well served the purpose of strengthening contacts and exchanges between various ethnic groups, as well as cultural exchanges between East and West.

Kublai had a high respect for the doctrine of

Confucius and Mencius. To win over Han Chinese intellectuals, he put them into important positions. He also asked Phatspa, a prominent lama of Tibetan origin, to develop a new Mongolian script based on the Tibetan script. A large number of books written in Chinese characters were translated into this script for the education of Mongol children.

The implementation of the Han Chinese system helped to heal the wounds of war that had lasted for several hundred years. Vitality returned to the fields and family courtyards. Prosperity was once again seen in major cities. People enjoyed a stable life and the social economy made one more step forward.

5. Killing the corrupt officials

Kublai had a firm trust in Ahama, a Chinese Moslem, and allowed him to manage the state treasury for twenty years, for he believed Ahama was "good at managing finances." This meant Ahama knew how to amass wealth from among the people for covering the huge expenses of Kublai and his government. Ahama, with trust from Kublai, was arrogant and aggressive. Making use of the power he had, he sent people out to do business in order to collect wealth. His ruthless embezzlement and wrongdoing aroused the dissatisfaction of the crown prince and many officials. The ordinary people, who suffered seriously from the corvee levied on them, also bore a strong hatred for Ahama.

In the third month of 1282, Wang Zhu, an officer in charge of a thousand houses at Yidu, secretly had a huge bronze hammer made and began to look for a way to fight Ahama. By taking advantage of the fact that Kublai and the crown prince were taking a trip, on the night of the seventeenth of the third month, Wang Zhu and monk Gao organized a discussion. They brought together more than eighty people and spread a rumour that the prince had come back to the palace and wanted to see Ahama. As soon as Ahama arrived, Wang Zhu rushed up and seized him, banging the bronze hammer he had hidden in his sleeve hard on Ahama's head. After people learned of the death of Ahama, they jumped for joy. Those too poor to buy wine pawned their clothes so that they could have some with which to celebrate. When Kublai heard of the death, however, he flew into a rage and put Wang Zhu and monk Gao to death. Before he was killed, Wang Zhu shouted at the top of his voice, "I've rid the world of a vicious man and after my death people will write about what I have done."

Kublai did order an investigation that revealed the wrongdoing of Ahama and his encroachment upon state property. Kublai thus ordered that his coffin be opened and that his dead body be smashed. Ahama's close followers were all put to death.

Now Kublai needed another man to run his treasury. In 1287, he gave the job to Sangge, who subsequently amassed personal wealth and sold official posts for money, arousing popular hatred. When Kublai was out hunting, Cheli, a court minister, boldly reported to the emperor the crimes of Sangge. Kublai, however, repudiated him for slandering his treasury minister. He told his guards to beat the sides of Cheli's head until blood oozed out from his mouth and nose. Cheli did not back off, but went on to say: "I have no personal grudge against Sangge and what I am doing today is for the good of the country. If Your Highness orders an investigation of Sangge and then kills me, I'll die without regret."

Kublai was deeply moved by this and gave the order to investigate, which proved Cheli right. When the private properties of Sangge were confiscated, they amounted half of the total property in the palace. Kublai ordered that Sangge and his trusted aides be executed.

Following the days of Genghis Khan, the Mongols regarded outward invasion and military conquering of others as their merit. Kublai inherited this tradition and fought long years against his neighbours. Each time, he would fight until he won victory. Continuing military expansion activities and the heavy corvees that were levied eventually aroused strong opposition from the people.

In the first month of 1294, Kublai fell gravely ill and soon died. His throne was succeeded by his grandson, Timur.

X   Zhu Yuanzhang: from Monk to Emperor

The peasant uprising, with the Red Turbans as the backbone force, finally overthrew the rule of the Yuan Dynasty after eighteen years of fighting. A man who had been a cowherd, a monk and then peasant leader, Zhu Yuanzhang (1328 – 98), emerged as the winner and ascended to the pinnacle of power as the founding emperor of the new dynasty: the Ming (1368 – 1644). He took the reign title of Emperor Taizu of the Ming in the first month of 1368.

The Ming was one of the most powerful and prosperous dynasties in Chinese history. Backed by a flourishing economy, an expansive territory and rich resources, it was a major world power of the time.

From the founding emperor to the last one, called Chongzhen (1611 – 44), who hanged himself on the Jingshan Hill north of the Forbidden City, the Ming was ruled by sixteen emperors for a period of 277 years.

1. A young monk who experienced tremendous hardships

Zhu Yuanzhang, originally named Zhu Chongba, was a native of Peixian County, Jiangsu, the same town where Emperor Gaozu of the Han Dynasty came from. His father, Zhu Wusi, was an honest farmer. Driven by the need to feed the family, the father later moved his family to Zhongli in Haozhou (east of present-day Fengyang County, Anhui).

During his early childhood, Zhu learned to read and write when he attended a private school for several months. Financial difficulties in his family compelled him to drop out of school. He began to work for a landlord by tending his oxen and sheep. Xu Da, Tang He and Zhou Dexing, who were generals that helped Zhu establish the Ming Dynasty, were all his childhood friends. Once they were so hungry that they slaughtered a calf and had a hearty meal of roast beef. It was when they finished eating that they realized what a disastrous offense they had committed. What was to be done? Zhu Yuanzhang, who had always been very brave, stood out to take full responsibility. He buried the hide and bones of the calf and then stuck its tail into a mountain cave. He reported to the owner that: "A calf got itself stuck in a mountain cave and I could not pull it out." The owner beat him and drove him away. His little pals thanked him profusely for handling the problem for them and from then on regarded him as their leader.

When he was seventeen years old, his hometown was attacked by an outbreak of pestilence. His parents and elder brother caught the disease and died within half a month. The villagers stopped farming and his home had no more grain to eat. Zhu then shaved his head and became a monk. At the Huangjue Monastery, he beat the morning bell and evening drum, burned incense and swept the courtyard, living the typical life of a novice monk.

Soon he found such a lonely and poor life too hard to continue. There were simply too many monks in the Huangjue Monastery and so the abbot sent some of them out to be for a living. As a new comer, Zhu Yuanzhang also had to go out begging for food. Later, after he became emperor, Zhu recalled how he walked the streets and lanes with a bamboo hat and a monk's begging bowl, spending the night in the wildness and experiencing untold hardships. He said, "I was just like a cape driven by the wind." He toured along the border region between Anhui and Henan and visited a number of towns, which brought him into contact with regional customs and habits, and well-known mountains and rivers and thus enriched his knowledge.

Three years later, Zhu returned to his hometown and once again entered the Huangjue

Monastery. Though he led a quiet and secluded life in the holy ground, in his heart he remembered the varied and colourful life outside the temple. He was no longer content with being a monk for the rest of his life, and was now ready to seek something bigger.

In 1351, the Yuan court forced labourers to dredge the old course of the Yellow River and people's indignation at this continued corvee service grew to a boiling point. Han Shantong, the leader of the White Lotus Sect of Buddhism, seized the opportunity to mobilize people by sending disciples to work among the labourers. They spread the word that "When a stone statue of a one-eyed man descends, the world will be in revolt." One day, people working in the riverbed dug out a stone sculpture of a one-eyed man on whose back were carved these words: "Never mind that I have only one eye. As soon as I arrive, the world will be in revolt." Of course the statue had been planted there by Han Shantong, but the labourers were not suspicious. So this finding excited them. News travelled fast and increasingly more and more people believed that a great turmoil would soon reign in the world.

Han took this chance to start a rebellion. The rebels wore red scarves on their heads and were clad in red clothes. They also carried red banners. Thus they became known as the Red Turbans.

In their wake, Peng Yingyu and Xu Shouhui also launched a Red Turban revolt in Hubei. Guo

Zixing revolted in Haozhou (today's Fengyang, Anhui) by killing prefectural officials and occupying towns. Zhang Shicheng, a salt dealer, also raised a banner against the Yuan Dynasty.... All across China red flags suddenly fluttered and rebels were everywhere. When news of this arrived at the Huangjue Monastery, Zhu Yuanzhang burned with enthusiasm and was ready to take action too. He also heard, however, that the rebel leaders could not agree with each other to work together, so he decided to wait and see what might happen. Just then, Tang He, his childhood friend with whom he used to tend cows and who was now an officer in Guo Zixing's rebel army, sent a letter to Zhu, inviting him to join their ranks. A fellow monk told Zhu that Tang He's letter was no longer a secret and that someone was about to report on him for a reward. This pushed Zhu to make up his mind and flee to Haozhou that very night to join Guo Zixing.

2. From soldier to commander

Three years of wandering had opened up his eyes. Reading in the temple had also helped him. So, although young, Zhu Yuanzhang was rather mature. He was good at making decisions and fought bravely and intelligently. He won the admiration of the Red Turban leader, Guo Zixing, who moved him to be an aide working in his headquarters. Guo also married his adopted daughter, Ma, to Zhu. As a result, Zhu quickly rose in the ranks and was given the nickname of "Young Master Zhu." It was then that he changed his original name, Zhu Chongba, to Zhu Yuanzhang.

Soon after the wedding, Zhu bid goodbye to his bride and went to his hometown to recruit soldiers. Folks at home came to see him and joined him as Red Turban soldiers. When Zhu returned, he came with more than seven hundred new recruits. Guo Zixing then rewarded him by promoting him to be a middle-level officer. Later, Zhu took a twenty-four-member task force to recruit a landlord force three thousand strong. After reorganization and rectification, he took this newly recruited force to attack the Yuan army barracks at Dingyuan (present-day Dingyuan, Anhui). They won and thus recruited another 20,000 men from among the captives. Now, with the support of generals Xu Da and Tang He, Zhu grew in self-confidence.

Zhu Yuanzhang paid great attention to the role of intellectuals. Feng Guoyong and Feng Guosheng, two brothers, led their army to join the ranks of Zhu. The two brothers were well versed in military strategy and Zhu learned from them ways of winning the people and land in the country. Feng Guoyong told him, "Jinling (today's Nanjing) has been a capital for several dynasties. If you can take it and use it as your base in conquering other places, eventually you'll have the whole country." Li Shanchang, a man known as a think tank, also came to

259

join him. Knowing that Li was extremely learned, Zhu asked him, "Now that the whole country is at war, when do you think peace will return?"

Li Shanchang replied, "In the last years of the Qin Dynasty, the country was in turmoil much like it is now. Liu Bang, coming from a commoner's family background, was broad-minded, put people to do the tasks they were best at, did not kill innocent people, and in five years he brought about peace and became the emperor of the Han." Zhu also came from a poor family background, similar to that of Liu Bang. Besides, they all came from Peixian County. So Zhu was in full agreement with Li. From then on, Zhu took Liu Bang as his example in everything he did. He most respectfully listened to the opinions of intellectuals.

As his army grew in size, things became more complicated. In his army many were captives from the Yuan forces and others who were formerly soldiers in private landlord armies. As a result many of them were lax in discipline. They looted and raped women wherever they went. In light of this situation, Zhu decided to rectify the army's style. After they took Hezhou (now Hexian County, Anhui), Zhu gave an order that all women who had been captured be released. After that, whenever they took a town, they would put up posters announcing their discipline and whoever broke that discipline was punished by death. General Hu Dahai's son did not observe the order to abstain from alcohol and

Zhu wanted to punish him. Someone tried to talk Zhu out of it. He reasoned that Hu Dahai was fighting in the front and, to be on the safe side, it would be wise to be lenient with his son. Zhu became angry at this. "I'd rather have Hu Dahai rebel against me than to break my own order of discipline," he said. In the end, Zhu personally beheaded Hu's son. Consequently, Zhu's army maintained strict discipline and its reputation spread far and wide.

Han Shantong, leader of the White Lotus Sect, discussed earlier in this chapter, was arrested and killed while he was still making preparations for a rebellion. His wife, Yang, hid in the Wuyi Mountains, Fujian, with their son, who was called Han Lin'er. In the second month of 1353, Liu Futong, a general from Han Shantong's army, found Han Lin'er and made him emperor. They took Song as the name of their kingdom and made Bozhou (today's Boxian County, Anhui) the capital. In the third month, Guo Zixing died of illness. In the fifth month, the young emperor appointed Guo Tianxu, son of Guo Zixing, to be the grand marshal and Zhu Yuanzhang, to be the assistant marshal. In the ninth month, Guo Tianxu was killed by traitors while he was leading an attack on Jiqing (now Nanjing). Zhu thus became the commander of the entire army built up by Guo Zixing as well as the marshal of the Red Turbans.

Once he had the entire military power in his hands, Zhu Yuanzhang led his army to inflict a thorough defeat of the Yuan navy. He then crossed the Yangtze River to attack Jiqing. In Jiqing, half a million people, both the military and civilian, surrendered. Zhu entered the city, put up posters to assure the residents of their safety and changed the name of the city from Jiqing to Yingtianfu. From then on, Zhu used Yingtianfu as his base and began to expand his forces. The purpose of changing Jiqing to Yingtianfu (roughly meaning city of responding to the will of heaven) was to indicate that he was there in response to the will of heaven, laying bare his intention of becoming the emperor. Although at that time he was still a subject of the young emperor of the Song, in reality he was already the leader of an independent force.

Though he had occupied Yingtianfu and its vicinity, Zhu and his army were still not strong enough. Seeking a solution to the question of how to gain a strong foothold amidst powerful neighbours, Zhu went to ask the opinion of Zhu Sheng, a veteran Confucian scholar. When Zhu Yuanzhang came into the house, the host was at a chess game with someone and totally ignored Zhu Yuanzhang, who had to stand dutifully and obediently watching the chess game. When it was over, Zhu Sheng, who had as if already guessed the intention of Zhu Yuanzhang's visit, wrote nine Chinese characters on a piece of paper that read: Build a wall high, store grain everywhere and don't hasten to become a king. After that Zhu Yuanzhang continued to build his army so as to raise its combat capability. At the same time, he worked hard to promote agricultural production, having the soldiers go in for land reclamation, farming and military training. He was making preparations for some grand endeavour.

Meanwhile, Zhu tried to recruit the services of all talented people. He brought in Liu Ji, Ye Chen, Song Lian and Zhang Yi, who were then known as the "four great masters" to serve as his advisers. He had special houses built as their dwellings.

To avoid drawing onto himself unnecessary trouble, Zhu superficially maintained the ruler-subject relationship with the young emperor and still carried the flag of the Red Turbans. In fact he even maintained the old slogans of the Red Turbans. After several years of effort, Zhu gradually consolidated his base area and built a strong army with adequate supplies. He was now strong enough to confront the other strong forces of that time.

3. Onto the pinnacle of power

Zhu's most powerful enemy was Chen Youliang, who began his career as a subordinate of Xu Shouhui, leader of the Red Turban's southern force. Later Chen's growing ambition drove him to kill Xu Shouhui and declare himself king of the Han, occupying a vast region that spread across Jiangxi, Hunan and Hubei provinces. He was ready to attack Zhu Yuanzhang. In 1360, commanding a powerful navy, Chen sailed down the Yangtze River to attack Yingtianfu, Zhu's home base.

Zhu called his assistants together for consultation. Seeing that Chen came with an overbearing air, some were scared and stood for surrender. Others called for a fight first and then a retreat if necessary. Only the newly-arrived adviser, Liu Ji, sat there speechless.

When the meeting was over, Zhu Yuanzhang asked Liu Ji to stay so he could hear his opinion. An avid reader and well versed in military strategy, Liu surpassed many others in intelligence. He said to Zhu, "Our enemy has come from afar, while we are staying here resting. They think they outnumber us. They are arrogant and therefore underestimate us. Wait until they enter well into our territory and then intercept them by an ambush. We are sure to win."

Zhu's spirit was lifted by these words and he formulated a plan to ward off the invading enemy.

Kang Maocai, a subordinate of Zhu, was an old acquaintance of Chen Youliang. So Zhu asked Kang Maocai to write Chen, feigning surrender and promising to work as an inside agent, so as to lure Chen further into the territory.

Kang Maocai said, "It is easily done. I'll send an old servant to deliver the letter. The old servant used to work for Chen Youliang and so will not arouse his suspicion."

When the old servant met Chen with Kang's

letter, Chen was not at all suspicious. He merely asked, "Where will Kang Maocai meet us?"

The servant replied, "At Jiangdong Bridge, which is a wood bridge."

Chen was overjoyed and treated the old man to an elabourate meal. Before the servant departed, Chen told him, "I'll take the force to Jiangdong Bridge. When I arrive, I'll call out 'Mr. Kang' several times. Then Kang Maocai should come out to meet me."

When the servant returned and reported on his mission, Zhu Yuanzhang immediately sent people to pull apart the wooden bridge and replace it with a stone one. Now everything was ready for Chen's arrival.

True to his word, Chen came with his navy to Jiangdong Bridge. There he saw a stone bridge instead of a wooden one. He began to become restless. On second thought, he decided that since he was here anyway, it didn't matter anymore whether the bridge was made of wood or stone. He called out "Mr. Kang" several times. There was no reply. Then it occurred to Chen that he must have fallen into a trap. Hurriedly he ordered the ships to turn around and retreat.

Just then yellow flags were hoisted and soldiers in ambush rushed out from hiding. Their shouting for kill echoed in the sky. Chen was at a loss what to do. Many of his soldiers were killed or thrown into the water. More than 20,000 were captured by

Zhu's army. With protection from his generals, Chen managed to escape. This battle, however, inflicted a fatal blow to Chen.

But Chen was not about to take the defeat lying down. After three years of recovery and preparation, he came with a force of 600,000, sailing in a great number of warships to attack Hongdu (today's Nanchang, Jiangxi).

Zhu assembled a force of 200,000 to help rescue Hongdu. Chen was compelled to pull off and station his navy on Poyang Lake, where the two opposing armies were ready for a final showdown. Chen's warships, tall and big, spread out for several kilometres, while Zhu's navy was armed with only some small boats that were by no means the match for Chen's.

General Guo Xing suggested that they fight the enemy with fire, which Zhu readily endorsed. This was because the large warships were linked together with an iron chain and so difficult to move. Zhu sent out seven small boats filled with dynamite. Each boat pulled behind it an even smaller boat. On the evening of the assault, a northeasterly wind began to blow. The dare-to-die fleet of seven boats sailed towards Chen's large warships and the fire from the small boats lit up Chen's fleet. The fire grew so strong that it turned the sky red. Heavy casualties on Chen's navy were registered. In their retreat, they were again ambushed, and Chen Youliang himself was shot dead by arrows.

Once the most powerful opponent, Chen You-liang was now defeated. Zhu then directed his army eastward against Zhang Shicheng.

Originally a salt dealer, Zhang raised an army in the years of turmoil and made himself king of the Wu, which took Pingjiang (now Suzhou, Jiangsu) as their capital. Changing sides many times, he was now against the Yuan and then for it. All he was interested in was to have his little kingdom, amass his personal wealth and enjoy a life of luxury, music and sex. His generals were mostly also men without grand goals.

In attacking Zhang, Zhu Yuanzhang took three steps: first, attack northern Jiangsu and the lower reaches of the Huaihe River; second, take Huzhou (now Wuxing in Zhejiang) and Hangzhou, and finally, attack Pingjiang. In the final battle, Zhang Shicheng was captured and killed because he refused to surrender.

Until then, Zhu Yuanzhang was ostensibly under the command of the young emperor. Now Zhu's desire to become emperor himself grew quickly. He decided that the young emperor was in the way of his becoming the sovereign ruler himself. So under a pretext of welcoming the young emperor to Ying-tianfu, he secretly sent people to sink the boat carrying the emperor. The young emperor was drowned in mid-river as he tried to cross the river at Guabu (southeast of present-day Liuhe, Jiangsu).

With Zhang Shicheng gone, Zhu Yuanzhang

compelled Fang Guozhen, leader of another force, to surrender. Now a vast area in the middle and lower reaches of the Yangtze River was under his control. From then on, he directed his main force onto a northern expedition in the hope of defeating the Yuan.

In the tenth month of 1367, Zhu Yuanzhang held a ceremony of pledging to heaven at Qilishan, north of Yingtianfu to challenge the Yuan regime. His plan was to take Shandong first and then take Henan. From there his army could march on to Tongguan. Finally his army would march towards Dadu (now called Beijing), capital for the Yuan. Once he took Dadu, he thought, his army would spread across Shanxi, Shaanxi, and Gansu.

The northern expedition army led by Xu Da and Chang Yuchun marched invincibly ahead, taking Shandong in just a few months. Then it took Bianliang (now Kaifeng) and approached Tongguan, forming a three-side seige of the Yuan's capital, Dadu. The Yuan Dynasty's Emperor Shun (1320 – 70) did not inherit the gallantry and military skills of his ancestors and was a man used to a life of debauchery. Realizing that Dadu had become an isolated city, he had no desire to fight and so he fled north, taking away treasures, wealth, concubines and palace maids. In the eighth month of the next year, Xu Da's troops entered Dadu, putting an end to the Yuan Dynasty that had been founded by the Mongols and had ruled China for ninety-eight years.

In the first month of 1368, amidst the good news of Xu Da's success in Shandong, Zhu Yuanzhang ascended the throne in Yingtianfu and, using the city as his southern capital, established a new empire, the Ming Dynasty. That year Zhu was forty-one years old, having been in the army for sixteen years after he took off his monk's robe.

4. Concentration of power by an extremely conceited emperor

As the new emperor, Zhu had to attend to everything and his job was very tiring indeed. Before the day broke, he had to get up to read and sign documents and meet with his ministers. He was kept busy all day long until midnight. There were no holidays. Take the ninth month of 1386 for example. In eight days from the fourteenth to the twenty-first, he received 1,660 reports relating to 3,391 requests for instructions. On average, he had to read more than 200 reports and give directions on some 400 cases. With so much paper work, he had to work at night. Why did he have to do so much? Because he trusted no one and was afraid of the power slipping into the hands of other people. So he had to look into everything in order to safeguard his rule. To keep the power in his own hand, Zhu took the following measures.

First, he took back control of the localities. In

the early Ming Dynasty, the set-up of local administrations still followed the old Yuan system of having a Secretariat that held the military, civilian and financial powers. Earlier, Zhu Yuanzhang was the chief of the Secretariat for the young emperor. Superficially, he supported the reign of the young emperor, but in reality, he held the emperor in disregard. Now that Zhu himself had become emperor, he was well aware of the shortcomings of allowing the Secretariat to hold the exclusive power of all local regions in all military, civilian and financial areas. So, in 1376, he created the system of three departments as a replacement for the Secretariat. The Department of Administration was in charge of civil and financial affairs, while the Department of Command and Department of Justice were in charge of military and judicial affairs. All three departments directly reported to the central court. With this change, the power that originally rested with the Secretariat was divided into three departments, which effectively prevented any possibility of over-concentration of power leading to independence.

Second, in the early Ming period, the Secretariat was headed by the left and right prime ministers and divided into six ministries. This arrangement empowered the Secretariat with decision-making rights on political, administrative, military and financial affairs. The prime ministers were only responsible to the emperor. They were so powerful that they could easily make the emperor just a figure head. The first left prime minister was Li Shan-chang and the right prime minister was Xu Da. Li was a cautious man, while Xu Da, as a general, had fought on the battleground for many years and therefore had no grudges against Zhu. In 1373, Li's son-in-law, Hu Weiyong, was promoted to be a prime minister. He wielded his power to form a small clique and was arbitrary in decision making, posing a challenge to Zhu's power as emperor.

In the first month of 1380, Hu Weiyong said to Zhu, "The water coming out the well at my home has become very sweet, which is a good sign for the prosperity of the country." Zhu was happy to hear this and decided to visit Hu at his home.

When the emperor's entourage pompously trooped out of the Xihua Gate of the palace, a man came running to the emperor's sedan. It was Yun Qi, a secret agent Zhu had dispatched to investigate the residence of Hu. Yun Qi was panting so hard from running that he could hardly speak. The emperor accused him of being impolite and had him beaten. Though he was bruised from the beating, he still pointed his hand to the direction of the residence of Hu Weiyong. Then Zhu suddenly realized that Yun Qi had perhaps discovered something amiss. He immediately told his sedan bearers to turn back. He ascended the palace tower to take a close look at the residence of Hu and vaguely sensed an ambush. He wanted to ask Yun Qi about his findings, but Yun was already dead from the beating. He then made arrangements for the proper burial of Yun and sent out secret agents to kill all three generations of Hu Weiyong.

In all, more than 15,000 people lost their lives during this wave of killing, which shocked the whole court. After that, Zhu abolished the system of prime ministers, and elevated the positions of the six ministers in charge of personnel (appointments and dismissals of officials), civil affairs (land, residents, taxation and finance), rituals (ceremonial rules, sacrificial occasions, schools, imperial examinations and reception of visitors), military affairs (selection of officers, governing of soldiers and weaponry), judicial affairs (law, justice and prisons) and works (engineering projects, craftsmen and artisans, cultivation of land, water conservancy projects and transportation). All the ministers directly reported to the emperor. Their sole job was to implement imperial orders, and all decisions were to be made by the emperor himself. The abuse of power by Hu Weiyong provided the emperor an opportunity to abolish the more than one-thousand-year-old system of prime ministers and thus become a dictatorial monarch, who took the powers that originally rested with both the emperor and prime ministers into his own hands.

Meanwhile, he had the central military leadership, the Grand Military Headquarters divided into five commands of left, right, middle, front and rear. In times of war, all the movements of the army and appointments of generals were to be made by the emperor, whose orders were carried out by the commands. Only the commanders from the commands were made generals to lead their forces to the front. Once a war was over, they had to return the seals as symbols of their leadership.

Through such reforms of the central and local governments and the military, Zhu Yuanzhang was able to bring all the administrative and military powers onto himself, establishing the highly concentrated rule of the emperor and making himself one of the most powerful emperors in Chinese history.

According to one story, once Zhu disguised himself in civilian clothes and went on an inspection tour. At a shanty temple, he saw a mural on the wall. The mural depicted a monk with a sack and had an accompanying poem that read: "The world is vast; everything is collected in the sack. You have to take things out when you take more in; what's wrong in slightly loosening the bag you have?"

The poem made a mockery of Zhu, who used to be a monk, and his taking all power into his own hands. Finding the ink had not yet dried, he told his subordinates to catch the painter, who was nowhere to be found.

5. Rule by force and killing of meritorious subordinates

When he had secured his position as Emperor Gaozu of Han, Liu Bang turned on his most meritorious generals, killing Han Xin, Peng Yue and Ying Bu, among others. Zhu Yuanzhang, who learned from Liu Bang in every way, did likewise, except that he went even further in killing almost all the generals and officials who were instrumental in establishing his empire.

The case of Hu Weiyong, mentioned earlier, was in essence made a vehicle for political struggle. All officials who the emperor believed posed any threat to his rule were killed, along with all members in their families on basis of all kinds of fabricated crimes. During a decade before and after Hu Weiyong's case, some 30,000 people were killed.

Another misplaced verdict was that of Lan Yu who, as a general, led expeditions to Mongolia several times. His outstanding performances won him the position of Duke of Liangguo. His merit made him arrogant. Dozens of officers who fought under his command proved to be brave and good at warfare. Zhu Yuanzhang was afraid that Zhu Yunwen, his grandson, who was made the new crown prince after the death of the original crown prince, Zhu Biao, the son of the emperor, could not keep these former generals in place and therefore there would be danger of an armed coup. So in 1393, Zhu Yuanzhang accused Lan Yu of planning a revolt and had three generations of his family killed. All those civilian and military officials who had served under Lan Yu were killed also. This wrong verdict led to the death of another 15,000 people.

Zhu Yuanzhang did not even spare Xu Da who, as his childhood friend, had gone through fire and water with him to help found the Ming Dynasty. Xu Da enjoyed high prestige and commanded universal respect. At age fifty-four, he was still in the prime of his life and career. These factors convinced Zhu Yuanzhang that to keep Xu Da around would be leaving a potential challenge to the rule of the Zhu family. Xu Da, however, was a cautious man and Zhu could not find fault with him. In 1385, Xu was sick with a sore on the back. Steamed goose was a dish such patient should never eat because the meat was thought to make such an illness worse. But Zhu Yuanzhang chose this time to bestow a steamed goose on Xu. The emperor commanded supreme power and if he wanted somebody to die, that person would have to die. With the goose given him by the emperor, Xu Da realized that the emperor was displeased with his childhood friend. So with tears in his eyes, Xu ate the goose and died not long after.

Other meritorious generals such as Zhou Dexing, Feng Guosheng and Liao Yongzhong were either told to die, whipped to death or killed. None of them escaped. Zhu proved to be someone who, during his struggles for power, people could get along with by sharing his weal and woe. Once he took the throne, however, he would not allow his comrades-in-arms to share his good fortune.

Zhu Biao, the crown prince, was raised to be honest and did not approve of his father's policy of "rule by fierce force." Whenever Zhu Yuanzhang killed one of his former colleagues, the crown prince would try to stop his father, and so they often quarrelled. One story has it that Zhu Yuanzhang wanted to punish the crown prince's teacher, Song Lian. The crown prince tried to talk his father out of the idea. This enraged the emperor who roared at his son, "He can only be pardoned when you are the emperor!" These words made the crown prince so terrified and worried that he went to drown himself. Fortunately people discovered this and pulled him out of danger.

Another time, the crown prince tried to reason with his father, saying that he should be more benevolent and should not kill so many people. Zhu Yuanzhang said nothing in reply to his son. The next day, he called his son over and told him to pick up a thorny branch. Finding the thorns pricking, the crown prince did not pick it up immediately. Zhu then made a double-edged remark, saying, "The branch has thistles and thorns so you don't dare to pick it up. Is it not a good idea for me to pull off the thistles and then give it to you?" Zhu's high-handed policy was like pulling off the thistles so that his successor would enjoy a stable rule.

The crown prince still did not appreciate what his father did. He said, "Because there used to be Yao and Shun (two benevolent and virtuous kings in ancient China), there were subjects of Yao and Shun." He meant that only when there were enlightened rulers, would there be docile and loyal subjects. Zhu Yuanzhang flew into a rage at his son's words. He picked up a chair and tried to hit his son with it. Being a scholar with a weak temperament, the crown prince fled. Soon after that he fell ill and died.

The death of the crown prince saddened Zhu Yuanzhang, but he did not change his policy of "rule by fierce force." He made the eldest son of the late crown prince, Zhu Yunwen, his heir-apparent. To pave the way for the young Zhu to eventually become emperor, Zhu Yuanzhang once again killed several senior ministers and generals. At that time, all the ministers went to court in the morning with heavy hearts. They would say parting words to their families and have arrangements made in case they did not return home alive. If they safely returned home that day, their families would celebrate. Careful officials said that if Zhu Yuanzhang ever pushed his jade belt, worn outside the robe and down bellow his belly, it was a signal for killing that would send officials shivering in fear. If he lifted the belt up, it was a sign of peace for that day.

Emperor Zhu Yuanzhang built up a network of secret agents to spy on and suppress anyone who dared to show dissatisfaction with his rule. In 1382, he established a secret agent organization, called the brocade guards, who directly reported to the emperor. Its staff was spread across the country and they adopted the most brutal forms of torture and ways of killing. Many senior ministers fell victim of the brocade guards, who continued their abuse until the end of the Ming Dynasty.

6. Rewarding the farmers

After the founding of the Ming Dynasty, Zhu Yuanzhang was kept busy with political reforms he needed to make so that he would not become just a figure head. He also devoted much of his time to encouraging farmers to promote agricultural production.

After two decades of war, what Zhu Yuanzhang faced was deserted cities, wasted land and bankrupt businesses. He often spoke about the destruction of war with his ministers. He took Yangzhou as an example, saying that this city used to be a prosperous metropolis but, when the war was over, only eighteen families remained there. The new prefect of the city had to build a makeshift hut for his temporary office. Zhu told them that the farmers had suffered the worst. All year long, they had to toil in the fields, live in thatched huts, wear poor clothes, and yet they still did not have enough to eat. They often relied on wild vegetables to fill their stomachs. He reminded his ministers that farmers should not be heavily taxed so that they could endure and survive the hardships.

As a result, he formulated policies that encouraged farmers to engage in agriculture and the opening up of wastelands. All newly-opened land was exempt from taxation for three years. He made the army produce its own food. Those stationed along the border spent 30 percent of their time guarding the border and 70 percent on agricultural production, while those stationed in inland areas devoted 80 percent to farm production. As a result, during the early years of the Ming, the military, which was one million strong, was mostly self-sufficient in grain.

He also had a census taken of measurements of the farmland and population so that landlords and local despots could not cheat on taxation and force corvee labour onto farmers by deliberately twisting the figures as to acreage and population. In regions that were hit hardest by the war, he took the measures to reduce taxes and provide relief.

Every evening at dusk, Zhu had people tour the streets and lanes, beating musical instruments made of wood and shouting at the top of their voices, "Maintain neighbourly relations; educate your children; be content and work hard at your job and commit no crime!" In the morning, garrison guards would blow bugles on top of the city wall, and shout, "To create a society is diffiuclt, but to maintain it is more difficult!"

These words revealed the heart and mind of Zhu Yuanzhang. As an emperor who was a former cow tender, monk and general with fighting experience in many battles, he was fully aware of the hardships and difficulties of making a living by ordinary citizens. Although he was the "son of heaven," his memories of the hardships he had gone through remained fresh. Therefore, Zhu kept to a frugal life and did not drink. When blueprints for the construction of the palace were shown to him, he reduced the scale of the pavilions, terraces and towers. The part involving the most delicate carvings was abandoned. Being strong and practical became the standard. His personal utensils were made of copper instead of gold. Someone presented him a bed with golden thread decorations. Zhu said that to him this was not much different from the jade inlaid seven-treasure chamber pot used by Chen Shubao, the last emperor of the previous dynasty. He told people to take the bed out and smash it. Everyday he worked diligently from morning till late in the night. When people suggested that he take a rest, he replied, "Since ancient times, if the people were diligent, the country prospered. And if the people were lazy, the country was weak. When I think of this, how can I take a rest?" He devoted all of himself to the rule by his family. In the fifth month of 1398, he fell ill from overwork. Thirty days later he died at the age of seventy-one. After his death he was buried in the Xiaoling Mausoleum at the foot of Zhongshan Hill, Nanjing.

7. Inner-struggle leading to war again

Zhu Yuanzhang, or Emperor Taizu of the Ming, thought he had pulled out all the thistles and thorns on his walking stick and that his descendants would enjoy a safe and stable period of rule. As soon as he died, however, his children and grand-children began a fierce fight among themselves.

The crown prince, Zhu Biao, died when Zhu Yuanzhang was sixty – five years old. According to family traditions, the eldest son or eldest grandson should succeed to the throne. As a result, Zhu Yun-wen (1377 – 1402) was made the crown prince. In the eighth month of 1398, he succeeded to the throne and took the reign title of Emperor Jianwen.

Altogether, Zhu Yuanzhang had twenty-six sons who were all princes commanding armies stationed in different localities. The new emperor, Zhu Yunwen, felt deeply that these uncles of his were a great threat to his rule. His uncle Zhu Di (Prince of Yan) was stationed in Beiping, originally Dadu, capital of the Yuan Dynasty. He was both intelligent and courageous, and the emperor was most worried about him.

Qi Tai, Huang Zicheng and other ministers who were advisors to the new emperor stood for reducing the power of the local princes and dukes so as to consolidate the central power. They argued that this should be the long-term policy, but these ministers lacked adaptability in dealing with political issues and went ahead with their plan in great haste, which only produced contrary results.

In the beginning, although Prince of Yan harboured great ambitions, he had no immediate plans for a revolt. However, when Emperor Jianwen, on the advice of his ministers, stripped four princes of their positions, the Prince of Yan became alarmed. As a result, he stepped up military drilling in preparation for a rebellion.

When news of this reached Nanjing, the Ming capital, Emperor Jianwen consulted with Qi Tai and Huang Zicheng. They came up with the idea of pretending that the northern border was in danger. They wanted to take all the crack forces under the Prince of Yan's command to the front. The prince did not want to hand over his command. Instead, he had an underground chamber built in the rear garden of his residence where he secretly had weapons made. To prevent the people outside from hearing the sound of casting weapons, he had several thousand ducks and geese raised whose crowing muffled the sounds of weapon making.

In the sixth month of 1399, several trusted officers under Zhu Di, Prince of Yan, were arrested. They were taken to Nanjing where they were sentenced to death. Zhang Bing and Xie Gui, whose job was to supervise the prince, began to deploy soldiers to arrest Zhu Di at any time. At that moment, Zhu Di pretended to have gone mad, loitering in the streets with uncombed hair, and snatching food and drinks from others. Sometimes, he even lay down in the ditches to sleep and thus got mud all over his body. Still the two were not assured. They went to the prince's home to see for themselves, saying they were there visiting the prince in his illness. It was midsummer, but they found Zhu Di fully clad in fur clothes trying to warm himself by a fire. He shivered with cold. In fact, underneath the fur coat, he held a bucket of ice. When they talked to him, he simply didn't make any sense.

Now convinced that the prince was really mad, they reported this to Nanjing. The prince of Yan, however, was still worried that the emperor might not believe he was really mad, so he sent Deng Yong to the capital to report on his illness. But by this move he outsmarted himself. Qi Tai, a court minister, saw through the trick, arrested Deng Yong and presented him for questioning by the emperor. Deng could not endure the torture and confessed that the prince was only feigning to be mad, while he was really busy preparing for a revolt.

As if suddenly awakened from a sound sleep, Emperor Jianwen issued an edict to Zhang Xin, a general commanding the army in Beiping (another name for Beijing), to arrest all officials in the palace of prince of Yan. Zhang Xin had originally been a subordinate of the prince. After receiving the secret edict from the emperor, he found himself in a dilemma. His mother asked what was bothering him and he told her the truth. Greatly alarmed, his mother said, "The prince of Yan has been kind to us and we should not requite kindness with enmity!"

So Zhang Xin went to the prince's palace and told him about the edict. Zhu Di, the prince, jumped off his bed and knelt in front of Zhang Xin. He kept saying, "I owe all my family to you."

Immediately, the prince of Yan stopped pretending to be mad. He wrote a petition to Emperor Jianwen, repudiating Qi Tai and Huang Zicheng as "treacherous officials" who were trying to sow discord among members of the royal family. He had decided to take his army south to Nanjing, he stated, to get rid of these treacherous ministers working by the emperor's side.

The war between the uncle and nephew continued for four years. Then in the sixth month of 1402, Zhu Di led his army to attack Yingtianfu (Nanjing). On the very same day, Emperor Jianwen gave an order to set the royal palace on fire. When Zhu Di, or the prince of Yan, came into the palace, he searched everywhere for three days but could not find Emperor Jianwen. He questioned palace maids and was told that the emperor had burned himself to death. They pointed to a place where Zhu Di had found a corpse that had been burned beyond recognition. The prince shed a few tears when he saw this and sighed, "Foolish, you didn't have to do this."

Was that burned body really Emperor Jianwen? Some said yes and some said no. Some said it was the body of the empress. Still others said that after he issued the order to burn the palace, Emperor Jianwen and his close followers went out of the city and fled to the southwest border province of Yunnan where he became a monk who roamed the land. Zhu Di himself also suspected that the emperor was still alive. To make sure there would be no remorse because of later troubles, he sent people to search for the toppled emperor. He even ordered Zheng He, a eunuch, to lead a massive fleet to look for the former emperor in countries across the South China Sea. But Emperor Jianwen was never found, which has become a major mystery in the history of the Ming Dynasty.

Zhu Di now became the emperor with the reign title of Emperor Yongle. To suppress resistance, he launched a massive massacre. He told Fang Xiaoru, a doctor of literature who used to serve Emperor Jianwen, to draft an edict for his ascension to the throne. Fang, who was loyal to his previous sovereign ruler, threw the writing brush on the ground, saying, "I will not write it. If you want to kill me, go ahead!" Zhu Di answered, "You may not be afraid of death, but don't you care for the lives of all your relatives in the Nine Families?" According to the ancient system, the "nine families" referred to the four generations on the father's side, three generations on the mother's side and two generations on one's wife's side. Fang Xiaoru said loudly, "I don't even fear the killing of ten families!" He took the brush, wrote four characters and threw it at Zhu Di who read it and found the four characters meaning "Thief from Yan Usurping the Power." This enraged Zhu Di who had the mouth of Fang cut from ear to ear. Zhu Di also had the members of his nine families murdered. He even added to the death list friends and disciples of Fang who might be described as the tenth family. In the end, 873 people were murdered. Zhu Di later had the Forbidden City built in Beijing and moved the capital of the Ming there. This former prince of the Beijing region thus became the first Ming emperor to sit on the throne in the Forbidden City.

XI The Twelve Emperors of the Qing Dynasty

The Qing Dynasty (1644 – 1911), an empire established by the Manchu minority from northeast China, was powerful with an expansive territory. In late 18th century, the national population of China had already reached 300 million, making it the most populous and strongest feudal country in East Asia. When the Opium War broke out between China and Britain in 1840, foreign powers began to invade China, which step by step fell into becoming a semi-feudal and semi-colonial country.

As the last feudal dynasty in Chinese history, the Qing was overthrown by the Revolution 1911. Its demise ended more than two thousand years of feudal monarchy rule in the country.

Before they crossed the Great Wall and came into China's Central Plains, the Manchus had already been ruled by two emperors. Later, with Beijing as its capital, the Qing continued to be presided over by ten more emperors. Together the twelve sovereign rulers sat on the throne for 296 years.

1. Nurhachi, who began
with thirteen sets of armour

A beautiful story has circulated since antiquity at the foot of the Changbai Mountains in China's northeast: one day three fairies came to take a bath in Buleli Lake at the foot of the mountain. Suddenly a magpie with a red fruit in its mouth alighted on the bank. It left the fruit there and flew away. Fukulun, the youngest of the three fairies, was the first to come ashore. She picked up the fruit and put it in her own mouth. While preoccupied with putting on her clothes, she somehow swallowed the fruit, which made her pregnant and she later gave birth to a baby boy called Aisin Gioro Bukuliyong-shun.

Apparently the story about the magpie and the fruit was created in an attempt to explain the rise of the Manchus, and it is probably the reason the Manchu ancestors took the bird as their totem.

The Manchus were an ancient minority tribe which already inhabited the northeast of Jilin Province and the region by the Mudan River in the Zhou (a. 11th century – 256 BC) and Qin (221 – 206 BC) periods. At the time they were called the Sushens. During the Sui and Tang dynasties (581 – 907), their name was changed to Mohe, and during the Five Dynasties (907 – 960), they were known as the Nüzhens. They came to be known as the Manchus after 1636.

In 1559, a Nüzhen family which for generations had been border officials for the Ming court, gave birth to a baby boy named Nurhachi (1559 – 1626). It is said that he was born after his mother had been pregnant for thirteen months and, as a new-born baby, he was big and strong. Unfortunately his mother died when he was very young. He had to dig for ginseng, pick pine nuts and help his father raise his brothers. He also collected local produce to sell to the Han people in Fushun or to trade with the Mongols, which expanded his knowledge and enabled him to be well versed in both the Chinese and Mongolian languages. He loved to read and had what today would be called a photographic memory. Nurhachi particularly loved war novels such as *The Romance of Three Kingdoms* and *Outlaws of the Marsh*. He was said to have served as a soldier in the army led by Li Chengliang, commander of the Ming troops in Liaodong and won the trust of the general. Once the commander accidentally discovered that there were seven red moles on Nurhachi's foot and decided that these were signs that he would become emperor. So the commander wanted to have him killed to avoid future trouble, but his beloved concubine informed Nurhachi of this and told him to run away. Then she committed suicide by hanging herself.

The Ming court adopted a policy of divide and

rule towards the Nüzhens, by supporting one tribe to fight another and deliberately sowing discord among the different tribes. In 1583, Nurhachi's father and grandfather were killed by Ming troops in a battle between two rival Nüzhen tribes. In the fifth month of that year, Nurhachi collected thirteen sets of armour left by his father and started a revolt. First, he attacked Nikanwailan, the Nüzhen tribal leader who had helped the Ming troops kill his father and grandfather. This raised the curtain for his grand career. In battle he always charged at the forefront of his army. Having killed Nikanwailan, he turned on neighbouring tribes and conquered them one by one. He built Hetuala Town (today's Xinbin County, Liaoning) by the Suzi River which he made the political center for his growing empire. The rise of Nurhachi aroused concern among the other tribes. In 1593, the Yehe and Hada tribes in Haixi and the Horqin tribe in Mongolia launched a joint attack in three columns against Nurhachi. Nurhachi laid an ambush at the precipitous section of the Guci Mountains. He sent out a small force to lure the enemy into his trap. The enemy suffered heavy casualties. Nurhachi and his army wiped out over four thousand invading troops and captured more than three thousand horses. He rode on this victory and unified the Nüzhen tribes in Jianzhou.

Nurhachi established an eight-banner organizational and administrative system that combined fighting and farming into one. First he set up four such units and then another four, each of which was identified by the colour of its flag: yellow, white, red, blue, then yellow-bordered, white-bordered, red-bordered and blue-bordered. Those in the eight banners were "warriors when they went out and farmers when they were at home" and "were engaged in farming and hunting in times of peace and fighting in times of war."

During the wars for annexing the Nüzhen tribes, Nurhachi seemed to be loyal and respectful towards the Ming court, but in reality he secretly built up his forces in preparation for a final showdown with the Ming rulers.

In 1616, Nurhachi ascended to the position of khan in Hetuala and named his kingdom the Great Kin (or Later Kin), openly raising the banner of opposing the Ming. Two years later, with the excuse of "seven big revenges" including that for his father and grandfather, he led a cavalry of 20,000 to attack the Ming troops. He took Fushun, a major strategic stronghold of the Ming Dynasty and strongholds in its vicinity, looting the places of its people, animals and materials.

When news of this reached Beijing, it threw the court into great shock. The Ming rulers decided to wage a massive offensive against the Later Kin. In the first month of 1619, 90,000 Ming troops began to march in four routes towards Hetuala, capital of the Later Kin. Nurhachi's policy was "I'll tackle one of the invading routes at a time no matter how many come." He led 60,000 Later Kin soldiers to fight the Ming force of 30,000 led by Du Song at Sarhu. It snowed heavily and was difficult for the army to march. But Du Song was eager to win the first battle and so he pressed his army on. When half of the Ming army entered an ambush laid in a mountain valley, the Later Kin troops rushed out, cutting the Ming army in two. Du Song, the Ming commander, died in the battle and his entire army was destroyed. Then Nurhachi engaged the other routes of Ming troops one by one. In a mere five days, 45,000 Ming officers and men lost their lives. After the battle at Sarxu, the Later Kin troops occupied the region between Liaoyang and Shenyang and their political and economic strength grew quickly. In 1625, the Later Kin moved into Shenyang, then called Shengjing, and named it as their capital, thus laying the foundation for the establishment of the Qing Dynasty in 1644.

In the first month of 1626, Nurhachi took an army 130,000 strong to attack Ningyuan, now Xingcheng of Liaoning.

Yuan Chonghuan, the Ming general guarding the city, bit his finger until it bled. With the blood he wrote his pledge to encourage his soldiers to unite as one and defend the town with their lives. Indeed, they warded off several attacks by the Later Kin army. On the third day of battle, Yuan Chonghuan used eleven cannons to shoot at the enemy. The Later Kin soldiers fell in large numbers and Nurhachi himself was also seriously wounded. He had to pull back to Shenyang.

In Shenyang, his wound worsened. With a heavy heart, he said, "I have always been invincible, but now I've lost to Yuan Chonghuan. What kind of person is he exactly?" In the eighth month of 1626, Nurhachi, hero of the Nüzhens, died with great regret at the age of sixty-eight.

A month later, Huangtaiji (1592 – 1643), the eighth son of Nurhachi, was made the new khan of the Later Kin.

2. Huangtaiji sowing discord among his enemies

Huangtaiji was a handsome man who was intelligent and eager to learn. When he was only seven years old, his father let him manage the affairs of his large family. Huangtaiji attended to everything, important or trivial, with great care and order, demonstrating his administrative ability. From a very young age, he had inherited the warrior spirit of the Nüzhens. He trained hard and proved to be an outstanding marksman on horseback. Once on a march, the army ran out of grain and had to depend on hunting for food. Huangtaiji killed two Mongolian gazelles with one arrow. As he demonstrated his resourcefulness and performed meritorious military deeds, he won his father's love and trust. So when Nurhachi died in the eighth month of 1626, he succeeded to the throne a month later.

In carrying out Nurhachi's behest, Huangtaiji continued to fight the Ming troops. He fought several battles with Yuan Chonghuan and, like his father, suffered defeat. In a tone of hatred and helplessness, he sighed, "This southerner called Yuan Chonghuan is really tough!"

Then who was Yuan Chonghuan?

Yuan was a native of Dongguan, Guangdong. At the age of thirty-six, he became a successful candidate for the highest imperial exam held in the capital. Yuan was full of strategies because he was an avid reader of military books. Originally a small official of the seventh rank, he volunteered to take a study tour of the Shanhaiguan Pass, the east end of the Great Wall, and its vicinity, since the country was being invaded there. Upon his return, he petitioned to the Ming court, expressing his desire to give up his civilian post and join the army to defend Shanhaiguan. The Ming court was at that time unable to find a commander for the post when Yuan's petition arrived. The court promoted him by several grades to become the commanding officer of the army at the forefront.

Yuan Chonghuan was the major obstacle to Huangtaiji's plan to march southward and take control of the country from the Ming rulers. He had to get rid of Yuan first! After much hard thinking, he decided on a strategy of sowing discord.

In the eleventh month of 1629, Huangtaiji took

the eight-banner army on a massive offensive against the Ming. This time, he tactfully avoided Yuan Chonghuan by making a detour and marching south through Mongolia in the west. His surprise move allowed him to quickly take Zunhua and Sanhe in Hebei. Then he attacked Shunyi and Tongzhou, two towns in suburban Beijing. He was just miles from the Forbidden City. When Yuan Chonghuan heard this he hurried to rescue the capital. His army marched for two days and two nights without rest and covered 150 kilometres until they reached Guangqumen, just outside Beijing. The sudden arrival of Yuan and his troops sent the Later Kin troops into great fear, thinking some magic force must have landed. Ming rescue troops also arrived outside Deshengmen, a northern gate to the capital. The two sides were soon engaged in a fierce battle. Cannon shots shook the windows of the imperial palace.

The battle lasted from morning to afternoon and Huangtaiji had to retreat several kilometres. The two camps now had some time to rest and recuperate. Huangtaiji took a few people to feign an inspection of the terrain and then returned to his camp. He summoned Gao Hongzhong and Bao Chengxian, two of his commanders, for a secret meeting.

Before that meeting, Gao and Bao had been guarding two eunuchs they had captured from an animal farm belonging to the Ming court. When the two commanders returned from Huangtaiji's camp, the two captive eunuchs were already in bed, but had not yet fallen asleep. Gao and Bao sat next to the two eunuchs and began to whisper.

Gao spoke first, "Our retreat today was a ruse designed by our ruler," he said.

Bao pretended to be surprised, asking, "How did you know?"

Gao explained: "Just now our ruler went out of the camp with a few accompanying soldiers. Two people came from the other side and they talked for quite a while. I couldn't hear everything they said, but could make out the essence of their conversation. General Yuan of the Ming had a secret agreement with our ruler and our victory is now in sight."

Bao seemed to understand, and said, "Then we will soon be in Beijing." His voice had great excitement in it.

Gao hurried to stop him, saying, "Shhh! Be careful. If this leaks out, all our previous efforts are ruined."

One eunuch, named Yang, was pretending to be asleep and heard every word they said. He was eager to escape so that he could report what he had just learned. The next day, Huangtaiji deliberately reduced the watch on the two eunucks so that they might escape. They ran back to the Forbidden City and told what they heard to Emperor Chongzhen.

Emperor Chongzhen had always been a conceited and suspicious man. Falling into Huangtaiji's trap, he had Yuan Chonghuan brought into the court and locked him up in prison, giving him no chance to explain. Hearing this, Huangtaiji was beside himself with glee, saying, "Now our victory is in sight!" He told his army to retreat to Shenyang.

During the eighth month the following year, Emperor Chongzhen issued an order to execute Yuan on the ground of treason. Yuan died at the age of forty-six. His wife, children and brothers were exiled to places 1,500 kilometres away from the capital. This ruse of Huangtaiji only became known when he wrote the True Records of Emperor Taizong of the Qing, after he had successfully unified the Central Plains.

Emperor Chongzhen's foolish action in killing Yuan Chonghuan was tantamount to breaking his own defence. And the unjustified death of General Yuan left people with great indignation. In 1916, 286 years after Yuan's death, a temple dedicated to Yuan was built in Xinyi Park (now Longtanhu Park), in southeast part of Beijing, so as to remember this national hero who was wronged to death.

In 1636, Huangtaiji declared himself emperor. He changed the name of his kingdom from the Later Kin to the Qing and the name of his ethnic group from Nüzhen to Manchu. He came to be known as the founding emperor of the Qing Dynasty with the reign title of Emperor Taizong of Qing.

Emperor Taizong, who himself was a politician tempered in the great cause of building a new dynasty, regarded the training and enlisting talent as a fundamental policy that would enable the country to grow strong. He said, "I run the country with talent as the fundamental resource. If you have money, eventually you're going to spend it all. But if a country has one or two real talents to serve it, it means the country will always benefit from them." To begin with, he emphasized reading, stipulating that all children between eight and fifteen years of age in the families of princes must go to school. Otherwise their parents would be punished. He also introduced exams to recruit outstanding people from among the Manchus, Hans and Mongolians for official posts. Fan Wencheng was a Ming official who had surrendered. Huangtaiji consulted him on everything before he made any decisions. At the battle of Songshan, he captured Hong Chengchou, a Ming general. Huangtaiji sent Fan Wencheng to persuade Hong to surrender. Hong repudiated Fan, saying he would rather die for the Ming than surrender. Then he stopped speaking and listened to Fan's speech. Just then some dust fell from the beam in the house onto Hong's shoulder. Hong scraped it off with his hand. When Fan Wencheng saw Huangtaiji, he said: "Hong Chengchou is not prepared to die. He cared too much for his clothes, let alone his life." So Huangtaiji went personally to persuade Hong. Taking off his marten overcoat and putting it gently on Hong, he said, "Are you cold?" Hong did not expect Huangtaiji to be so amiable and to admire talent to such a degree. He thus surrendered to Huangtaiji. There is another story about how Hong was convinced to surrender. Huangtaiji learned that Hong Chengschou loved women and so sent several beauties to him without achieving his purpose. Then he sent his beloved concubine, Lady Zhuang, to Hong. This lady was the most beautiful woman of that time. To Hong who faced the wall with his eyes shut, she spoke in a voice as soft and comfortable as a spring breeze. She said, "General, you refuse to eat, but aren't you thirsty?" Then she provided him with a small teapot. Hong took a mouthful of the liquid. It was not water but ginseng soup. The beautiful lady gave him more and in the end Hong drank the whole pot of ginseng soup. Then he began to eat. So in the end, Hong could not resist the inducement of a beauty and good food, and so he surrendered.

Absurdly, news circulated in Beijing that Hong Chengchou was already dead and Emperor Chongzhen began to prepare for a memorial service for Hong. The preparations stopped only after news of Hong's surrender was confirmed.

For Huangtaiji, Hong's surrender was like the acquisition of the most treasured thing in the world. On the same day as Hong's surrender, Huangtaiji presented him with many valuable gifts and arranged an opera show to celebrate the occasion. This aroused resentment among some in his original ranks, who said, "Hong is just a surrendered commander. Why does our emperor treat him so generously?"

Huangtaiji asked them, "You have gone through so many hardships for so many years. What's your purpose?"

They answered, "To win the Central Plains."

Huangtaiji smiled, saying, "That's right. But we don't know anything about the Central Plains. We are just like blind people. Now we have someone to guide us. Why shouldn't I be happy?"

The generals and soldiers decided that Huangtaiji was right.

Later Hong proved irreplaceable in helping the Qing troops to enter the Central Plains and take south China.

All his lifetime, Huangtaiji remained a diligent man. His long years of fighting and endurance in bad weather finally wore him down. The death of his beloved concubine also saddened him. In the night of the ninth day of the eighth month of 1643, he died while sitting on the bed in the palace in Shenyang, at the age of fifty-two.

3. Emperor Shunzhi entering the Central Plains at the age of six

On the ninth night of the eighth month in 1643, disaster fell in the Palace of Clearance and Tranquillity in Shenyang, capital of the Qing Dy-

300

nasty, when Huangtaiji, or Emperor Taizong, suddenly died. Immediately, the death threw the palace into confusion. Huangtaiji's sudden death did not allow him time to make a will and princes began to fight for the throne. The main contenders were his son, Haoge, and his brother, Dorgon. Equally powerful, neither of them wanted to concede to the rule of the other. And a bloody fight within the palace was about to break out. Just then, Dorgon decided to support Fulin (1638 - 61), the six-year-old ninth son of Huangtaiji, for the throne. As a result, the struggle inside the family was averted.

What exactly made Dorgon to decide to give up the throne? Some say he was afraid of a fight within the royal family and yet did not want to leave the throne to the youthful Haoge, so he came up with the compromise that allowed the Prince of Zheng, Jirhalang, and himself to help the young emperor run the court. Lady Zhuang, the most beautiful lady who was concubine of Huangtaiji, had an illicit relationship with Dorgon even while Huangtaiji was still alive. When Huangtaiji died, Lady Zhuang was only thirty-two and her son was six. A widow with a baby boy usually had no chance of seeing her son succeed to the throne. Lady Zhuang, however, was able to keep the relationship between herself and Dorgon burning, resulting in Dorgon's decision to meet Lady Zhuang's request for making her son the new emperor.

On the twenty-sixth day of the eighth month

that year, Fulin became the emperor in Shenyang. The next year, he changed the reign period to Shunzhi and his reign title Emperor Shizu of the Qing. He was, however, better known as Emperor Shunzhi. His mother, Lady Zhuang, was given the honorary title of Empress Dowager. A boy of six, of course could not preside over the court and the power of running the country naturally fell into the hands of Dorgon.

In the first month of 1644, Li Zicheng, a leader of a peasant uprising, set up his kingdom at Xi'an and called it Dashun. On the eighteenth day of the third month, Li's forces fought their way into Beijing. Emperor Chongzhen of the Ming hung himself on Coal Hill (now called Jingshan Hill) the next day. The Ming Dynasty fell. At this critical junction, Wu Sangui, the Ming general who was commander of the garrison at Shanhaiguan Pass, surrendered to the Qing court. Then the Qing troops under the command of Dorgon and Wu's forces launched a joint attack on Li Zicheng's peasant army. Li Zicheng was forced to flee back to Beijing on the twenty-sixth day of the fourth month. Three days later, he hastily ascended the throne in the Hall of Heroic Warriors in the Forbidden City and took the title of Emperor Dashun. However, the next day he had to flee Beijing. Shunzhi thus became the first Qing emperor to sit on the golden throne in the Forbidden City.

From the later years of Nurhachi and through

seventeen years of the reign by Huangtaiji, the Manchus and their army had loitered on the northern side of the Great Wall looking for opportunities and ways to cross this man-made barrier and build their power base in Beijing. But for them the Great Wall proved to be an unsurmountable barrier. Now, however, their descendant Fulin easily went through the Shanhaiguan Pass on the wall and realized their dream, soon after he became the sovereign ruler.

Why was this boy emperor so lucky? It is said that his luck was related with Chen Yuanyuan, an outstandingly beautiful lady.

Wu Sangui, the Ming general who was stationed in Shanhaiguan, intended to surrender to Li Zicheng, the peasant leader after the Ming Dynasty fell. But when he heard that his home in Beijing had been searched, that his father had been beaten up and that even his most beloved concubine, Chen Yuanyuan, had been taken away by Liu Zongmin, a general under Li Zicheng, Wu was overwhelmed with wrath. He vowed to fight Li Zicheng and thus surrendered to the Qing troops, leading the latter through the once impregnable stronghold. As a result, Wu Sangui proved instrumental in the Qing troops' victorious march into the hinterland of China. And all of this was because of a lady. Who was to blame then? Li Zicheng was an outstanding peasant leader. Once he and his troops defeated the Ming and entered Beijing, he became conceited and loosened discipline on his troops. Thus they paid a heavy price, which was something he had never expected.

Having occupied the Central Plains, the Qing court adopted soft tactics towards the people in order to gain their support. But once the Qing became fully established, Emperor Shunzhi decreed that all the Han people had to shave their head (shaving the hair on the front part of the head and keeping a long tail on the back), saying, "If you keep your hair, remove your head; if you want to keep the head, remove the hair." Many Han people, in order to safeguard their ethnic dignity, lost their heads. Emperor Shunzhi also allowed farmland to be taken away from the Han people to be converted to "royal villages" and "imperial villages." He banned the formation of any literary society. In order to wipe out the remnant forces of the Ming Dynasty, the Qing troops kept rolling into the south, killing wherever they set foot. At the end of their "ten-day rape of Yangzhou," the river water was red with blood.

It was Dorgon who led the Qing troops into the Central Plains and it was he who was there in Beijing making everything ready for the young emperor to enter the city and take the throne. In other words, he proved most meritorious and thus was made the prince regent. Later he was given the honorary title of "Father of the Emperor." Riding on his performance, Dorgon grew conceited and arrogant. He abused his power and took no heed of the young emperor. He even married Lady Zhuang, the mother of the emperor, who had been given the honorary title of Empress Dowager Xiaozhuang. The daring Dorgon went further with this absurdity by traditional standards and published an edict in the name of the emperor, publicizing his marriage with the emperor's mother. The edict is compiled in the first volume of the *Unofficial History of the Qing Dynasty*. It reads: "The Empress Dowager became widowed during the prime of her life and leads a lonely life. I, as the Son of Heaven, have tried to provide her with everything under heaven. However, I can only provide for her material needs, but not what she needs in terms of feeling and passion. Now that I have been leaving the Empress Dowager in misery because of the loss of her husband, how can I tell all my subjects to be filial to their parents? My uncle, the prince regent, is now a widower. His high position and handsome physical outlook give him no match throughout the country. Empress Dowager is willing to bend her position and marry him. In respect to Empress Dowager for her kindness, I have decided to respect her decision. All proper formalities should be conducted by the department concerned." Unlike the Han people, to marry one's sister-in-law once she was widowed was not an unusual practice among the Manchus. But the edict above was planted on the emperor.

In the last month of 1650, Dorgon fell off his

horse and died during a hunting trip. On the twelfth day of the first month of 1651, Emperor Shunzhi, now fourteen, began to personally run the court in the Hall of Supreme Harmony. Two months later, acting against his mother's wishes, he ordered that the tomb of Dorgon be destroyed and that the corpse be whipped, on the grounds that he had received a report that, while alive, Dorgon had "plotted to take the throne." In reality, the emperor did all this to give vent to his anger with Dorgon for marrying his mother by taking advantage of his young age.

Emperor Shunzhi was a devoted Buddhist and took the monk Yulin as his teacher. He also took the Buddhist title of "Xingchi." Harbouring a secret love for the wife of his younger brother, he eventually took this woman as his concubine and called her Lady Dong E, after his brother's death. When the lady died, the emperor was struck with such sorrow that he even said he wanted to become a monk.

On the sixth day of the first month of 1661, Emperor Shunzhi died in the Hall of Cultivation of the Heart. The cause of his death is a mystery to this day. According to one story, Emperor Shunzhi was so grieved by the death of his beloved concubine that he quietly gave up his throne and became a monk on Mount Wutai, a Buddhist holy mountain in China. "The leaving of Shunzhi" thus is one of the three mysteries of the Qing Dynasty.

4. Kangxi, one of the most successful Chinese emperors

Emperor Kangxi (1654 – 1722), with Xuanye as his personal name and being the third son of Emperor Shunzhi, took the throne in 1661 after his father's death. He named his reign period Kangxi in 1662. The second emperor the Qing after the empire expanded into the Central Plains and built the capital in Beijing, Emperor Kangxi was the most successful ruler among all emperors in Chinese history. With sixty-one years on the throne, he also had one of the most long-lasting reigns.

As a boy, Xuanye was handsome and had a thunderous voice. One day when he was six, he went to the palace with his brothers to see their father. The emperor asked him what he wanted to do when he grew up. The boy answered with a firm voice, "I'd like to do what you're doing, father. I want to run the country." From then on people always referred to him as the "young and aspiring Xuanye." When he took the throne in 1661, Emperor Kangxi was only eight years old and he was assisted by four ministers. Among the four, Suoni was old, Ebilong would always follow the thinking of Aobai, and Sukesaha was a weak person, which resulted in Aobai being the only real decision maker. Aobai formed his clique for his own interests.

He planted his most trusted followers in the government, while keeping those who held different views out. He even had innocent ministers killed. He also continued the policy of forcibly seizing land from the Han people.

In the seventh month of 1667, the fourteen-year-old Kangxi began to personally administer the court. Aobai still abused his power in a dictatorial way without paying much attention to Kangxi. To get rid of Aobai, Kangxi selected ten teenage young men from the royal family to learn martial arts and wrestling in the palace in preparation for future needs. He sent out agents to keep a close watch on Aobai.

One day in the fifth month of 1669, Aobai did not come to court, claiming to be sick. Kangxi went to his house along with several guards, ostensibly to visit him. Kangxi and his guards charged into his bedroom. Aobai hurriedly jumped into bed pretending that he was really ill, although he did not even have time to take off his boots before he did so. Just then, one of the emperor's guards discovered something protruding from Aobai's bed. He took off the cover and saw it was a knife. This exposure caused Aobai to turn pale with terror. Emperor Kangxi, however, smiled. "It is a good habit for us Manchus to always keep a knife near the body," he said, brushing the topic aside. According to rules, however, it was a crime for a subordinate to have any weapon when he met the emperor.

On the sixteenth day of the fifth month, Kangxi, now ready with all necessary arrangements, summoned Aobai to court. As in the past, Aobai walked into the court with a great air. In the Hall of Supreme Harmony, he did not kneel in front of the emperor but, holding his head high, asked, "What is it you want to see me about?" Kangxi smashed his hand on the table and roared, "Aobai, do you know your crime?" Aobai smiled coldly. "In eight years, I have taught you how to run a country," he said. "What crime have I committed?" The emperor replied, "For years, you cheated me. You formed your own clique and kept the power in your own hands. You have killed ministers at will. Dare you say you have committed no crime?" With one motion, a group of young wrestlers came in from the two sides and threw Aobai on the ground. Before he realized what had happened, he was taken prisoner. Diehard supporters of Aobai were also punished by death one after another. Kangxi was only sixteen years old when this took place.

Next, Kangxi suppressed the rebellions by three princes, conquered Zheng Keshuang, grandson of Zheng Chenggong, in Taiwan and unified China. He issued an edict to stop seizing land from the Han people, to build irrigation networks and to encourage farming. He had people compile a 10,000-volume *A Collection of Books of Ancient and Modern Times* and the famous *Kangxi's Dictionary of Chinese*. Under his rule, China became the most pow-

erful and unified country in the world. From his reign, the Qing Dynasty entered the golden period of "prosperity under Kangxi-Qianlong."

Kangxi was a successful ruler and historians have compared him to the broadness of Liu Bang, the founding emperor of the Han Dynasty, and to the resourcefulness in enlisting the service of right people for the right posts of Li Shimin, Emperor Taizong of the Tang Dynasty. Kangxi also hired foreign teachers in order to learn Western science, technology, philosophy and customs.

Emperor Kangxi had thirty-five sons, which gave him difficulty in picking one of them to succeed him. As he wavered in coming to a decision on the question of succession, his sons began to fight among themselves for the throne. Eventually, the title of emperor fell on the head of his fourth son, Yinzhen.

5. The mystery concerning Yongzheng's ascension to the throne

Emperor Yongzheng's personal name was Yinzhen (1678 – 1735). As the fourth son of Emperor Kangxi, he succeeded to the throne after his father's death in 1722. The following year, he took Yongzheng as the reign title for his rule and thus he became known as Emperor Yongzheng.

He was a notable figure and historians have had

varied opinions of him. The most talked about topic in this regard is how he distorted the edict of his father to become the heir.

Kangxi saw the birth of his first son when he was only fourteen. His eldest son was born to a low-ranking concubine and thus was not qualified to succeed to the throne. The second son, Yinreng, was born to the empress and so was made the crown prince on his first birthday. Unfortunately when he grew up, he lived an unbridled, arrogant and luxurious life and had to be stripped of his title as the crown prince thirty-three years later. Then six months later, Emperor Kangxi restored the title of crown prince to him. Yinreng, however, did not change his behaviour and three years later, he once again lost the position of crown prince. Later, Emperor Kangxi's favour shifted to his fourteenth son, Yinti. He sent this son to be a border general in the northwest in the hope of giving him an opportunity to acquire experience for eventually taking the throne from his father. The fourth son, Yinzhen, was a cunning man. In the struggle for succession, he adopted a policy of being openly relaxed yet working intently in secret. He covered up his strong ambition to become the crown prince and pretended to be above such a desire for succession. He socialized with monks so as to discuss Buddhist scriptures with them and seemed to live a life free from ambition or desire. His hope was to slacken others's vigilance and win the favour of his father. In secret, however, he worked hand in glove with two key people, Longkeduo, who was his uncle (his mother's brother) and a commander of the infantry guarding the capital, and Nian Gengyao, his cousin who also held military power.

Gravely ill, Emperor Kangxi summoned his fourteenth son, who was still stationed on the border, to rush back to the capital. The edict of summons, however, was withheld by Yinzhen and Longkeduo. While dying, Emperor Kangxi still did not see his fourteenth son arrive but found that his fourth son ready to succeed him. He was gripped by anger and threw a string of Buddhist beads at the fourth son. Yinzhen was very crafty. He caught the beads and knelt down to thank the dying emperor, saying that the beads thrown at him were a gift of trust from his father. This further infuriated Kangxi, who died in great anger. After he breathed his last, Longkeduo began to read the distorted edict that thus allowed Yinzhen to become the legal successor. At the same time, he sent his trusted aide to take a letter to Nian Gengyao, then serving as the viceroy of Sichuan and Shaanxi, instructing Nian to prevent the fourteenth son's return to Beijing.

Matheo Ripa, an Italian missionary who served in the Qing palace for thirteen years, wrote about the events in Beijing at that time in his diary. According to Ripa, cavalry men galloped in the street. Shouting and screaming was heard here and there... a typical scene of a coup. Till this day, the ascension to the throne by Yinzhen remains a mystery.

Once he became the emperor, Yongzheng began to deal with those brothers who had contended for the throne, killing some, shutting up others. As for the two people who helped him acquire the position and knew the secret, he adopted the policy of showering them with gifts and positions first and dealing with them later on. First, he encouraged them so that they grew arrogant, which then gave him reason to remove them. He listed ninety-two crimes of Nian Gengyao, forcing him to commit suicide. He also listed forty-one crimes of his uncle and sentenced the old man to "life imprisonment." The series of abnormal measures that Yongzheng took aroused people's suspicion that he must have come to the throne by distorting the edict. As there were so many stories about how he came to the throne, Emperor Yongzheng had a book entitled *Wakening with Great Benevolence* written about his succession. But the book was full of errors that only raised more queries and aroused more suspicions.

In the course of suppressing the opposition and strengthening his power, Yongzheng established the military privy council under his personal leadership. He placed this council above the court as a cabinet. He often sent agents to watch the court officials and search their houses, thus winning him the nickname: "Emperor of House Searching."

However, Yongzheng was a diligent emperor. He continued to put down rebellions in border regions, punish corrupt officials, and reform the taxation system so that taxes were collected according to the acreage of land people owned. This latter measure reduced the burden of poor farmers and promoted production. During his reign, the economy experienced speedy growth.

Learning from his father's hesitation in choosing a crown prince, Yongzheng adopted the method of secretly appointing the crown prince, which meant that he didn't consult with the ministers but picked the candidate himself. And he had the name of the crown prince written on two copies. One copy was locked up in a box kept behind a huge horizontal plaque with the inscription "Open and Just" that hung in the Palace of Celestial Purity, and the other copy was carried around by himself. After his death, it was to be taken out and read aloud by the chief eunuch.

On the twenty-first day of the eighth month in 1735, Emperor Yongzheng fell ill in the Yuanmingyuan Park. The next day, the emperor was said to have become fatally ill and on the twenty-third he was already dead. The course of his sudden death can not be found in the official records, which has caused people to speculate. One interpretation goes so far as to suggest that the emperor's head was chopped off by an assassin and his body was buried with a man-made head of gold. This "gold head" is another great mystery of the Qing Dynasty. According to this rather complicated and surprising story, the emperor persecuted so many people for what they had written and had many of them wrongly put to death. One of these was Lü Liuliang, a prolific writer. After his death, he was accused of writing things against the Qing rule. Emperor Yongzheng thus ordered that his coffin to be opened and his corpse destroyed. His children and the families of two students of his were all killed. One of them, however, managed to escape. She was Lü Siniang, the granddaughter of Lü Liuliang. In preparing for revenge, she learned superb fighting skills. She disguised herself as a palace maid, slipped into the palace, sneaked into the bedroom of the emperor and killed him.

Many scholars find such far-fetched stories unbelievable and, citing such books as the *True Records of the Qing Dynasty* and *Manuscripts of the Qing Dynasty History*, argue that the emperor died of natural cause.

Plans were made to open the tomb of Emperor Yongzheng in 1981, but the project has been postponed. One of these days, excavators will answer the question of whether or not the head of Emperor Yongzheng was cut off by Lü Siniang.

6. The dissolute Emperor Qianlong

Hongli (1711 – 99) was the fourth son of Emperor Yongzheng. In the eighth month of 1735, Emperor Yongzheng died. According to his instructions, the chief eunuch took out the box put behind the horizontal plaque bearing the words of "Open and Just" that hung in the Palace of Celestial Purity, opened it and took out the secret edict. It read: "I have decided to make my fourth son the crown prince who will succeed me upon my death." The next year, Hongli named his reign period Qianlong and he became known as Emperor Qianlong.

According to one story, Qianlong was an adopted child. His mother by birth was the wife of Chen Guan, a senior court minister. At the same time as the concubine of Prince of Yong (who later became Emperor Yongzheng) gave birth to a baby girl, Mrs. Chen delivered a boy. Upon the insistence of the concubine, the boy was taken away from Mrs. Chen and replaced by the girl. After Emperor Qianlong took the throne, he visited the south of China six times to secretly meet with the Chens in Haining.

The six decades that Emperor Qianlong sat on the throne are considered to be the most prosperous period of the Qing Dynasty, as well as the period when it began to decline. Twice the emperor sent armies to put down rebellions on the border and so he consolidated the unification of the country. He widely recruited men of learning to complete the writing of the *History of the Ming Dynasty*, *A Complete Library of the Four Treasures*, *A Comprehen-*

sive Study of Civilization Throughout the Dynasties.

The emperor himself was a man of learning and was good at composing poetry and writing calligraphy. A trip to the Forbidden City will show the visitor many poems and couplets in the handwriting of Emperor Qianlong.

He was also an emperor who wallowed in licentious pleasure. Once on a visit to the Yuanmingyuan Park, he struck up an affair with the sister-in-law of the empress. At the beginning they simply teased each other, then they fell in love and finally they ended up sleeping together. When the empress found it out, she couldn't openly release her anger. She died finally after long suppression of her indignation and depression. A year later, Qianlong made Wulanala empress. Once the emperor said that he was going out to study society in civilian clothes so as to disguise his real identity. His real purpose was to visit women. The empress tried to gently persuade the emperor to refrain from visiting other women, but the emperor repudiated her for being "mad" and stripped her of her position as empress. In depression and disappointment, she soon died also. For thirty years from then on, the emperor married no woman with the official title of empress.

During his reign, he left the capital to visit different parts of the country twenty-one times, spending a great fortune to the criticism of his subjects.

Once, while on a tour, he read a report in his sedan chair that the peasants in Sichuan were waging a rebellion. He sighed, and said, "Tigers and rhinoceroses have all come out from the shed while beautiful jade is being smashed in the box. Whose fault is this?" None of the accompanying officials dared to make a sound. But He Shen, a sedan servant who was in his early twenties, said, "Your Highness, the local officials have unshakable responsibilities!" Qianlong nodded in satisfaction at this answer, saying, "Well said." Thus He Shen, who was good at being a sycophant, became a trusted official of the emperor, eventually becoming the prime minister. While He Shen was prime minister, embezzlement and bribery were the fashion of the day. "Three years as a government official bringing one 100,000 taels of silver" was what people said, a true portrayal of the corrupt officials. At the time, whoever wanted to have anything done had to pay bribes to He Shen. Tributes to the court all went through He Shen, who kept the good ones and forwarded the leftovers to the court. According to estimates, in the later years of Qianlong's reign 80 to 90 percent of the tributes from different localities ended up with He Shen. All the time, however, the emperor treated He Shen as his most loyalful official. He even married his daughter, Princess Hexiao, to He Shen's son. With a mouth good for only saying things the emperor loved to hear, He Shen amassed unlimited wealth. What he was doing was no secret to many people. Yongyan, the crown prince, for example, knew it. Since his father trusted He Shen so well, the crown prince for the time being had to keep silent on the matter.

Qianlong became emperor at the age of twenty-five and turned the throne over to his son when he was eighty-five, having been emperor of exactly sixty years. Since his grandfather Kangxi sat sixty-one years on the throne, Qianlong knew it was inappropriate to outdo his grandfather. He Shen was terrified when he learned that the emperor was going to give up his throne. Kneeling in front of the emperor, he insisted, "Your Highness is in such good health with such energy, you should preside over the administration for a few more years." But Qianlong told him, "I've made up my mind and it is not open for any further discussion. But you don't have to worry, for I can always tell the court what my opinions are." Indeed, Qianlong acted for three more years as the Supreme Emperor and, like a huge umbrella, continued to protect He Shen, China's number one embezzler. On the second day of the first month of 1799, Emperor Qianlong died at the age of eighty-nine, having been the most long-lived emperor in Chinese history.

7. Emperor Jiaqing rid the country of the most corrupt official

Yongyan (1760 – 1820) was the fifteenth son of Emperor Qianlong who, in 1796, succeeded to the throne with the reign title of Emperor Jiaqing.

Jiaqing took the throne when he was thirty-nine. His father was still the Supreme Emperor. So Jiaqing had to listen to everything his father said and left the major issues for decision-making to He Shen to report to and decide on by his father. He Shen sent trusted aides to help the emperor copy poems, but in reality they were there to watch every move of the emperor. Emperor Jiaqing was well aware of He Shen's real intentions, yet he kept quiet and pretended not to know of this.

Then, in the first month of 1799, Emperor Qianlong died. A few days after he took the administration into his own hands, Emperor Jiaqing had He Shen arrested. He personally listed twenty major crimes that He Shen had committed. When He's house was searched, his property was found to be worth one billion taels of silver, which equaled twenty years' revenue for the Qing court. Two weeks after the house search, He Shen was sentenced to death. The huge sum of wealth and treasures that He Shen had amassed were shipped to the court and into the possession of Jiaqing. So people said, "He Shen fell into the ditch and Jiaqing became rich."

Succeeding to the throne in the prime of his life, Jiaqing had great aspirations. He was diligent and maintained strict discipline for himself. He removed corrupt officials and advocated frugal government. He issued edicts to cut palace expenditures, abolished tributes, put an end to the practice of visiting the south and sent relief to disaster-stricken people. As a result of the unlimited squandering and corrupt politics in the late years of Emperor Qianlong's reign, the nation was already boiling with popular indignation and the Qing empire had already taken a turn towards its decline. Sharp struggles were taking place inside the palace. On the twentieth day of the second month of 1803, Chen De, a poor city resident, sneaked into the palace. With dagger in hand, he approached Jiaqing's sedan with the intention of assassinating the emperor. He was caught and killed along with his son. On the fifteenth day of the ninth month of 1813, a peasant rebellion force led by Lin Qing launched an attack on the palace from their base in the suburbs. Emperor Jiaqing became terrified at these events. Believing that the trees in the palace could provide cover for the assassins, he ordered that the trees be cut down. Later emperors followed his decision and that's why it is rare to see any trees in the Forbidden City today.

During his twenty-five years of rule, Emperor Jiaqing's most noticeable act was his banning of opium. On the twenty-fifth day of the seventh month in 1820, Jiaqing died at the mountain summer resort of Chengde, north of Beijing, at the age of sixty-one.

8. Daoguang became emperor by both intelligence and gallantry

Minning (1782 – 1850) was the fourth son of Emperor Jiaqing. He succeeded to the throne the day his father died, and came to be known as Emperor Daoguang.

Minning started to read at the age of six and had an unusually good memory. He was also quick at learning military warfare, to the delight of his grandfather Qianlong. One day, Qianlong went on hunting and took his grandsons along to compete in archery. He promised that all those who hit the target three times successively would be given the prize of a yellow vest. Minning, then aged eight, shot three arrows at deer and all of them hit the targets. Qianlong was so delighted that he composed a poem in praise of this brave and well-trained grandson.

On the fifteenth day of the ninth month of 1813, when Lin Qing and his peasant rebels attacked the Forbidden City, it was Minning who led the garrison guards to shoot down with rifles those who jumped over the city wall. His actions won the praise of his father, Emperor Jiaqing. His intelligence and bravery won him the admiration of both the grandfather and father and this laid the foundation for him to eventually succeed to the throne.

In the seventh month of 1820, Emperor Jiaqing

became gravely ill while on a hunting trip to Rehe. He summoned his ministers, telling them, "In keeping with the tradition of my ancestors, I have written 'It is decided that Minning is to be the crown prince.' and I have put it behind the plaque of Open and Just." So after his death, Minning took the throne.

Daoguang was known for his frugal life. He allowed only four dishes to be served for his meals. He also sometimes wore clothes with patches on them to court. Officials followed his suit and for a while it was considered a glorious thing to wear clothes with mended patches.

But such a "great sage" could not tell who was loyal and who was not. Cao Zhenyong, in whom he placed great trust, was a cunning court veteran. People asked him what were the tricks to becoming an official and he said, "The only thing you have to do is to nod your head and say little." Wang Ding, who was a straightforward person and a senior minister, exposed wrong behavior of Muzhang'a in front of the emperor. Muzhang'a knew he was wrong and did not dare to argue. Emperor Daoguang, however, smiled and said, "You're drunk!" He then had his eunuchs help Wang Ding out of the court. The next day, Wang Ding again exposed Muzhang'a, but he only infuriated the emperor who got up and left. Wang Ding pulled on the emperor's robe and went on with his presentation, yet the emperor remained unmoved. Upon returning home, Wang Ding hung himself, in imitation of the ancient people who tried to arouse a ruler's attention by killing themselves. Muzhang'a sent someone to talk to Wang Ding's son, Wang Kang, saying that if he dared tell the court how his father died, he would lose his official post. Under pressure, Wang Kang reported that his father died of illness. It was a great tragedy that Wang Ding lost his life out of loyalty and achieved nothing in the end.

During Minning's reign, the Opium War broke out. The emperor's suppression of General Lin Zexu, who stood for resisting the British aggression, his putting incapable and corrupt officials such as Muzhang'a and Qishan into important posts, his policy of surrendering to outside pressure and his hesitation on key issues at critical moment led to China's defeat, which gradually turned China into a semi-colonial country. It must be admitted that Emperor Daoguang was diligent and frugal, but he was not a man with administrative abilities and he was responsible for much of what later happened to the country.

Daoguang died in the first month of 1850 at the age of sixty-nine.

9. Emperor Xianfeng owed his succession to his teacher

In his old age, Emperor Daoguang could not make up his mind whether he should make his fourth son or sixth son the crown prince. One day he took his children hunting in Nanyuan. Before they left, Du Shoutian, the teacher of Yizhu, the fourth son, told him, "Just watch your brothers shoot. Don't ever shoot yourself. If the emperor asks you, tell him this..."

So Yizhu sat there all day as instructed by his teacher and killed no game whatsoever.

As they began to leave at dusk, all the princes had accumulated a great catch except for Yizhu. Emperor Daoguang was angry and criticized Yizhu, who answered with the words of his teacher: "It is not that I cannot shoot. If I did, I am sure I would not be empty-handed. But it is now spring, a time for the birds and animals to raise babies and I cannot bring myself to kill them. Besides, I don't want to compete with my brothers in this respect."

Daoguang turned from rage to delight on hearing these words, and said, "You're being so kind and benevolent. If you were to run the country, I would have no worries." Upon his return, Daoguang wrote the secret edict and put it into the box. This took place in 1846.

On the fourteenth of the first month of 1850, Daoguang died. His fourth son Yizhu (1831 – 61) became Emperor Xianfeng.

Becoming emperor at the age of twenty, Xianfeng had great aspirations. Unlike Emperor Yongzheng who ruthlessly dealt with his brothers who had contended with him for the throne, Xianfeng made his sixth brother, Yixin, Prince Gong. He also made the other brothers princes. He corrected his father's mistake of excluding Han ministers and appointed a number of Han officials. History, however, brought the young and aspiring emperor into a gigantic whirlpool, as the Taiping Peasant Uprising and the Second Opium War came one after another during his reign. By relying on forces led by Zeng Guofan, a Han landlord general, he suppressed the Taiping Uprising. As for the foreign invasion, he took a compromising policy, throwing China further into a semi-colonial status.

Xianfeng had neither the aspirations of his ancestor Nurhachi, who began his career with thirteen sets of armour, nor the stamina of Huangtaiji, who commanded the eight-banner forces with a heroic spirit. His aspirations were off as he wallowed in the luxurious and debauched life of an emperor. The same went for the eight-banner warriors and royal family descendants. Throughout his life, Xianfeng was only interested in women and he led a promiscuous life. The second year after he became emperor, he gave an order to select beautiful girls for his palace. One of these beautiful girls could sing and was good at winning men's favours with her womanly skills. Thus she won Xianfeng's interest. Later this woman, called Lan'er, became so powerful that she ruled China for forty-eight years "from behind the curtain" on three occasions, as Empress Dowager Cixi. Xianfeng also broke with the ancestral teaching of only allowing girls from official families of Mongolian and Manchurian origin into the court. He had many girls of Han origin. Four of the Han girls were particularly in the favour of the emperor. They were known by the names of Peony Spring, Apricot Blossom Spring, Warrior Forest Spring and Crabapple Spring, and collectively known as the "four spring girls." They were kept in Yuanmingyuan Park outside Beijing for the pleasure of Xianfeng.

In the ninth month of 1860, the allied forces of Britain and France fought their way into Beijing. Emperor Xianfeng fled, taking with him Empress Ci'an, Lady Nala (Lan'er or later Empress Dowager Cixi) and the four spring girls, as well as over a hundred other family members to the mountain resort at Rehe (now Chengde).

While they were in Beijing, the British and French forces looted Yuanmingyuan Park on which the Qing court had spent so much money and time to build, and then set it on fire. The Qing court once again sued for peace by paying indemnities and ceding land. Still, Emperor Xianfeng did not dare to return to Beijing and spent his time in licentious pleasure so as to fill his sense of loss in heart and spirit. Gradually his health gave way. On the twenty-second day of the eighth month in 1861, he died at the mountain resort.

Before his death, the emperor summoned eight advisory ministers, including Zaiyuan, Duanhua and Sushun, to ask them to help the young emperor in his job. The emperor had discovered the ambitions of Lady Nala. Afraid that she would become arrogant and above the law because her son would soon become emperor, Xianfeng wrote a will for Empress Ci'an, telling her to "maintain family law according to the ancestors' instructions" when necessary.

Xianfeng died at the age of thirty-one after being emperor for twelve years.

10. Tongzhi, the "naughty child emperor"

Zaichun (1856 – 75) was the eldest son of Emperor Xianfeng. He became the sovereign ruler with the title of Emperor Tongzhi the same day his father died. He was only six years old.

Tongzhi was a bright child. His mother, Empress Dowager Cixi, was busy fighting for political power and had neither time nor interest in raising her child. Becoming emperor at six, Zaichun spent all his time in the world of eunuchs who, in order to curry favour with the child emperor, did everything he wanted. As a result, the emperor was not at all interested in studies and won himself the nickname of the "Naughty Child Emperor." When his teacher tried to teach him to recite *The Analects* of Confucius, he could not remember a single word and the teacher called him a "fool." In front of Cixi, however, the teacher praised him as having intelligence "above all others."

When Xianfeng died, Cixi who had been a lady concubine was only twenty-six. Now she became the empress dowager because her young boy was the emperor. Good at political tactics, she secretly arranged for people to petition Empress Ci'an (official wife of the late Emperor Xianfeng) to "reign from behind the curtain." Senior ministers Sushun and others rejected the petition on grounds that "The Qing Dynasty had no such precedence." For a while, the two sides engaged in such heated argument and high-pitched quarreling that the young emperor became so scared he wet his pants right in court. Knowing that she was no match for the ministers, Cixi stepped up her activities in secret. She had An Dehai, one of her trusted eunuchs, beaten up and sent to the inner palace in Beijing as punishment. In reality she sent him back to Beijing to take a secret letter to Yixin, the sixth uncle of the young emperor, asking him to come to Chengde. Yixin, a man who had the support of foreigners because he had helped to sell out China's interests, was seeing his influence and power base expanding. Cixi's activities aroused the vigilance of Sushun and other ministers. With the excuse that a brother-in-law and sister-in-law should not meet in private, they tried to prevent the two from banding together. Yixin, however, cleverly disguised himself as a sorcerer and secretly met with Cixi. The two discussed plans for a palace coup. Yixin then hurried back to Beijing and the showdown between the two empresses and the eight senior ministers was about to begin.

Soon the two empresses announced their intention of returning to Beijing. On the twenty-sixth day of the tenth month, the two empresses and the young emperor left for Beijing by a short-cut. Sushun, however, had to travel together with the bier of Emperor Xianfeng and therefore his entourage took the main road, which took them longer to reach Beijing. On the first day of the eleventh month, the two empresses entered the city of Beijing. Yixin, came out of the palace to meet them, announcing the arrest of Zaiyuan and Duanhua, two of the eight advisory ministers who had accompanied the two empresses to Beijing. Then he sent people to gallop on horseback to arrest Sushun and others. That evening, shortly after Sushun and his party had gone to bed in Miyun, a suburban county, the guards who had come to arrest them broke the door open, pulled them out of bed, and took them to Beijing.

Empress Cixi called a secret conference of ministers who were royal family members, crying in order to win sympathy, she told them how Sushun and the others had bullied her and her son. Suddenly the six-year-old emperor said, "As servants, they dared to bully their boss. They should be killed." Thus, on the eighth day of the same month, Zaiyuan and Duanhua were ordered to commit suicide, Sushun was beheaded, and the other five ministers were either stripped of their jobs, demoted or sent to serve in the army. The struggle between the court ministers and Empress Dowager Cixi came to an end with Cixi emerging as the victor. On the second day of the twelfth month, for the first time, the two empresses sat behind the curtain. Empress Ci'an was modest and not interested in interfering in politics. She was there because Empress Cixi wanted her to be there as window dressing for herself. All decisions were now made by Cixi. From then on China entered a long period of rule by Cixi.

Cixi, adopting a policy of "employing foreigners to fight the rebels," left the suppression of the Taiping Peasant Uprising and the Nian Uprising forces in the hands of foreigners with their advanced rifles and cannons, thus alleviating a crisis for the Qing court. A group of people interested in Westernization, represented by Yixin at the central level and Zeng Guofan at the local level, emerged. They opened up military and industrial works by following the examples of the industrial revolution of the West.

When he grew up, Emperor Tongzhi also led a rather absurd life. He often went out of the palace in civilian clothes, taking along two trusted eunuchs to visit the brothels in the southern part of Beijing. Soon he caught venereal disease and died on the twelfth day of the first month of 1875, at the age of nineteen.

11. Guangxu was made emperor because of his young age

After the death of Tongzhi, Cixi called a meeting of ministers to select a new emperor. Empress Ci'an proposed that, since Yixin proved instrumental in their coup, his son Zaicheng should be made the new emperor. Zaicheng was then sixteen years old and Cixi believed he might not be easily controlled at that age, so she did not endorse this proposal by remaining silent. Yixin, of course, could not recommend his own son, so he proposed that one of the nephews of Tongzhi be made emperor in keeping with the Qing tradition of passing the throne to the son's generation rather than to brothers. Cixi understood that if Yixin's proposal was adopted, she would become the new emperor's grandmother and lose her power to rule from behind the curtain. So she cut Yixin short by saying that Zaitian (1871 - 1908), son of Yihuan, should be made the new emperor. Zaitian's mother was the sister of Cixi and he was only four years old at the time. It would be easy to keep a baby of that age under control. Afraid of Cixi, no one dared object.

When the straightforward court historian, Wu Kedu, heard that Cixi wanted to make her sister's son the emperor, he decided to show his opposition by killing himself. So he took some opium and went to see Cixi, telling her, "You want to make your nephew the emperor simply because you want to continue to rule from behind the curtain. I'm going to die, but before I die, I want you to know that you will be hated by people because of what you are doing!" Cixi, however, was no ordinary woman and so she went ahead with her plan.

With Zaitian sitting on the throne, Cixi began a second round of ruling from behind the curtain. Thirteen years later, the new emperor, known as Emperor Guangxu began to personally run the court. To maintain her control on the emperor, Cixi had him marry her niece, known as Emperess Longyu. Emperor Guangxu never loved this woman. Though they shared the same bed, he never made love to her. At the same time, two sisters, Lady Jin and Lady Zhen, became the concubines of the emperor. Throughout his lifetime, Guangxu only had one empress and two lady concubines, making him the emperor with the least women among all the sovereign rulers of the Qing Dynasty.

After he began to personally administer the court, Guangxu wanted to revitalize the country through reforms, but he met strong opposition from conservatives led by Cixi. Early in the ninth month of 1898, Cixi sent a trusted aide to Tianjin to meet with Ronglu, instructing him to launch a military coup to remove the emperor by taking advantage of the emperor's planned visit to Tianjin at the end of the tenth month to review a military parade. When

Guangxu was tipped about this plot, he immediately consulted with the reform activists Kang Youwei, Liang Qichao and Tan Sitong. During the night of the eighteenth of the ninth month, Tan Sitong went to see Yuan Shikai, commander of the New Army, hoping he would protect the emperor during the parade, kill Ronglu and place Cixi under house arrest so as to promote reform. Yuan immediately expressed support for the emperor and said matter-of-factly, "To kill Ronglu is like killing a dog." Then he reported the conversation to Ronglu who hurried to report it to Cixi. Cixi took action first, by placing Guangxu under house arrest at Yingtai in the Forbidden City. Lady Zhen, the favourite concubine of the emperor, was also put into prison because she supported the emperor's reforms. Ronglu led an army of three thousand to search for and capture all reformers. Tan Sitong was killed along with five other reform advocates. Kang Youwei and Liang Qichao managed to flee the country. Reform thus ended with the Empress Dowager Cixi ruling from behind the curtain for the third time.

In late summer and early autumn of 1900, the joint forces of eight Western powers took Beijing. Cixi forced the emperor to flee with her towards the west. Before she left, she had her trusted eunuch Cui Yugui bring over Lady Zhen from her cell to a water well. Cixi, pointing at the well, said, "I order you to die. Now jump!" Lady Zhen was a strong character and started to argue with Cixi, who urged the eunuch, "Hurry, push her down!" The beautiful, talented Lady Zhen, who shared the same views as the emperor, was thus killed by being drowned in the well.

Grief, solitude and hatred tortured the emperor. In a diary written in the tenth month of 1908, he wrote: "I am very ill, but I still have the feeling that the Old Buddha (a term reserved for Cixi in her late years) will die before me. If that is the case, I will give the order to kill Yuan Shikai and Li Lianying."

Li Lianying was the most trusted eunuch of Cixi. When he got his hands on the diary, he immediately reported this to Cixi, who said through gritted teeth, "I will absolutely not die before him." Then she decided to have Li take the emperor's food and medicine to him as of the twenty-first day of the tenth month of 1908. Wasn't it clear that she wanted the emperor to die quickly? In the afternoon of the same day, Emperor Guangxu's illness took a fatal turn and he died in the evening. The mighty Cixi, however, only lived two days longer than the emperor. She breathed her last in the dusk of the twenty-third day of the same month.

Guangxu was emperor for thirty-four years, but he could not realize any of his goals as he was under the tight control of Cixi. He died at the age of thirty-eight.

12. Puyi, the last emperor

When Puyi (1906 - 67) took the throne in 1908, he was only three. The reign title for this last Chinese emperor was Xuantong.

When he saw so many people kneeling in front of him at the ceremony to mark his ascension to the throne, the three-year-old emperor did not understand what was happening. He was so scared that he began to cry, demanding, "I don't want to be here. I want to go home!" His father, Prince Regent Zaifeng, held him with both hands and tried to calm him down, saying, "Don't cry. It will be over very soon."

The ceremony for the twelfth emperor of the Qing Dynasty to take the throne was soon dismissed. As they were leaving, the ministers whispered to each other, "Why did the emperor say 'I want to go home'?" "That the prince regent said 'It will be over very soon' is not a good omen!"

Within three years the Revolution of 1911 broke out. On January 1, 1912, a provisional government of the young republic was formed in Nanjing with Sun Yat-sen as the provisional president. On February 12, 1912, the Qing court announced the abdication of the emperor and the Qing Dynasty came to an end. Puyi, however, still lived in the rear palaces of the Forbidden City. His life continued in the same palatial styles, as he was accompanied by palace maids and eunuchs. He even appointed an empress and lady concubines in keeping with the wedding traditions of past emperors at the time his wedding was held.

Nevertheless, Puyi was a young man who longed for new way of life. He cut the long pigtail on his head, which the diehards of the Qing traditions regarded as their lifeline. To make bicycle riding easier in the rear palace, he had the high thresholds removed.

In June 1917, Zhang Xun, a warlord, came to Beijing with his forces. Working together with royalists such Kang Youwei, they staged a drama to restore the Qing Dynasty. On the first day of July, Puyi announced his return to the throne, but he had to abdicate twelve days later under the strong opposition of people throughout the country.

On November 5, 1924, General Lu Zhonglin from an army commanded by Feng Yuxiang told Puyi to leave the palace at once. Puyi left and took up temporary residence in the palace of Prince Zaifeng (his father).

On March 1, 1932, Japan made Puyi puppet head of their so-called Manchuguo (Manchuria). Later Puyi took the title of Emperor of Manchuguo. In August 1945, Puyi was taken to the Soviet Union as a captive. He was sent back to China in August 1950 and placed in the Fushun War Criminals Prison. In December 1959, he was released under a special government amnesty and he then returned to

Beijing. He died of illness on October 16, 1967, at the age of sixty-one.

Chronological Table of Chinese Dynasties

Xia	c. 21st-16th century B. C.
Shang	c. 16th-11th century B. C.
Western Zhou	c. 11th century-770 B. C.
Spring and Autumn Period	770-476 B. C.
Warring States Period	475-221 B. C.
Qin	221-207 B. C.
Western Han	206 B. C. -A. D. 24
Eastern Han	25-220
Three Kingdoms	220-280
Wei	220-265
Shu	221-263
Wu	229-280
Western Jin	265-316
Eastern Jin	317-420
Southern and Northern Dynasties	420-589

340

Southern Dynasties	420-589
Song	420-479
Qi	479-502
Liang	502-557
Chen	557-589
Northern Dynasties	386-581
Northern Wei	386-534
Eastern Wei	534-550
Western Wei	535-557
Northern Qi	550-557
Northern Zhou	557-581
Sui	581-618
Tang	618-907
Five Dynasties and Ten Kingdoms	907-960
Song(Northern and Southern)	960-1279
Liao	916-1125
Western Xia	1038-1227
Kin	1115-1234
Yuan	1271-1368
Ming	1368-1644
Qing	1644-1911

图书在版编目(CIP)数据

中国皇帝故事:英文/程钦华编著. —北京:
外文出版社,2000
ISBN 7-119-02047-1

Ⅰ.中… Ⅱ.程… Ⅲ.故事-中国-当代-选集-英文
Ⅳ.I247.8

中国版本图书馆 CIP 数据核字 (1998) 第 05635 号

责任编辑　胡开敏
封面设计　王　志
插图绘制　李士伋

外文出版社网址:
　http://www.flp.com.cn
外文出版社电子信箱:
　info@flp.com.cn
　sales@flp.com.cn

中国皇帝故事

程钦华　编著

黄友义　译

*

ⒸⒸ外文出版社
外文出版社出版
(中国北京百万庄大街 24 号)
邮政编码 100037
北京外文印刷厂印刷
中国国际图书贸易总公司发行
(中国北京车公庄西路 35 号)
北京邮政信箱第 399 号　邮政编码 100044
2000 年(36 开)第 1 版
2000 年第 1 版第 1 次印刷
(英)
ISBN 7-119-02047-1/I·458(外)
04000(平)
10-E-3198P